CONNECTING

THE

WATERS

CONNECTING THE WATERS

The Gifts of Three Boats

a memoir

DAVE MANGIN

Yeah, Dad, I really bit a hog in the ass on this one.

CONTENTS

Preface by the Author

This book is not finished. It is part of an endeavor that began in a barn in a small Central Wisconsin village, near North America's subcontinental divide. Like the uncertain destination of rain pouring upon a rock on the crest of that glacial moraine, it is unclear where this adventure will take me. For certain, it is part of my path. It has already rewarded me with insight, strength, means of coping with loss, and a path toward a brighter future. The journey is the destination, and it may only conclude with me ready to move onto the next chapter of my life when I taste the briny waters of the Atlantic from a vessel of my creation that I power, perhaps aided by benevolent winds and currents.

We are entering a new age. One in which we create at least one more degree of separation between us and the world and people that sustain our lives. This separation began with the industrial revolution, when some aspects of the occupation of man moved from fields, forest, and sea to factories and cities. People subjected themselves to the forces of machinery and human imposed perdition and began to abandon the natural laws of nature. The separation occurred in the factories so that conveniences and efficiencies outside of them could remove people from the trials of daily or household toil. Technology advanced and we became more distant from nature. Then came mechanized automation, then the information age. The separation is accelerated by leaps and bounds as our technology grows. And as we are now (and have been for some time) at a point so far removed from the elements that sustain us that it is not only our kids but we ourselves that ask, "What is real? Artificial intelligence and other forces of modern life are rewriting our sense of normalcy, our perceptions, and our reality. Damn right I am wary of this, even if many of their benefits are to be embraced.

So, what is real? How do we know what to trust, value, and how to navigate this newness in a way that is healthy, sustainable, ethical, fulfilling? I think it best to maintain a foot on the ground. By rooting ourselves to natural, real-life exchanges, experiences, and lessons, we are able to establish a baseline for what is trustworthy, common ground from which to negotiate the best paths forward with society, and a code to guide us in our work, recreation, and moral and environmental ethos.

Where do we find these real experiences? The best place, for me, is nature. The timeless systems that have evolved over billions of years and are far more stable, resilient, complex, and efficient than our economic system. They provide us insight to the natural laws that our modern economy is ultimately governed by, even if the two are often at odds with each other. Another way is through creation of something from scratch. As our hands interact with raw materials, lessons are learned and craftsmanship is sharpened. Expectations are developed for the scale of our homes, ease of lifestyle we might sustainably afford, and the investment of natural resources required to sustain us.

For me, the best combination of creation and natural experience is achieved by building and using boats. And for a complete story, I would recommend seeking out the headwaters of a river system and starting a journey there. Follow the waters to the ocean, and you'll find reality along the way. That is the story that I begin to tell here. I hope you feel encouraged by the following pages to carve out stories of your own. Finally, please share the reality you find, so others may be inspired by and find commonalities and new perspectives with it. This, after all, is how we evolve.

The Backstory

*The first river you paddle runs through the rest of your life. It
bubbles up in pools and eddies to remind you who you are.*
—Lynn Culbreath Noel

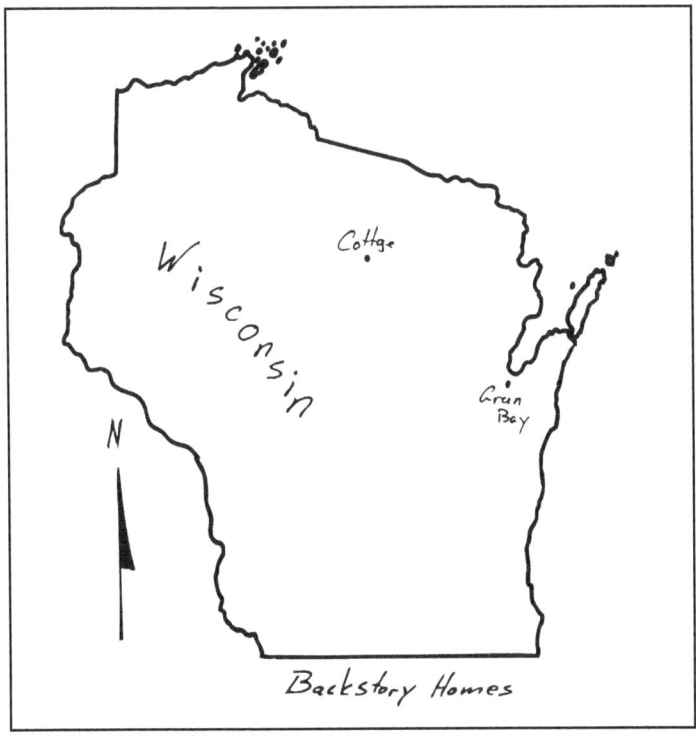

My heart needs something beautiful and productive to believe in. I've found it in the workings of the wild, but not so much in the constructs of man. My challenge to myself is to become one of the few who build something that is harmoniously fluid and efficiently serves a purpose.

This is nothing new, as every generation rebuilds the world according to its own conceptions. The words and actions used to do this never fully illustrate the extent of the leaders' awareness, much less a true picture of what is there. Just as mere words will never do justice to a sunset, our achievements will never perfectly mirror the perceptions that inspire us. But when people choose to blindly follow in the footsteps of their forefathers, they operate under a terrific misunderstanding that the rules inherited from their predecessors are more important than the laws of nature, or that the description is better than the sunset itself.

That is why each generation, before taking the societal steering wheel, should step outside the economic vehicle they are about to drive to see if the principles of its founding are solid—you know, kick the tires and look under the hood. How should the engine of this machine be tweaked to better accommodate the world as it changed under the guise of our forefathers? We cannot answer this question until we step out of the shelter of our ancestral traditions and face the realities of the world around us, harsh as they often are. If they truly are of value, these traditions will be adhered to and will be more precious as a result. This stepping out is surprisingly difficult to do, as we have done a great job of insulating our everyday lives from these realities.

—Journal Entry, September 9, 2007

Dave Mangin

Finding My North Arrow

It must have been July or August; I was about 5 years old. Summer had been around long enough for its warmth to be taken for granted, but autumn was not yet foreshadowed in the shades of green *Up North,* at the cottage in northern Wisconsin. The day's breeze died as the sun headed for the horizon, and my parents asked if I wanted to go out with them in the canoe. That vessel having been off limits to me in the past, I accepted their invitation to go for an evening paddle.

My mother is not a huge fan of the water, and it would be a couple of years before I even had the chance to flunk swimming lessons, twice. That may explain why I had never been in a canoe before. My mom took her place in the bow seat and I clamored aboard, feeling the canoe rock with each foot placement that strayed from the vessel's centerline. Eventually finding a comfortable spot on an extra life jacket in the middle of the canoe, my dad ordered us to hold on as he drove the canoe into the water and took up his favorite perch on the back deck of the boat.

Ignorance of my inability to swim made me perfectly unafraid of the water, so there was nothing to hold back my curiosity. I sat as I was told in the center of the canoe for about a minute before I edged toward the side to get closer to this new, dynamic environment. My mom's unease increased as I leaned over the side, rocking the canoe on its watery berth to drag my fingers through the water. The reproach I received was a small consequence to the sensation of my fingertips sweeping the cool surface. The calming simplicity and quietude set a perfect stage for contemplating phenomena such as the feel of the water riding up the front of each digit and the waves sent out behind them. These miniature wakes mingled with others until the disruptions were engulfed in the larger ripples sent off by the canoe itself.

My dad finally spoke up from the stern, his low raspy voice declaring that I had better stay in the middle of the boat. I sat there, separated by the canoe's high freeboard from this captivating playground. I watched and wondered at the whirl-pools my mom sent spinning away from her paddle with each stroke, feeling the canoe advance through the water with each passing swirl that was sent off on its own behind us. Those little currents each came to a playful, peaceful end as its angular momentum dwindled and it finally reunited with the surrounding depths.

The wind having died, the ripples from the canoe's hull and the liquid tornadoes were the only marks upon the water as we sliced its surface. Trees hanging over the shoreline were perfectly mirrored off the watery plane. The lake was its normal amber color as I gazed directly overboard, but we were surrounded by the brighter reflection of the blue sky. I anticipated our entry into the darker green reflection of the trees, but their shadowing haunt upon the water always remained a short distance off the bow. I could not understand why we never passed into the dimmer hues they cast upon the surface.

The surroundings held a stillness, a tranquil canvas onto which the sounds of evening began to play. The throaty declarations of bullfrogs echoed throughout the lake, and crickets began chirping. No mosquitoes molested us, although we occasionally passed through harmless clouds of gnats.

Becoming restless from my inactivity on the floor of the canoe, I began creeping again toward the gunnel. My arm draped over the side, and I reacquainted my hand with the soothing water. Despite, or because of, my understanding almost none of it, I was riveted by everything going on around me. Everything was so close and vivid, including my mother's nervousness as she scolded me back to the center of the craft. Like clockwork, I would edge to the side of the canoe to get closer to the water until I was rebuked back to my seat. Boredom would overcome my conscience, and I'd again make my way toward the tippy parts of the canoe, until my parents grew tired of the cycle, and we returned to shore.

I did not know it then, but I was struck. The marvels of light, sound, surrounding forest, and the wonder of the water's characteristics each cast a thread into me that became secured to the deepest parts of who I am. This is the earliest recollection I have of a connection with the surrounding nature of things. I was part of that world, learning the properties of its forces first hand. With each question of its dynamics sprang an urge to explore and understand everything about it. That captivation continues today, and increased understanding of these natural forces brings richer meaning to my life—both on the water and off. This evening on the water at the cottage planted the seed that would grow into my most enduring passion. The metallic taste of anxiety it left in my mother's mouth is one she would have to tolerate many times in the future as I followed this passion of mine on solo canoe and camping trips, backpacking adventures, and other *flingers,* as my dad came to call them.

Longing for connection with natural forces set the orientation for my deepest passions. Like most people, I would eventually be faced with societal issues of economic security and a job that pulls me from such intimate interaction with natural environments. My eventual separation from the wilder world would instill an emptiness and rage within me that would take years to understand. It is still unclear how we can meld our post-modern economy with the environmental one, but I can't seem to stop trying to figure it out. At any rate, that evening paddle established my north arrow for peace, beauty, and connection.

The Cottage

That evening on the lake with my parents marked a starting point. I do not think this beginning could have occurred anywhere but Up North. Compared to my life growing up in Green Bay, WI, the cottage was a gateway that gave access to places like the Pine Forest bordered by its two crystal blue lakes; ominous swamps with no trails in or out, where pillows of sphagnum moss swallow every footstep; or the crispness of a brilliant winter day in the hardwoods when the mercury reads 25 below. The soft light of candles and the hard ring of lantern light create an air of security in the cottage on nights when thunderstorms knock out the power.

It was an untouchable haven, separate from the rest of my world that was governed by classroom assignments or the orders of three older siblings, where my energy had to be somehow contained behind a desk for 6 hours a day, where I was forced to stifle creative energy in order to focus on math and reading. Compared with the freedom and lessons of the northwoods, the mundane routine and restrictions of the city rang hollow. It was here at the cottage that my personal education began. I began to know myself.

Every three or 4 weeks we packed everything possible into the back of the truck in preparation for a trip to the cottage. The splash of the garden hose would soak my jeans as I rinsed and filled the water jugs for the weekend away. We would spend 45 minutes looking for the right extension cord or length of rope and eventually decide it must already be up north. I would pile into the back of the truck where I would sit between my two brothers on an old car seat mounted on 2x4s. My sister rode up front with my parents, and Dad would settle into the driver's seat. We were finally ready to embark on a 3-hour trip that broke every chain that bound me to the city. Progress was measured by landmarks we passed: the *Indian Rock*, a stop in Antigo for gas and any last-minute thing we forgot, the deer farm, and forest lined fields. Someone would let out a holler as *the towers* came into view off Highway 17. The truck would finally turn onto County Trunk B to begin the ascension into The Harrison Hills and the forests of Lincoln County.

After backing the truck into its spot in front of the cottage, Dad came around back to open the tailgate for us. I would be the last one out of the truck and into the humidity of the woods, legs numb from the trip. Jumping off the tailgate and into the sand and leaves of the driveway, I remember the air feeling different. Thicker, with a fresher, more vibrant smell.

I would pitch in with the task of unloading the truck after watering a nearby tree. If not dark yet it would be close, and I was usually ready for the sack by the time the fridge was stocked, clothes stashed by my sleeping spot in the loft, birdseed dumped into its tray on the deck, and three wheelers unlocked. Saturdays I got up early, but still later than my brothers, to see what was to come with the day. One time I asked my dad, "What are we working on today?" I wanted to get it done fast because I had fox holes to dig, forts to build, trails to blaze, water to wade, arrows and BB guns to shoot, and fires to build. Dad responded, "Nothing. You can do whatever you want."

This was just the sort of freedom I needed to run at my pace, learn from my own mistakes, and experience the world on my terms. No soccer practice, no religion class, no homework, no having to sit still or quietly. Since I could roam on my own and not bother anyone (except with sound effects as I burned around on my invisible dirt-bike), I was not told how to live or operate or be productive. I knew what I wanted to do and the world that I played in set the ground-rules: Ice is cold, fire hot, water wet, rocks heavy, knives sharp, trees high, brush piles soft, and days too short. This is where experiential learning occurred. It's where I grew up.

We went up to the cottage in winter too. Dad would pull me on a sled with the three-wheeler; I would go snowboarding in the woods, jump off the deck into the snow, wander out onto the lake under the light of a full moon, and come inside to warm myself and dry my clothes by the fire. I could move at my own pace. I would return to Green Bay with a fresh perspective on issues I faced there, with more focus to do what I was supposed to, with a few sharpened skills and maybe a skinned knee.

Turbulence of Adolescence

When not up north, I dreamed about being in the woods. In middle and high school, I read books on wilderness survival and observation by Tom Brown, Jr. I went fishing in the Fox River and dreamed of wild adventures like paddling a canoe down the Mississippi River. These distractions from my school and daily life, however, seemed to be just that—some prohibited fantasy separate from the *real world* that felt a bit constrained.

I did not realize how perfectly normal it is to have boyish energy to run, play, and explore. Young males are not designed to sit still, but to develop skills and strength for working, building a home, and securing a family. It is our society that tames and tries to unnaturally cage our instincts. I was forced to stifle the urge to bounce around the room. I was guilty of having too much energy and having a hard time focusing on school work. I also had to mask the insecurity that sprang from this energy. I had to do what I was supposed to, not what came naturally.

Track and soccer served as outlets to let it all hang out and put on a mediocre athletic performance. I could then play the roles in the rest of my life. I was polite to customers while working at the drug store, combed my hair, respected adults, and worked hard at physical tasks. I got by in school, but not without stressing over uncompleted homework, worrying about having enough friends, and pretending to fit into the roles cut for people my age. Then I would hit my release valves. I ran my ass off at soccer practice—I played for 9 years and was absolutely horrible at it. I went fishing in the Fox River to be alone; I got into bicycling; and I got into drinking. These things, good or bad, were all outlets that allowed me to be almost normal the rest of the time.

And there was something else growing in my conscience. The time I spent in the woods or on the river bank had their influence on my disposition toward the environment. If wilderness and nature are so precious, why do we keep destroying them with our measures of beauty, success, manliness, and luxury? The clash between my two worlds was first experienced when fishing in the river by my parents' house, across from a paper mill that did its part to make the river too contaminated for swimming and the fish too toxic to eat.

I was about 10 years old when I first vocalized this concern. Max McGee and Jim Irwin were broadcasting the football game on the Packer Radio Network. My dad and I had the old Ford locked into 4-wheel drive, plowing through a snowstorm on the way back from the cottage. We alternated between listening to the game and talking about things.

I pointed out how people did all these things that experts said were so bad for the environment. People knew the doomsday stories but were still driving their cars and using aerosol cans with CFCs, and factories were pumping toxins into the air and rivers. I asked why people did not care more about the environment. My dad said that people start out caring about the environment, but then it's easier to sell out and follow along the same way as everyone else. I told him that I wasn't going to sell out. "Everyone sells out," he said. My eyes blurred with tears: "Well, I'm not gonna sell out!" My dad shook his head.

Of course, I sold out. I was selling out even as I told him I wouldn't, since we were guzzling about a gallon of gas every 10 miles in the big ford truck. I sold out on these ideals of clean living every single day by participating in this culture. I gave no shortage of thought to ecological living, the wild, and the world I was exposed to at the cottage or when fishing in the Fox River. But it was a completely separate one from my city life. Even though I considered the impacts of my life on the world around me, the cottage, which represented the natural wilderness I otherwise only saw on television, still seemed disconnected from the city.

As I began to see the sources and destinations of all our *stuff*, I found myself losing faith in the compensation of our society for the amenities we enjoy. The Fox River is still unswimmable, the climate is changing, woodlots are turned to subdivisions, oil is being extracted in increasingly devastating ways, and waste overflows landfills. I have been hitching a free ride. *Cheating*, as I have come to see it. Even now I sever naturally holistic ties by chaining myself to often-unfulfilling work rather than forming meaningful bonds with the world. But hey, a guy's got to make a living, right? At some point, if I were to find resolution to these issues that tore me up inside, some very fundamental changes would have to be made. But I was already turning my back on the wilderness and trending toward selling out to societal norms. I eventually took this as a matter of course and turned away from the struggle between society and nature. I tried ignoring this conflict that seemed to be an inescapable aspect of living in this post-modern economy.

Solitary Sunset Fear

As best I can tell, one isolated incident occurred when I was 17 that redirected my attention to that inner conflict of society vs. nature. Like the sunset with my parents on the lake, I would only credit this next episode as a turning point years after I learned to interpret the effects of it a decade later. In this one moment at the end of my junior year of high school, all my life's social and personal discrepancies came out at once as I was overwhelmed by an inner voice. The shock and fear of it threatened to drive the dreams and purpose from my heart.

I had borrowed the car to go camping over Memorial Day Weekend with a mess of friends. Friday afternoon I took my place in the convoy of high school buddies heading into Wisconsin's Northwoods. The weekend started on the wrong foot when I saw a beer bottle fly out of the car behind us. At that age, I had steadfast values, even if they were a bit misguided and I was unsure where to go with them. On the spectrum of indecency, littering was far more severe than polluting oneself. It would be another 30 years before I realized both types of defilement are essentially the same.

We soon made it to the campground, part of a steady stream of cars. Everyone staked out spots for their tents, and people settled around the fire to eat, drink, and let the lunacies begin. I approached the guy who threw the bottle out the window on the way up to this place. He took it as patronizing of me to say anything, so I backed off. While I knew I was being a thorn in the side, I had grown up enjoying the outdoors responsibly, often picking up after people who left their trash behind. Here, responsible behavior was the exception. A bit defeated, I sat back and watched the folly of the party unfold for the rest of the night.

Next morning, litter and hungover kids were strewn about the campsite. We were apparently there for one reason because we had started drinking again, in the hopes of relapsing to same condition as the night before. The manager came by to tell us we were not welcome back the following year. Restless over the mess, guilt crept in. I drew a few looks when I started picking up garbage, as if cleaning up the defilement in which we wallowed was contrary to everything this party stood for. Young and self-conscious, I exchanged my trash bag for a beer, and the party raged on.

Such a scene would eventually become commonplace in my social circles. I would come to host parties where bottles were shattered on the kitchen floor, cinder blocks smashed on basement walls, tables overturned, beer spilled, holes punched in walls, and more, but it was all within my own living quarters. According to the code I had established, it is perfectly acceptable to trash your own home and then take care of your own mess, but every other space should be left better than when you arrived.

The night wore on, and the crew around the fire began thinning. Most made it to their sleeping bags to struggle against the head spins as they lay down in a drunken haze. I decided the next morning that I had enough of this obscenity. The antics here resulted in nothing cool or productive, just trash and gross stories. There was no adrenaline of skiing behind a car or riding bicycles, nothing was being built or even torn apart in productively focused demolition. It was too much. I packed up my gear and took off.

With most of Sunday and Monday left to kill, I went further north and west to the cottage. I stopped and fished along the way, rolled the windows down, cranked up the radio, and enjoyed my freedom. I thrived in my solitude. Spring was springing, and I basked in the season's splendor. I pulled off at a stream crossing and waded in with my fishing rod, catching a nice rainbow trout that I decided to clean and fry for dinner. I slowly slipped into my own pace but still had things to distract me from myself. There were no cell phones or social media yet, but I had to plan my route, look for fishing spots, read the river, and focus on driving. Classic rock on the car radio helped to further set the care-free mood.

Arriving at the cottage late in the afternoon, I went swimming first thing to wash off the final remnants of the party. There is nothing quite like a running start and diving off the end of the dock, looking down at the reflection of your airborne person just before breaking the cool surface. I swam out to the raft, dove in a time or two, and scrubbed myself clean.

Back up in the cottage I tried frying the fish, *tried* being the operative word. The lesson of the meal was to make sure the oil is preheated before dropping the fish in. I thought of dumping it, but having chosen not to release it alive, my conscience would not let it go to waste. There had been enough of that for one weekend. I scarfed it down in a fashion that still did not justify its death, but it did provide sustenance. Slightly improved now at this middle stage of life, cooking was definitely one of my weaker areas as I grew up.

The day was growing short. The shallow angle of the sun's rays softened to gold that illuminated the covered deck. I wandered down to the lake again where I decided to watch evening drop in. I declined a float in the canoe; otherwise the setting would have been identical to the evening I welcomed with my parents over a decade earlier. On shore, I soon had a nice fire burning with tall flames piercing the evening glow. The lake's surface settled into a glassy reflection of the hemlocks and birches that grew from its shore, and the gold light began to take on more color. At least I couldn't mess up a sunset the way I did that trout.

The sun sank lower in the sky, and I tried settling into my fireside seat to take it in. But instead of relaxing, I was anxious. Without the distraction of activity, music, or the anticipation of meeting up with people, I felt alone. I was alone. I had nothing to occupy my hands or my head, and I was growing worrisome.

With no one else there to justify my existence, a loneliness crept in that I never felt before. I was empty and meaningless, daunted, perhaps, by the power of nature and the largeness of my surroundings. I needed someone to talk to, to be with and to make my world fuller. It was like standing blindfolded at the edge of a windy, exposed precipice with nothing around for reference of scale or to measure myself by. What the hell was going on? This anxiety was ridiculous. I tried to convince myself that it was nothing, that I must be a pretty small *boy* if I cannot even spend one night alone in the woods not even in the woods, at the cottage. What was wrong with me? But I could not convince that panic to go away. The sun was now nearing the treetops on the far side of the lake. I looked to its golden light, the quietude around me, the calm of the lake, and the light of my fire. It was giant, and I was nothing. I felt naked and exposed. But what was it that was so big? What was I exposing myself to? A wave of desperation engulfed me. I involuntarily jumped up, kicked out the fire, ran up to the cottage, shut down the power, locked up, and sped away from that vast wilderness of unexplored reality as fast as the car would take me. I cranked the radio and sang along at the top of my lungs for distraction.

I blasted away before I could question my decision to bail. I might have been able to go inside the cottage or retire to the deck, or even turn on the TV, but instead I bailed from everything altogether. My hurry was interesting too because by the time I got out to the county road, only 2 miles away, I already felt relieved. I was not escaping a place, but a circumstance. Once in the car I had music and the anticipation of being with people to insulate me from whatever it was that had terrified me on the lake. But what freaked me out so badly? What kind of a candy ass was I? I could hunt, fish, cook (sort of), swim, build fires and shelters, and take care of myself. Why was I afraid? I turned away from something that was staring me down, that seemed to penetrate the depths of my soul. I lacked the resolve to stare back.

I drove the 2.5 hours back to my parents' house, a scared boy seeking shelter from the world. Back to the security of the city and my living room. I walked in the house and my dad asked what I was doing home so soon. I told the truth about not wanting to party anymore but left out the fact that I had been so scared at the cottage. This anxiety arose from nowhere, so I wrote it off as a weakness. I spoke of it to no one and tried to make sense of it on my own, a process that would take years to work through. In the meantime, I took solace in the soft carpeted floor of the well-lit living room in front of the reassuring buzz of the television.

From that day, I dreaded the fear that crept in around sunsets. It coincided with big questions. My life had no direction aside from high school and the inevitability of college. I knew my values, but to what end would they be applied? What was my mark on this earth going to be? Further, with that episode of running from myself at sunset, my independence was being called into serious question. I was perfectly fine in the close quarters of night. It was the approach of twilight that scared me. Although the sunset fear eventually accompanied me to the University of Wisconsin Stevens Point where I attended college, I was distracted from it by things like parties, mountain biking, and the discovery of rugby.

Collegiate Folly

Having spent most of my life away from connective environments and experiences, work was something a person muddled through in the hopes of the weekend coming quickly and the dream of retirement. You put your time in at the office so you can escape to someplace wild and natural for a quick respite before returning on Monday. So that is how I approached school and how I envisioned the eventuality of a career. I went through much of my youth and college years engaged in the institutional forms of education and work that are standards for our culture. But in those regimented traditions, I was ignoring something within myself. I was not listening to my gut.

There was one formative evening early in my college career that tweaked the direction of that entire chapter of my life. We were partying in my dorm room after the Packers came back and squeaked out a Monday Night Football victory over the San Francisco 49ers. The stereo was blasting and I was yelling something to my roommate when a guy looked up at me and said, "You should play rugby." I said I was too small, but he pointed out that he was the same size as me. I got down off the table I was standing on, looked him in the eye, and saw it was level with mine. Sure enough, he was as short as me.

I weathered the next day's hangover and decided to follow through on what I agreed to the night prior. Walking out to the rugby pitch, I approached a small crowd of guys, all shapes and sizes, and introduced myself to someone who looked like he might be the coach—a bald guy with a British accent (Professor Michael Williams is from Wales. He played on their national team at one time, and moved to Stevens Point to teach, subsequently becoming the English Department Chair). There were some pretty big guys. One had more hair on his broad back than I had on my head. Another sported a mohawk, and more than a few looked a little crazy—or just stoned. Tom, the guy who talked me into this mess, came over and said hello. That was pretty cool of him. We ran drills and at times broke into two groups, pack members in one and backs in the other… whatever that meant. I tried rolling along with the group of bigger guys but was ushered over to the group of backs by the Mohawk Guy. Then Willy raised his voice, saying we had a good practice, and declared through his accent the words I would come to dread: "All right now. On the line, please."

The next 15 minutes were lung screaming agony. All sorts of insane jumping up and running as fast as we could to some imaginary line and back. I heard someone yelling from down the line as we'd take off again: "HIAAT! C'mon, Point, dig in and go! Whewww! Yeah!" He was one of the fastest guys on the team, definitely the most spirited. I moved down the line during one respite, and I ran with him at every practice. Tackleberry, he came to be called. Tom and Tack are still two of my best friends. And so rugby became the quintessential way for me to blow off steam for the next 4 years.

One event from this phase is pretty summative of the period. Arctic Fest, an annual 20+ team tournament on the backwaters of the Wisconsin River in which ruggers basically took over the entire town, came up quickly. My brother John came up from Madison to check it out. His girlfriend had attended UWSP, and he heard Arctic Fest weekend was one weekend a lot of people just stay inside. Of course, he came up to see it for himself. That Saturday night at Buffy's, our favorite bar, we were experimenting with different ways of smashing bottles on the floor. I was getting frustrated because every time I slid an empty off a table to stomp on it, John would beat me to it and smash it under his boot. I had my foot raised and was about to get in a good one, though, when I saw him out of the corner of my eye suddenly lurch forward. A bouncer pushed him from behind, grabbing the back of his shirt, and drove him toward the door. As I marveled at this spectacle, the exact same thing happened to me by another bouncer. As is always the case, experiencing the spectacle first hand was far more interesting than watching it. Being plowed through the crowd of bar patrons, the sea of people parted before us as I was being thrust off balance toward the exit. This whole thing was thoroughly enjoyable.

We were just about to go through the door when a guy fell in front of us, directly in the doorway. Rather than trample him, I stuck my arm out and stiff-armed the door jamb, instantly stopping our forward progress. I looked over my shoulder and said to the bouncer, *Let's give this guy a chance to get up, eh?* He half got up, half slithered to the side, and I looked over my shoulder again. *Ok, now let's go!*

I was pushed out the door, and the first thing I saw was John's bottle of beer spinning on the ground, dribbling its last contents. John was picking himself up from the ground. Laughing, we high-fived, picked up his beer, and went to the next bar.

Those sprints, getting pummeled by people outweighing me by 100 pounds, the parties, and the hangovers were just the sort of punishment lacking in my life now that my brothers were no longer living with me. Rugby served as a distraction from the inevitable prospect of a real job, this debauchery among misfits perhaps representing my rebellion against the concept. For the time, I was living the dream. No responsibility, but something else would be rediscovered as my collegiate phase unfolded.

Reacquainting with a Passion

I have always liked playing with water. From creeks that my childhood friend Paul and I would dam with sticks, rocks, and leaves, to syphons I played with in the kitchen sink, I liked the way water operated. The way it flowed, puddled, stuck, lubricated, cooled, warmed, froze, melted, boiled, condensed, hydrated, dissolved, quenched, carried, swept, blasted, permeated, merged, felt, diluted, and sustained life were all fascinating to me. I especially liked the way things floated upon it. I would make rafts out of twigs and popsicle sticks to float in the curb of our suburban street after a torrential rain. Another friend and I would carve small boats out of balsa wood that I could play with in the sink. The most profound influence on me were the hours I would sit on the shore of the Fox River, under a railroad trestle and across the river from two smokestacks standing as steeples in commemoration of the Industry of Man and reminding me why I couldn't eat the fish I was pulling from the water.

All those years growing up at the bottom of a bay of one of the world's largest freshwater lakes and I didn't have a boat.

No matter to me, as my brothers and I found our freedom up north where we had the canoe on the small lake below the cottage. No matter, that was, until late in my college career when I experienced the taste of rapids, paddling new and strange waters, seeing them from a disposition much wilder and more secluded than the roadside. Riparian environments added a layer of remoteness from civilization and vehicular transport that was more novel than hiking a trail to the back country. They are among the richest society of biological diversity, thriving at the interface of land and water. The newest converts are most devout, and I took my baptism into wild waters hook, line, and sinker.

Respite From the Folly

As the horizon appeared on my educational career, I grew scared. I was not ready to enter society to make my mark. Hell, I still didn't know what mark I wanted to make. But somewhere in the recesses of my psyche lingered a subtle whisper, to heed those inner callings for wild places and to follow my passions, even if that pursuit is put on pause for some time.

Working hard is something I have always been good at, but every occupation I could conceive either caused harm to our natural world or was part of a broken system that didn't seem to cover the damage it does. I wanted to change the system but had no idea what this might look like. A slew of my friends were graduating that spring and May seemed to be a continuous string of parties. We'd go to a bar for one friend's celebration in the morning and hit our third shin-dig by sundown. Finding myself stroking midnight at yet another bar, I looked around, wondering what I was doing to myself. I went home, poured over the DeLorme Atlas and Gazetteer of Wisconsin, and picked out a route. It was time to break out on my first solo canoe trip. I chose a 25 mile stretch of the Prairie River, a class A trout stream that winds through the flatlands of glacial outwash in Northern Wisconsin. I knew it to be narrow and fairly swift, but its current should be manageable … at least I hoped.

I packed my limited camping gear, and the next day I rented a canoe. The river runs near the cottage so I knew the roads in this area well. Still, I had little knowledge of the river. I counted the bridges I had to cross and mentally noted landmarks that would foretell a stretch of rapids. After that I discarded my map. I also left my watch at home. These things were symbolic of the structured world of classes, deadlines, and debauchery I was hoping to leave behind.

I drove an hour north and dropped my gear on the river bank. About 20 miles south, and I parked the car at the County Road C bridge. Then I headed out on foot under a bright sun and blue sky, trying to thumb a ride back upstream. I had never tried hitchhiking before, and I wasn't sure if it would work or how dangerous it might be. A picture-perfect day in May. The sun was warm, and before long I was sweating through my t-shirt. A beautiful day for a walk if nothing else. My gear was a long way up the road, and the locking of my car doors was the point of no return. I would walk all the way to the canoe if I had to. I was doing this. My first ride pulled over after about an hour on this largely vacant county trunk, just as I was beginning to have my doubts about the whole thing. The driver fished the river quite a bit and was stopping at a gas station on the main road for bait. From there I was on a state highway the rest of the way to the put-in, and it only took 10 minutes for a retired guy to pull over. He used to be an engineer and was involved with the dam that had recently been removed from the river. Both men were connected to the stream in their own way, and the air of adventure bolstered good conversation.

The hitch-hiking worked splendidly, and I came to enjoy it as a way of meeting people and getting about the state in later years (then it was ruined by my own affluence and the purchase of a car). I have been picked up by quite an array of different characters. The conversation is always interesting, since both parties are complete strangers who will never see each other again anyhow. Some pretty personal information gets divulged, almost like a therapy session.

Upon making it back to my canoe, I organized my pack and shoved off. I enjoyed a bagel and some trail mix as a mid-afternoon snack. I had the water all to myself, save for a few insects hatching off its surface. I floated for a couple of hours, steering round rocks and logs, and gently paddling the slow sections. Just as the sun was turning from yellow to gold in the west, I passed a break in the trees that revealed a hay field laying at eye level with me. It would be a good place to camp if it weren't so early in the evening, but then I reconsidered. *I'm not on any schedule. I can camp wherever I please.* So I did. I pitched my tent near the river and cooked a packet of broccoli-cheddar rice over a fire. I learned that I really do need a lid for my pot, since my cheesy rice was peppered with ashes. After dinner and watching the sun sink through the trees, I read some Robert Service by firelight and retired for the evening.

The glow of the dying fire reflected off the ceiling of my tent as I recounted the day from my sleeping bag. I had successfully arranged the car and the gear by hitchhiking for the first time. One test down with several stressors yet to face. Would I have enough time to get to my car tomorrow? Is this trout stream navigable the entire length of this run? How will I manage the rapids? Would my car still be there when I arrive at the take-out? These worries kept me awake, and my anxiety increased the more I thought about them. I remember my last thought, a couple of hours later, finally settling on the fact that there was nothing I could do but go with whatever came to pass, so I may as well not worry about it. With that, I finally fell asleep.

I awoke early the next morning to a clear sky and heavy frost. I struck my crispy tent straight away to get a jump on the unknown length of river in front of me. I had been sweating as I walked along the highway in a t-shirt just the day before. And by the time I got on the water this morning my hands were stiff with cold. Welcome to Wisconsin weather. Of course I didn't have any gloves with me. I dreaded the thought of paddling with my knuckles exposed to the cold air, but I knew things would warm up with the sunrise. Upon the water, I noticed how comfortable my feet were on the bottom of the canoe that was warmed by the water. The steam rising from the river's surface also heated the air. As a result, my stocking feet and bare hands were quite cozy being so close to the relatively warm river. The fog, coupled with the predawn light, softened the landscape of fields and forest, while the frost lent a delicate feel to the scene. Every alder twig and blade of grass was encapsulated in its own intricate sheath of crystal, creating infinite sparkles as the sun finally broke the horizon.

My gear was ample without filling the whole canoe, and it was tied in well for the hairy spots in the river. I was proud of this pack that had everything I needed, to be exploring and thriving under my own preparation.

Less than a mile downstream from my campsite, I paddled directly under a bald eagle perched in a tree looking for breakfast. The river parallels Highway 17 for a while, and I approached a fast stretch strewn with boulders and chutes around snags. I knew this beautiful stretch that ran under huge pines and hemlocks from trout fishing, although to flow through it so swiftly was quite a new experience. I was impressed with how precisely the boat could be positioned for entering the small drops. I further explored different paddle strokes and their effects on the hull.

Morning wore into midday as I wandered downstream. Somewhere in here was once the logging town of Heineman, which burned down in the early 1900s. There were some old wooden pilings half hidden in the tag alders that marked the spot. After crossing under the Heineman Rd Bridge, I knew the Prairie Dells were coming up. This was the canyon that was dammed until recently. I had seen this gorge from the shoreline once, and it posed a bit of a threat with steep walls, boulders, and ledges.

I came around a bend and could hear the rush of whitewater. As far as I could see downstream, though, there was none. I suspiciously slowed down to the pace of the current. Then I realized that just ahead of me there was flat water, but I couldn't see the base of the distant trees or shoreline. I was staring at a horizon, which must mean a drop. Do I stop and scout it? As I got closer, I could see the river on the far side, so it couldn't be too big. I stood up to try to see any rocks exposed below the drop and could see none. I had the impression this wasn't super huge, so I knelt in the middle of the canoe and went for it. The bow was over the drop before I could see the whole thing, about 3 feet. I leaned back in the canoe as I went over, and my bow remained mostly dry as it rebounded from near submersion. I passed through as smoothly as could be.

Below the drop the water changed. The river was fast and shallow with rocks strewn about. I was able to paddle around them as the sound of the falls filled my ears. But I could hear more ahead. The river narrowed and accelerated some more. The canyon walls closed in. The gradient of the river was evident as it spilled over ledges and was forced through curves and around more boulders. There was enough flowing to paddle smoothly and navigate the channel but not so much to create haystacks below the drops. As I flowed on through, a bystander might even have been fooled into thinking I knew what I was doing! Below the last drop under the tallest of the canyon walls, the river spilled into a deep pool. The hull splashed into it, and I was again in calm water.

A cry of exhilaration poured from my chest. A fly fisherman just downstream casually eyed me. I embarrassingly nodded as I drifted past, floating on down through the calm waters. I was the only one who could appreciate the thrill that the foolishness of not scouting the river had afforded me.

I figured there wouldn't be any major falls and that I could handle whatever came my way. And if I dumped, I'd simply get wet and let the river flush me out if that's what needed to happen. Yes, it was a risk. But a measured one that I was more than willing to take. It was precisely what this trip was for, and well worth it.

I got a little lonely in the early afternoon as I was paddling through a less interesting stretch of tag alders and marsh, but I arrived at the car soon afterward. Alas, the doubts that haunted me the evening before turned out to be baseless; it sat there unmolested. If I only had a dollar every time that was the case. I packed my gear and made my way back to Point, to rejoin the folly I was making of my misfit nature.

That trip sealed it. I still had no idea what I was to do with my life, but I knew I would soon have a canoe.

Boat 1: Ripple

There is a road, no simple highway
Between the dawn and the dark of night
And if you go, no one may follow
That path is for your steps alone.

—Bob Hunter

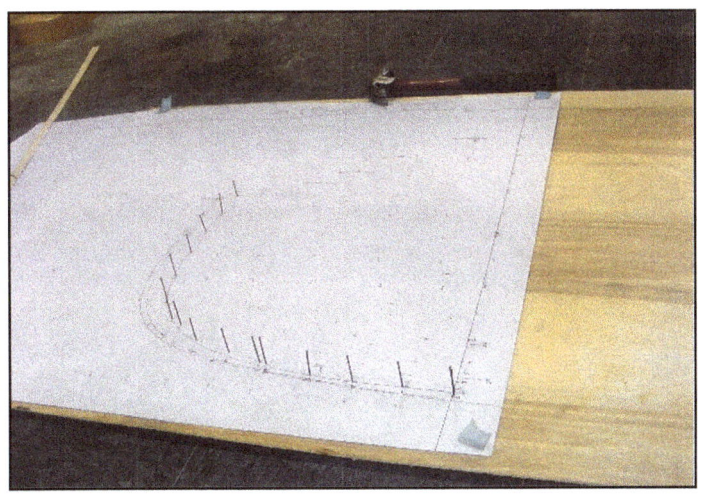

Graphing the table of offsets.

Creating Ripple: Partying Down in Lew's Garage

Pouring over the Process

That was the beginning of the summer of 1999. For those few months I lived with John and his girlfriend, just outside of Madison, where we worked for the same masonry contractor. He was going through an apprenticeship and I was working my way between college years as a laborer. In the previous semester at college, my principal mechanism for procrastinating was to spend hours looking up canoes and primitive survival arts online, wondering if I would ever have it in me to develop such skills or build a canoe myself. Then I stumbled across Newfound Boatworks and their cedar strip canoes. These were quite possibly the most beautiful human creations I had ever seen. Looking farther into the company, they sold kits and gave instruction on how to build these boats. Some type of black magic must be required, or so I imagined, to make them come together. But as days went on and I was drawn into this and other cedar strip websites the question arose if I could ever do this myself. Someday, when I had a job, a shop, the time, and the skill set, maybe I would be worthy of such an undertaking.

Work that summer was subject to the weather. When clouds gathered, a mason would use his trowel to draw a circle in the dust next to his mud board. "When there are four raindrops in that circle, I'm calling it a day." And most everyone would follow suit as the weather turned wet. On one of our rain days,

John and I went to a bookstore. I found myself thumbing through the book *Canoecraft* by Ted Moores, captivated for over 20 minutes. My other brother, Lew, once commented that looking at a book for more than 15 minutes was an indication that it would be a worthwhile purchase. But in these days of fortifying generic mac & cheese with instant rice to stretch my dollar, I wasn't sure I should spring for this book. Reluctantly, I pried the $17 from the pocket of my dusty jeans to cover the cost. Still, I was sure that if I ever took on a project like this, it would only be after years of practice as a woodworker and I had developed skills I could at this point only dream of. I would also need to acquire a fortune's worth of tools and a shop in which to build this thing. Yeah, right. Someday, maybe, if I'm lucky; when I'm about 60, ready to retire, and too old to enjoy it. But at least I had this book and could start learning about all the skills I didn't have.

The history of canoes was very interesting, and I saw that there were designs included in this book too. The plans consisted of a table of offsets for each model, and the construction methodology was about the same for all of them. Here is a brief idea of what goes on: A canoe is built on a set of molds that are stationed (station molds) along a plank mounted like a workbench (called a strongback). The molds, drawn from the table of offsets, are merely plywood pieces cut to exact shape of the inside of the hull, like a series of bulkheads that are located every foot along the boat's length. Strips of cedar are laid edge to edge over the molds to close the hull, like artificial skin over the ribs of a dinosaur skeleton. They are nailed to the molds temporarily, and their fitted edges are glued together permanently. When the hull is completely *stripped* the nails are pulled, all-night fairing and sanding parties thrown, the outside fiber glassed, and the hull removed from the molds. Slightly less intense all-night sanding parties are resumed for the inside, followed by more fiber glassing, then some trim and seats are thrown in. Well, things are a little more involved than that, with decks, stems, varnishing, getting materials, and in my case building the strips and molds.

After pouring over the process for a few evenings, I realized I could do the first step, selecting a design from the book and using the corresponding table of offsets to plot out the curves of each station mold on a piece of graph paper, effectively establishing the blueprints. On the next rain day I sourced the paper I needed and enjoyed the precision of plotting and drawing late into that evening. The station molds themselves, cross sections of the canoe at each foot along its length, were merely plywood pieces cut to the curves I had already plotted. Well, I could afford this and Lew (also living in Madison) offered the use of a bandsaw where he worked to complete the task. I did it in case I ever had a shop of my own to work in, and if I ever became enough of a woodworker to embark on such a journey.

Lew also had a garage behind his house. Out of morbid curiosity, he encouraged me to use it and get this thing going. I had read fairly far into the process at this point and things seemed doable, with maybe a step or two that I'd have to figure out, like steam bending and this sorcery of fiberglassing. One day at lunch I grabbed a piece of cardboard and sketched the strongback and its supports (the plank mounted horizontally for the station molds to attach to). The thin strips of cedar that comprise the hull would be easy enough to secure to the molds. I looked at this scrap of cardboard in my hand with the rudimentary sketch on it. This seemed doable…

I wanted badly to take on this project and had already found fulfillment in the time and consideration I had devoted to it. But if I took it on, I just knew I'd screw it up, and the whole thing would be a waste of money, time, and resources, not to mention an embarrassment to me in front of my family and anyone who knew about this debacle. But something in my gut told me I'd figure it all out. I felt that if I shied away from this now I might never do it, and cowering from meaningful challenges would become habit forming. My mind was telling me it was a ridiculous, irresponsible thing to take on, but my gut was screaming at me to go for it. *Goddammit, I'm gonna do it*, I thought to myself. This is going to be a lesson in why I shouldn't *bite a hog in the ass,* as my dad would say, but at this point it'll be easier to pursue this project than to ignore it. Afterall, I would find the money someplace and probably either finish it or flounder by the end of the summer.

That feeling of resolve was peculiar. Beyond the fear of imminent failure, I felt excitement over the prospect of the challenge, and a sort of relief to be following my gut. Something inside told me this was going to work, although I couldn't quite bring myself to believe it. It was like when I chose to run the rapids on the Prairie River. Once I was committed, the insurmountable fears of the imaginary unknown gave way to active response to the real situation. Sometimes following my passions has been the most impractical thing I could do, but the resulting stress from these conflicting options goes away once I start following my gut. The results have been some of the most rewarding and educational experiences of my life.

Partying Down in Lew's Garage

I scrounged tools from the smattering I owned, my dad, and a friend or two and piled them in my Nissan Sentra. Then I strapped lumber to the roof and moved into Lew's garage. It took forever to get the station molds aligned on the strongback, making sure they were at the right intervals on the plank, aligned to the center line, square, and plum in two directions. Once complete, I could sight down the strongback and envision the compound curves made by strips that would eventually span the gaps between station molds. This thing was taking shape! No longer just on paper or in my imagination, I had a physical creation to show for my efforts to demonstrate forward progress.

I burned up an old router of my dad's in milling the strips and used an old case of beer bottles to help establish the table for another router I borrowed. I moved on to installing the first actual pieces of this canoe, the curved stems at either end of the boat. A steamer was required to achieve the sharp curve of these laminate pieces, and the book showed a variety of models that would cook the wood into the requisite pliability. The one I settled on was a galvanized bucket with metal duct work protruding from a wooden lid on top. I picked up some pieces of dryer duct and made a T that was fitted to a 4" hole in the lid. As an extra measure for air sealing, I tore the weather strip off the door of my car and stapled it around the rim of the bucket. Surprisingly, when I balanced this contraption atop Lew's electric stove and plugged the ends with nasty socks, it worked! I got the stem pieces cooked and clamped to the forms at the ends of the strongback. One more horizon of new techniques was now overcome, with so many ahead that I still couldn't see the far horizon of this project.

Strongback.

Misfits with Common Ground

Mid-summer came round and that meant a party at the cottage thrown by my brothers and their friends. Stories from the different years of this tradition have become legends among members of that circle. Like the fiasco I escaped from back in high school, there was a lot of drinking, typically some wrestling, and usually some shenanigans that sprung from a bike race around the lake, king of the raft out on the water, or some other special event in any given year. Unlike the high school party where I remained on the fringes and fled, here I'd find myself in the center of the action, engaging by my rules. No littering, head shots, spilling beer, or using a hangover as an excuse to back out of anything.

This particular year I found myself by the fire late Saturday talking with one of Lew's oldest friends, Rob. They had known each other since middle school and Rob had become a good friend of the family. The conversation drifted through dispositions on society to the notion of breaking away from the usual concept of career, city, and economy. This was the first time I had actually bonded with a friend of my brothers at a mutual level, rather than lurking around as a young punk trying to hang with the big kids. As we fantasized about the notion of abandoning the norms we knew and forging our own path, we started talking about Jimmy Buffett, of all things. Turns out we were both Parrotheads. Going beyond the Caribbean escapism of his popular tunes, we delved into the insight and depth of his older, lesser known material. Rob recommended checking out one of his books, *Tales from Margaritaville*. We said goodnight in the early hours of the morning, just before the birds started singing. We had definitely struck a chord with one another. Rob headed back early the next morning, but I heard him open the patio door to the cottage soon after sun-up. I lifted my head from my pillow in the loft as he tossed a book up to me. It was a copy of *Tales from Margaritaville*. "If you want to follow that vagabond lifestyle, this'll feed the urge," and he headed out before I could say much of a goodbye. He was right.

Regaining the Post-Respite Rhythm

Back in Madison, I was now in the downhill side of summer and had to get a move on this canoe. It was difficult to understand a process I was only reading about and had never seen. The book I followed was great, but there were no online forums or videos to consult for details of the techniques that were so foreign to me. YouTube was just a figment of someone's imagination at that time. At some junctures, I wouldn't be able to visualize more than a step or two ahead as I muddled through things like shaping the stems to receive the strips or making cheater strips for parts of the hull with compound curves. Sometimes when the path wasn't clear, the only thing I could do was to take the next step and then go from there. Inevitably, as I took that first step, even if it were the only one I could see, others became clear as I progressed to them. At summer's end I had the first few strips on, but I had to go back to school in Stevens Point, almost 2 hours north. Only just begun, this thing was a far cry from finished. But I hadn't floundered yet!

Strips upon strongback.

35

Back at school I didn't talk about the project much with my friends. I wanted a short list of people seeing me take the fall as this thing blew up in my face, or when I abandoned it. I even kept it from my parents so they wouldn't try talking me out of it. They saw the project on one of their visits to Lew's place but kept their doubts to themselves. I can only imagine that my mom was quite concerned, and I think my dad sat back with curiosity to see what would come of this. That fall rugby, drinking, and hunting took precedence over the project, so it sat idle for a semester. It was in danger of drifting into the lost land of things started and never finished. I knew it, and something told me that if I let this go that I would turn my back on other things that are important to me. Between fall and spring semesters at school, I borrowed a kerosene heater from my dad and in the darkness of winter break reacquainted myself with the undertaking. Through the slowly growing daylight hours of winter, I incorporated the canoe into my routine. After attending class and going to work, I would drive to Madison to pursue the completion of this vessel through the nighttime hours. The first few trips to the shop were discouragingly unproductive and took a ton of effort. With time a routine was struck, and actual progress was made. The trips to Madison no longer required such deliberate effort, but became habit.

The canoe took shape as the hull was slowly closed in, upside down on the strongback. The momentum of the project took hold and it became my central focus, with my class attendance as the greatest casualty. I had a collection of CDs to accompany me, most notably the Grateful Dead, Jimmy Buffett, and Sheryl Crow. About half my evenings were spent in silence, however. I was fulfilling a dream and it felt amazing. The quietude was soothing, even reassuring as I focused my attention on the task in front of me. The smell of cedar, the stark shadows from my work light, and kerosene vapors (air quality was horrendous in this makeshift shop) set the character of these months of work. I lost myself in the late hours and toil of tapering thin pieces of cedar to a snug fit. I absolutely loved it. On March 20, 2000, on my third attempt at getting the right shape, I inserted the final strip to complete the hull.

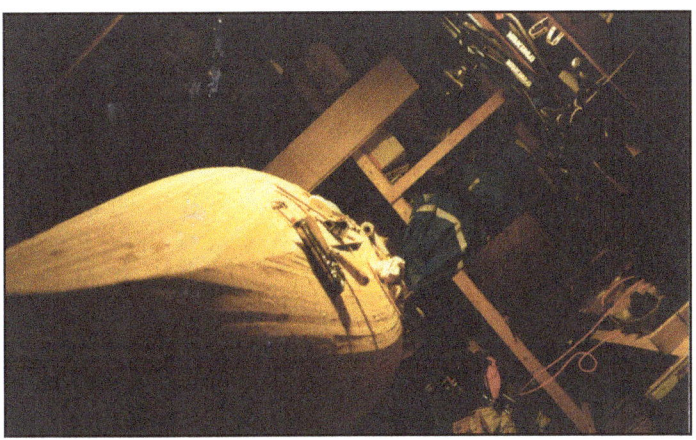

Ripple whiskey strip.

Now to remove the staples that fasten the hull to the strong-back. The row of station molds set the first impression of what the boat would eventually look like. Now that the strips filled in the hull, it added skin to the skeleton, revealing some absolutely gorgeous curves. Once the staples were removed, the only thing left to hold this flimsy structure together would be the glue between the strips. I supposed this would be an opportune time for the project to derail. I called the office manager at Newfound Boatworks for consultation. I was worried about the stress some of the strips were under as I installed them, creating an awful lot of tension in the hull. I was afraid that as I popped the staples from the strongback that the strips might spring loose, that the hull would explode. The office manager was taken aback at this question:

"What!!?! EXPLODE?!!? Um, no, I have never heard of that happening…"

I pulled the staples and the hull held together just fine.

After several evenings of sanding the ridges and hard spots out of the angular joints of strips, the canoe looked clean and sheer. If nothing else, it sure was beautiful. The last major chasm of ignorance that lay between me and the fruition of this craft was fiber glassing. I had figured out everything up to this point and understood the process for all the components of trim. This was the black magic part. In my mind, only people born with the skill could actually do it. I spent another hour on the phone with the folks at Newfound Boatworks getting a tutorial on the topic and read a few different takes on the process, considering things like hardener type, effects of heat, applying too much epoxy, under-saturating the weave of fiberglass, and other roads to dismal failure. Materials were ordered and had already arrived, with the only thing left being to jump in and do it. I was absolutely petrified. I mixed a small batch of resin and hardener and applied it to a scrap of fiberglass. It was easy enough to paint the resin onto the white cloth, and a bit of a wonder to watch the white fibers disappear as their saturation with epoxy turned them clear. Now for the boat. Same process, only more square footage. I ran into a few glitches but nothing too major. I ended up doing just fine-for my first time. To this day I still catch reflections of old bubbles, runs, and waves in the glass on the inner hull of the boat, but I smile at those bits of character and the lessons they taught me.

The days warmed, and after a few more coats of epoxy it was time to remove the canoe from the strongback. To this point, the project was a mass of parts, bonded to the concrete floor of the garage. It looked cool; hell, it even looked like an inverted canoe. But it had been dependent upon the station molds and strongback for its shape and form. To remove it would make it its own entity, one step closer to actually being a canoe. I figured that despite taping the edges of the station molds, they were still bonded to the hull of the canoe by so much of the glue that had oozed out between the strips, and only that held the hull together. Maybe the hull would fold in upon itself when I tried to pry it free? This thing still could not possibly work.

I went to the strongback and wiggled edges of the hull loose where I could. In some places it was really lodged to a station mold, so I unscrewed the mold from the strongback. I went to one end and lifted on the stem-no movement. I applied more upward pressure. The hull cracked and made a couple snapping sounds, and I knew that at any moment it was going to crumple like a ball of tinfoil. After these coronary inducing noises, the hull wiggled slightly, like a loose tooth. I went to the other end and did the same, with slightly less acute trauma to my person, even though the general level of stress kept rising. The tooth loosened more. My heart was racing; I couldn't think straight, and I just wanted this to be over. I hastily walked to the other end of the form, blindly grabbed it under the stem and with maniacal recklessness gave a sharp pull upward. SNAP!!! I forced open my clenched eyes, and the surprisingly light-weight canoe hull was in my hands, hovering above its home of 8 months. Nothing was shattered or exploded. Nothing folded in half or split apart. The hull, although flimsy, was its own entity, its shape perfectly preserved as it had been upon the strongback. That was where I invented the *Stationary Swamp Tromp Victory Dance*. I shamelessly had a little party of whoops and hollers as I danced around Lew's garage in celebration over this milestone. Looking back on the moment, how rightfully so.

Over the coming weeks, I spent several overnights in Lew's garage, sanding and glassing the inside. Lew came out to the garage late one evening and watched me sanding the inside of the hull. I had fallen into a routine of making it to Madison once or twice a week, sometimes only for the midnight hours, to work on the canoe. He sounded a little concerned as he pointed out, "Dave, you shouldn't work on this project past the point of it being enjoyable. This is not the sort of thing you want to burn yourself out on and grow to loathe."

The truth was, I loved being able to pour my effort and resources into an endeavor of my own. A project that was fun to work on and whose end product I could enjoy for a long, long, time. I loved the life lessons and craftsmanship this process was teaching. I knew that both would come back to reward me in the future. I loved the sacrifices I made. The opportunity cost gave the boat a sense of life investment and more substance. It was not simply handed to me like so many other things. For the first time in my life something was completely mine because I intimately knew everything that went into it. Working on this canoe became my passion. At these times, the question of who I was or what I was supposed to be never came up. I was in my element.

My parents were now following the process, and my mom, understandably, was wondering how I was able to pull it off. She asked once, "Dave, do you really have the money for this project?"

"Of course I can afford to build a canoe. I just won't be able to pay the phone bill."

It was ok, since the phone was only disconnected for a week or so, although that order of my priorities was not shared by my roommates.

The only thing destroyed in this process was a load of my brother's laundry—Why I was using the washing machine for an epoxy mixing station, or when the spill even occurred are beyond me. There's also a good chance I drove away with the household cordless phone atop my car, but that one has never been proven. I can't fully claim that one since we're only about 95% sure it was my fault.

Anyway, I got to work on the gunnels and installed them through the course of a 16 hour workday. Concurrently, I built the seats and center thwart. With those installed, I made up my own technique for decks and impatiently applied a few coats of spar varnish. I took the book's advice and had a name plate engraved at a local trophy shop—the book said this was a prudent measure. "You built it, you earned it." I agree.

Backwater Baptism

I christened Ripple on April 20, 2000, on the backwaters of the Wisconsin River near Stevens Point. My dad drove over for the event, although I was a bit less than enthused to have anyone else witness one of the most fearful events of my life. I fully expected this canoe, once placed carefully upon the water, to sit quietly for a moment before spontaneously rolling over and sinking to the darkest depths of whatever abyss it might be able to find. Well, an audience would make for a better story later on, I guess. He watched as I rolled the canoe off my shoulders and onto a pillow of water. It felt surreal that this thing should float so buoyantly, and level to boot! I very carefully climbed aboard and in udder disbelief at not rolling over, falling through the hull, or succumbing to some other calamity my imagination might invent, tried a paddle. I figured something was bound to go drastically wrong, but it glided silently, straight and true.

I got up at 4:00 the next morning to return to these strange backwaters of the Wisconsin River to explore more islands and inlets. This maze of sloughs and points made me feel like I was in the wilderness, yet it was less than 10 minutes from town. How had I never known about this before? Spring was in fresh bloom, and the world was coming alive once again with waterfowl, deer, eagles, muskrats, herons, and beaver. Dawn and dusk had always been spectacles to behold, but far more so from the water. My eyes were opening to explore the wilder, more intimate haunts of our waterscapes.

At the end of the semester I apologized to one of my favorite professors for skipping almost a third of his lectures.

"Sorry Dr. Brush, for missing so many classes of yours, but I've been busy with a project down in Madison."

"Oh, really? What have you been working on?"

"Well, I built a cedar strip canoe."

"REALLY?!? I just bought one! Aww, does it paddle nice... and the lines...how long did it take you? What are your seats made of...?"

As it turned out, he was almost excited about this thing as I was. Never mind the missed class, Dr. Brush understood that this project was a dream I was seeing come to light, an opportunity not afforded to some people through their entire lives.

The most striking and immediate notion I had upon building and christening this canoe was the sense of ownership. In looking at any detail of her construction, even to this day, I am reminded of the episode of Ripple's creation story that lent itself to that nuance, intentional or not. I still recall the reason and purpose behind the waviness of the hull between the accent strips of walnut against the softer cedar, the bubbles and ripples in the inner coat of fiberglass, and the small gap between deck and gunnel. The screw holes in the bow stem from the original brass strip bring about the recollection of the trickle the screw heads made as one passed along the waterline.

Because I chose not to use a kit for construction, I designed my strongback, cut out my forms, and ripped the strips. I routed beads and coves into respective edges of every single strip on that makeshift router table. I wanted this to be my project without dreading the regret of any shortcuts when all was said and done—even if the strips from a kit would have been a more consistent thickness with no saw-marks or knots. I have come to see the blemishes I built into the craft as a form of character, a viewpoint that let my guilty conscience ease back a little.

Other memories were added along the way. The uneven nature of the first waterline scribed to the hull from a wavy floor, the divet in the remaining brass ring upon the stern deck from a vibrating strap en route to a Boundary Waters trip. Others do not understand the details of these aberrations, or even notice them. But they're part of my history with this boat. If I were to sell this canoe, these stories would be lost, the new so-called owner having no clue they even exist. They'd just claim rights to this boat because they handed me a wad of cash, or more likely increased the number in my bank account by a few digits with their phone. True ownership is so much richer than mere possession or occupancy. It's a camaraderie that enriches our lives and reminds us of our life lessons from the creation or years of use of our things.

The other side of the education this boat provided was one of becoming intimate with who I am: my strengths, weaknesses, fears, and potential. Ripple helped reveal who I am and who I could become with the skills I acquired through the building process and doing something I honestly didn't think I had in me.

This was my first breakthrough. It would set a precedence of pouncing on opportunities as they arose to fulfill other ambitions. At the very least, a shred of pure color was streaking into my character that until this point seemed like one big, bland compromise.

Then Ripple and I ventured on waters throughout the state and beyond. These excursions were almost exclusively solo and became journeys inward as well as outward. I have explored dozens of lakes and rivers for hundreds of jaunts of self-discovery in this canoe. It has been exhilarating, sometimes scary, sometimes desperately lonely. But those journeys were always rewarding, and now my kids have paddled this boat. I still get out with Ripple and reacquaint myself with her personality on the water, like that of an old friend with whom I stay in touch. For a long time, she was hands down my daughter's favorite… until her newest sibling.

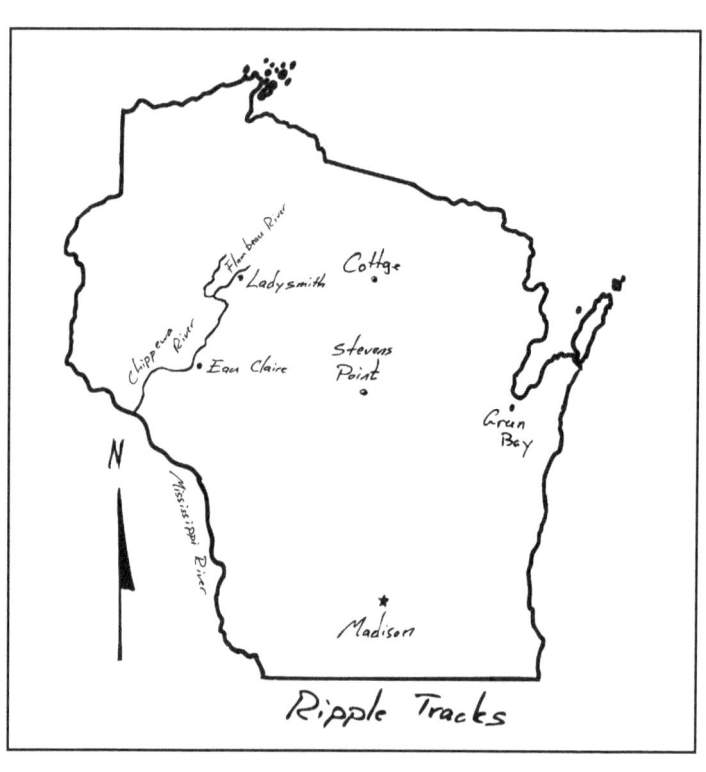

Experiencing Ripple: Paddling Wisconsin's Contributions to the Gulf Coast

Northwoods Trailer Solitaire

Jimmy Buffett quoted in one of his lesser-known tunes that he comes from where the rivers meet the sea, and that's why he's so wild and fancy free. Similarly, coming from the birthplace of the waters in Wisconsin has marked me in its own way. These headwaters have two destinations: the Gulf of Mexico via the Mississippi River, and the Atlantic Ocean by way of the Great Lakes and the St Lawrence Seaway. As I paddled more fluvial wonderlands of the state, I realized I dreaded turning my back on the water to return to my abode while the river continued on without me. I wanted to experience all the places where that water travelled. Also, the more places I paddled, I bore witness to the effects of our progress on these ecological havens.

I graduated from The University of Wisconsin Stevens Point in the spring of 2000 with a degree in Land Use Planning and a couple other things. Through no fault of that institution, I was unprepared to start a career. My privileged approach to education was to take it for granted and coast through, not applying myself. I became proficient at distracting myself with things like drinking, rugby, and Ripple. And now something was off. It just didn't feel right to jump into the work force as a cog in a great machine that I didn't really understand or agree with. So I applied for internships instead of permanent positions. I visited a suburb of Milwaukee to interview for a position with their planning and zoning department doing a street tree inventory for the summer. I arrived early and drove through the neighborhoods a bit. The large homes on serpentine streets with their neatly boxed off yards I thought would do better with green corridors running between the lots, narrower streets, and more pedestrian paths. The interview went well, and I was just about offered the position on the spot. As we all stood and shook hands, one of the city planners suggested I take a spin around a bit to see the results of work they had already done. I chose not to tell him that I already did so and saw things that, in my estimation, needed fixing. In that moment I knew I wasn't going to take this position, setting myself up for a job that would maintain this status quo of our notion of success. I smiled, thanked them for their time, and walked away.

Another interview I attended was for a seasonal position to manage the parks and boat ramps of Rusk County, WI. They were desperate for help and in fact did offer me the position on the spot. Logic would have dictated that I set myself up for a comfortable life in the burbs. Instead, I followed my gut to a summer of cleaning outhouses, picking up cigarette butts in campsites, and mowing lawns. In a grappling match between the pragmatist and the idealist within me, score another for the idealist.

I had gone to school, kept my nose clean, and coasted through my classes. I was drifting with the current of society, but the path seemed like it didn't quite fit. I was aware that I was unsettled. Hell, I was reminded of it every evening at sunset. By all means, I should have slid into the internship that would lead to a local government job that afforded a great suburban home and benefits. But instead of continuing to get carried along by the current, laughing the whole way through without caring who or what aspects of the wild earth were cast aside by my prosperity, I stiff-armed the vocational doorway before I was swept through it. I had some serious figuring to do in order to prepare myself for my role in this society. I had to get to know myself.

This was going to be the loneliest summer of my life, as I was desperate for direction and faced my indecision in solitude. I didn't know what to do for a living, but I refused to embrace a workforce I didn't believe in, where I felt so out of place.

I chose instead to move into a dilapidated aluminum house trailer in the boondocks of Rusk County, on the Flambeau River. This decision even made my dad nervous, so he insisted on coming with me as I moved in. After unloading my things (I was proud of the notion that I could fit my belongings in the back of a single pick-up), my dad and I went into the small town of Ladysmith to grab dinner and a beer and shoot a game of pool. He crashed with me at my new pad that night and left me with a case of Blatz Genuine Draft as a parting gift the next morning.

This trailer not having been lived in for 2 years, its rust-colored water took a while to make its way out of the tap. I chose not to use it. Rather than spread my few possessions throughout the house, I laid my mattress on the floor of the living room, set my table next to it with my lamp, and placed my book shelf made of 2x4s along an adjacent wall. This arrangement turned out to be a set-up I would re-establish multiple times and places in the future. I moved my few dishes to the kitchen area and placed my dad's case of beer in the fridge.

My lifestyle there was a bit unorthodox by current standards. I chose not to use the running water of the trailer-more for concern of my health than anything else, so I brought in jugs for drinking and I used the river for bathing. I was still faced with the uncertainty of my future. With no parties or rugby distractions, this question haunted me continuously. My stress would escalate to a crescendo of panic at times, and I'd snub it by going to bed at 7:30 just to get the day over with. I would rise early the next morning feeling great, as I was brought back to the moment. There would also be time to go running or paddling before work. Other times the panic came on in the middle of the afternoon. Working and living in the country, I learned to find beauty in my immediate surroundings in order to bring me back into the moment. It might be the wind wafting the lacy branches of a white pine, or the heads of geese poking above the grass of a roadside field that brought me back from my panic. Taking solace in the beauty and wonder of the present put my future back where it belonged, out there and not immediately upon me.

The Sunset Fear, Revisited

One of my books of that summer was borrowed from a college friend through the rugby circle: *Surfing the Himalayas*, by Frederick Lenz. This guy was snowboarding in the 80s before most people had heard of the sport. He followed his passion to Nepal, where he literally ran into a monk who became his mentor as he discovered and explored the philosophy of Buddhism. Frederick spoke about a loneliness that would overcome him in the Himalayan wilderness at times, especially when he was solitary at sunset. In those instances he longed for companionship, some society to mingle with or women to talk to. His mentor, Master Fwap, spoke a bit esoterically about the notion but explained that as the sun lowers in the sky, it is a time of power when we have access to larger realities. Lessons that we need to heed may become more apparent to us. And that is how I took it. That sunset fear I had experienced 6 years before and had chased and questioned ever since finally made a bit more sense. The panic that arose was the result of inner struggle and conflict that had been growing and was unacknowledged through the course of my youth. From that time on, whether that summer in Ladysmith, at Christmas in Ecuador, on the floor of a boat shop in upstate New York, or in the loft of a barn, any loneliness or desperation that crept in could be taken as a teacher of something that I had been missing. I could lean in and snuggle up to the fear and explore its depths to reveal the change required of me to bring my life into better balance. At long last, I had not beat the sunset fear but learned to utilize it as a prism of opportunity. I may still have been desperate for direction with regard to my future, but I was no longer fearful or lonely out of solitude.

The Ripple Effect

I embarked on numerous canoe trips that summer, afternoon or evening outings at first, on the Flambeau or Chippewa Rivers. For each riparian exploit, there is a consideration of logistics that is required. I need to somehow finagle my keister with my gear to the put-in, shuttle my vehicle between the put-in and take-out, and once at the end of the run, get my gear and my person back home again. There are no rules on how this is done. However, unless a person is motivated enough to carry a canoe on foot to the put-in and then from the take-out back home, a vehicle of sorts is necessary. Multiple runs to and from the put-in/take-out are required to get the requisite equipment to its necessary place. And while vehicles and things are being shuttled around, equipment is abandoned at either the put-in or take-out. So the two main questions are: a) How to shuttle the vehicle that carries the canoe/kayak, and b) How to secure the gear that is left on the side of the river someplace.

When more than one person is involved, there are generally two or more automobiles that are available for dropping off at the put-in and take-out. On solo excursions like in Ladysmith, I would use a bicycle with a car. Or, jogging works as well.

There was a connection to the landscape that I experienced a number of times through a routine of exercise and being outdoors. I would ride my bike into the office in Ladysmith to check in and start work, ride home at the end of the day, and get dinner going in my electric crock. Rice, beans, and cheese served up with corn chips was standard fare. Then I'd jump in the truck and drive downstream to Flater's Bar at the junction of the Chippewa and Flambeau Rivers. Rather than stop in, I'd park my truck and jog back up to my trailer where my dinner awaited. After that delicacy (my cooking was marginally improving), Ripple would be rolled onto my shoulders and we would head for the river. Before paddling, though, I needed a bath.

Bathing actually became its own ritual that I looked forward to every day. Wading out to the middle, about waist deep, I would turn to face the current with my toes gripping the cobbles of the riverbed. Cold water cupped in my hand would be run up one arm, then the other, to help me acclimate to the cold. Leaning forward to maintain balance, I lowered myself into the current until it rode up over the bridge of my nose. Gazing upstream in the dimming evening light, the world would wash down toward me at eye level. I was, in every sense of the word, immersing myself in the environment, and it was absolutely glorious.

The evening would be capped with a paddle/drift down to Flater's. Those couple of hours extended into the darkness of night as the transition from evening unfolded. The world came alive as deer emerged from their day's rest, racoons would scurry along the banks, and the flat watery reflection of the deepening hues of the sky were perfectly reflected off the water. An errant boil or two were some of the only revelations of this liquid media, along with the V-shaped disturbance in the water from an occasional muskrat or beaver. My metabolism easing back, I would begin to move at the pace of the water that bore me. An easy sense of calm would wash over that I eventually dubbed *The Ripple Effect*. At Flater's, Ripple would be mounted upon her gunnel pads to the roof, and I'd brace myself for the harsh sound of the truck firing and lights destroying the peace surrounding me as I made my way back to the trailer.

That sense of peace, revealed when moving at the pace of my environment, is what I wanted to derive from and promote with my livelihood. But where in the modern world is that possible for a beer drinking rugger like me whose idea of productivity is exhausting himself through the use of his hands and body in daily toil?

A Path Obscured without a Map

About mid-summer, I was at our cottage party with my brothers and their friends. I felt the familiar awkwardness of age and world view discrepancies with some of the crew. Ripple caught some attention, especially from my fellow Parrothead Rob, and we got to chatting again. He mentioned how he thought it was pretty cool that I built the canoe, how it'll last a long time to be something I pass down after I'm gone. Sort of a legacy. I supposed he was right. Just another perk of building Ripple, that perhaps she'd pass some of the lessons to others that I was able to uncover with her. By the fire, and over the course of a few hours that covered a lot of ground about society, we talked about how people are losing the ability to do things themselves, and again, how to get away from it all. We fell into easy conversation any time we were together after that evening.

I exercised my routine of county park maintenance for the remainder of the summer, in addition to working out and paddling. At the end of that summer, I paddled from the house trailer where I paid a whopping $120 rent for the 12 weeks I was there (on account that I still hadn't used running water), down the Flambeau to the Chippewa River, and on to the city of Eau Claire. My anxiety over the future hit an all-time high on the second day of this trip. I was on broad, slow water, baking under the sun. The banks were high and often obscured much of the surrounding landscape. The air was stagnant as my mood, and I had very little to distract me. Do I apply for jobs that go against my gut feeling? Go to work in the trades and have as little impact on this system as I can manage? Grad School (if by some stroke of magic I could get in)? Peace Corps? I finally figured I'd go back to tending mason for a few months to rebuild my checking account and go from there. Nothing to do but go with the current and wait out the doldrums until either something came along or I had some sort of brainchild that made me something other than a kid who didn't fit in with societal expectations. The problem was, it felt like I couldn't find the trailhead to this path.

Little did I know that this *was* the trailhead. I had faced down the sunset fear and tamed it into a tool I could use to find direction. What I lacked was a map, but what good would that even do if I was not yet familiar the landscape? It would take years of living and experiencing various facets of our economy and society that would enable me to draw my own map of the playing field and learn some of the rules. It would then be up to me to form a strategy for improving the landscape of our world. Here I was, with a college degree, longing for that last step of the process when I was just starting the first. No wonder I was scared.

I took a break at a portage around a dam to get some food and check in with my brother from a pay phone. Food in my belly and the sun on the wane, I put back in with considerably higher spirits. Coming into the waters of Lake Wissota, I raced a sloop against beam seas with the sun reflecting gold off the tops of advancing thunderheads. I made the dam and portage and set camp below on the lawn of a pumping station. Everything stowed, I dove into my tent just as the sky opened up in a thunder burst that lasted most of the night.

Next morning I paddled through the city of Chippewa Falls in dwindling rain singing Johnny Cash's *Ghost Riders in the Sky* at the top of my lungs. Skies cleared; I caught a small mouth bass, and I continued on to my ultimate takeout at the Eau Claire Dells Pond. I felt great, with 70s and sun sparkling on the waters around me, even if clouds were again on the horizon. How poetic a moment for my life in general. I'd take the storms as they came. For the moment, I reposed with sun and following seas.

The following May I decided to continue upon those waters from where I had left off. After paddling through the Eau Claire Dells Pond, I portaged *through* a paper recycling mill. Picture a 20 something kid in torn khaki shorts, a Hawaiian shirt, and sandals carrying a cedar strip canoe past people in white lab coats, hair nets, and ear protection working at machines the size of small houses in a mill the size of a football field. I made my way downstream, camped on an island, and next morning paddled out to the Mississippi River. The growing bluffs lining the river were nothing compared to the stone sentinels along Minnesota's eastern border. I made my way into the confused currents where the rivers combined and looked upstream as these towers stood in a row to watch over the greatest river basin in the land for as far as the eye could see. This new water was immense. Deep and wide, with a shipping channel marked by green and red buoys. Bigger water.

I turned downstream for a short spell to Highway 35. There I stowed Ripple and my gear in some bottomlands and hitch-hiked back up to my truck in Eau Caire. I was picked up by a guy who happened to know my cousin, of all things. He even drove me straight to my truck so I didn't have to walk through town. Funny, the connections that are forged and discovered as we embrace a bit of spontaneous interdependence of one another.

I made it to the Big Muddy. It felt like I would be back to continue the trip at some point, although I neither cared nor worried about when.

Sharing Ripple: Central City Meets
Central Wisconsin

Uncharted Waters

That summer of 2001 found me trying something new, as I accepted a boating instructor position at a summer camp that serves youth from Central Milwaukee. The experience opened my eyes to a whole new realm of issues I saw with our status quo. Social justice quickly became something else I was passionate about, as if I needed another dose of idealistic outrage at the wrongs imposed upon places, and now people, by this great machine of ours. One thing severely lacking for the youth attending this camp was connective experience to the natural world around. The camp director, after seeing my canoe, wondered if it might be possible for me to build one with the campers. Good Idea. It seemed to me that if the kids could see a boat building project through to the finish that it might provide some of the benefits for them that it did me. Maybe they needed this experience of creation, learning, and pride of true ownership even more than I had. There was no way, though, for the project that took me 6 months of consistent work to be completed in 6 weeks of camp.

An experience at the end of that summer provided a glimpse into a bigger part of the Ripple story than I could have imagined at the time. One of the teen counselors approached me about leading a canoe trip for the teen cabins. We came up with a 3-day jaunt on the Wisconsin River that required some serious string-pulling to bring together. We conducted advanced canoe lessons for the teens, including an afternoon trip to a park in Stevens Point so the kids could paddle in some current. We arranged to use almost every canoe the camp owned, plus two canoes from a different camp.

The kids each received laminated maps and compasses in the hope of learning navigation; we cooked our own food; and campers were in charge of their own gear. This was a huge accomplishment for kids who are so far out of their normal element.

The put-in was supposed to be at the end of a public road shown in my Gazetteer, but when we got there, passage was closed by a gate. Rather than portage a quarter mile to the river, we drove upstream to a riverside park for our put-in. Everyone made it to their canoes by late afternoon, and we paddled into a lowering golden sun on our western course. We approached a southern turn in the river, and I noted that the original put-in was just ahead. As we rounded the bend, there was a public beach sprinkled with middle-aged people engaging in conversation and enjoying themselves… with no clothes. *I had forgotten about the legendary nude beach at Mazomanie.* It existed after all. Well, that moment was an education for all. I'm not sure who was more surprised, the very white folks on the shore and in the river, or the black kids they saw from inner-city Milwaukee.

The rest of the trip was pretty straight forward but very long. Blisters were more common than drama, though, and everyone pulled together to make it a terrific success. *Perhaps sharing this kind of experience is something I should consider doing more…*

Dry Docked in the Cloud Forest

After summer camp I bounced between supplemental classes and the trades as I applied to the Peace Corps. My last few months in the US were spent in Ithaca, NY with a gal I was dating. I worked at Cayuga Wooden Boatworks and got to know a great crew of people led by Captain Dennis Montgomery. Then my departure date came up in February. I left the middle latitude winter and was stationed in Ecuador for 2 years.

The tropics were something completely different than I had experienced before. After a few months I wasn't sure what to do when the weather didn't start changing. I journalled more than once that there's just something I don't trust about a place that never gets cold. I lived in a house above a host family, with a four-room apartment all to myself. Again, with more space than I cared to fill, I hung a shelf from one wall of the main room that served as a pantry, built a table to cook at, and put a book shelf over another table where I ate, read, and did my journalling. I had one light that I used, but that drew too many insects. I opted for candlelight. In all, I lived for almost all of those 2 years without electricity in one room of a four-bedroom apartment.

Being on the equator, the sun set at about 6:00 every evening. That left a few hours each day for reading, writing, and thinking. Working on projects by day and myself at night, I developed a cozy routine. As projects got established with community members who became like family, I tried out a new activity called backpacking. I delved just deep enough to conjure up two new philosophies toward this new pasttime: what goes up, as in the terrain, just keeps going up; and that I don't need less or lighter gear. I just need a bigger backpack and to get stronger.

Aside from the community projects established with various people, I spent a lot of time in solitude. I reconsidered the questions and suspicions I had back in the states. Rather than being reality checked, my notions of environmentalism and social justice were reinforced, as I saw the same script played out in different ways in this developing nation. I also gave more serious thought to my future. I thought about the best things I had experienced in my life and how to expand them. The urge to keep following the waters still surfaced every once in a while, and I spent considerable down time reading up on hull design, wooden boat construction, and sailing rigging.

I also conjured up a concept that came to alternate between shaping my interpretation of and driving my approach to the world for over 20 years.

Art and Rugby Conception

With a little over a month left in my Peace Corps service we had what is known as the Close of Service (COS) conference. Our training group of 2 years previous rendezvoused at a beach side surfing and resort town called Canoa. About 30 of us gathered for a few days of paperwork, preparatory debriefing on the challenges of readjustment to the States, good food, and of course, a party. Stories abound from that weekend, but there is one small episode I would like to relate.

The second evening was our formal dinner. The hotel at which we stayed was very nice—the Ritz compared to what I would have sprung for (A friend and I spent a night in hammocks on the beach en route to this gathering, but that is a story for another book altogether)—and this was the evening of our formal banquet. A catering service provided a feast of steaks, salad, and fish. A particularly noteworthy morsel was a section of hollowed out cucumber served upon each person's plate, filled to its serrated rim with guacamole.

A good friend of mine sitting across from me, Caroline, noted the artistry of the creation. Caroline lamented eating a thing of such beauty as it is destroyed in the process. This opened the door to a concept I had been pondering for quite some time, and I jumped at the opportunity Caroline had laid out for me. For once, all the ideas in my head stayed out of the way of the words coming from my mouth as I stated with uncharacteristic eloquence something along the lines of the following:

> Caroline, not only should you enjoy the aesthetics of the creation in front of you, but you should relish the flavor and life giving sustenance it affords. Food and vitals such as this are the climax

of human endeavor, for they combine the two most basic and omnipotent elements in human experience: Art and Rugby.

You see, Carrie, everything we do in this existence is some combination of art and rugby. Rugby is the maintenance, toil, and bare sustenance of our livelihood. Art is the aspect of an activity or endeavor that enhances our lives to bring meaning, beauty, culture, and growth into our lives. Laundry duty, for example, is mostly rugby. We simply must grin and bear it as a necessary part of our lives, or pay someone else to do so. Other rugby-esque endeavors include washing dishes, mixing concrete, eating lousy, unhealthy food, going to the bathroom, and, all too often, breathing. In my view, rugby can be an outlet for rage through fighting, listening to hate music, or even warfare. Things done mostly for art, however, may include painting, listening to classical music, drawing, planting flowers, etc. The best is when the two combine in a balanced entity that is both graceful and util.

Don't get me wrong, this is not totally my idea. Dualities in nature have existed since the beginning of recorded history. Dark and night, male and female, form and function, yin and yang... all are ways of interpreting our world according to a system of measures or values. I simply took the idea and made it my own by applying two very real entities from my own life.

At this point Brandon, a highly respected friend of mine, piped in. He is well read, intelligent, creative, and completely unashamed to breach nearly any conversational topic in any circumstance, particularly sex. Brandon pointed out that "Dave, I agree with the idea of duality in our lives, but I don't know if art and rugby are exactly the two that work the best." My response was more or less as follows:

Of course not, Brandon. Every person's duality is different. The entities are something you know intimately and which are highly integral components of who you are. For you, Brandon, it may be Photography and Masturbation.

Brandon was dumbfounded by the genius of the idea. He exclaimed, "Yes, that's exactly what it would be...At the same time!" I responded again:

Of course at the same time, Brandon. Every human endeavor is some balance of the two, and when each entity is maximized, the ultimate pinnacle of human achievement is realized. Like in Carrie's guacamole creation. It is delightful to behold by the eyes as well as the taste buds, but it is also highly nutritional. The ultimate balance of Art and Rugby has thus been realized, or in your instance, masturbation and photography.

I realized in the table wide silence that followed that all eyes were pinned on me. Had my nerves not been numbed by the alcohol I'd ingested over the previous days, I would have turned three shades crimson and finished my meal with my eyes pinned to my plate. Such was not the case, however, so I took up my glass of wine, sat back in my chair, and enjoyed a long draught of its boldness enhancing goodness. Nurse Sara spoke up and questioned my need for more visits to the nurse's office for head examinations. The twinkle she had in her eye, however, showed that she was only covering for a deeper level of wonder (whether at my sanity or the genius rolling around in my attic, I've no clue). My buddy Kyle, with whom I had already discussed the dualistic nature of our world, nodded in support of my soap box declaration.

> The art of this hors devours is its physical beauty and the tasteful combination of texture and well blended foods, in concert with the appealing flavor of its fresh composition. Its rugby is the sustenance it lends your body. Both the guacamole and the receptacle in which it is served (the cucumber) are extremely healthy for human consumption. As such, may we enjoy this bit of soul strengthening indulgence.

I find ancient philosophies and folklore interesting, but I cannot say I go out of my way to study them. I was informed on some principles of the art Tai Chi at different times, and it sounded a little nebulous, as did the philosophy of Daoism of which it is part. I commented that it seems to be about opposites and how they balance each other. The person I was talking to, who I don't think was merely pretending to be more informed than me, said that was a pretty good summation of it, in a word: *balance.*

It is probably some sort of ego thing again, or I suppose it could be laziness, but I have not studied the yin and yang since then. I wanted to expound on this idea in my own head before I was overly influenced by the school of thought (definitely an ego thing). I really like the concept of the checks, or complimentary nature, of two oppositional forces. I shied away from the Yin and Yang because they still seemed a bit foreign to me and did not do much to spark my interest. Because I tend to see the world through analogies of things I regularly engage with, rugby has provided a metaphor for many experiences I encounter. This on its own did not cover a whole range of enterprises and items. There needed to be a complimentary entity. As my general approach to just about anything involved the rugby I was familiar with, it was ok that refined things I was not so familiar with were related to through a concept I had a similar unfamiliarity. Art-perfect. These two entities do well to describe the forces I see governing our lives.

The balance of rugby and art exists within everything we do. With a pinch of rugby brought into boat building, I had the resolve to boldy wield a spoke shave for efficient reduction of my stem. With the proper balance of art, I was able to derive the sweeping curves of Ripple's gunnels. The proper balance is sought in everything we do to make things easier, more effective, more graceful, or get results faster.

When a bit of art is thrown into a batch of aroused rugby, magical athletic feats can happen. In playing ping pong, I have surprised myself at my precision and reflexes. I find myself not thinking so much as reacting. Becoming part of the situation at hand and thriving in the long, fast volleys (these volleys usually end when I realize how well I'm doing, surprise myself, and start thinking too much about the situation). Outstanding tackles, terrific passes, and nimble running moves can happen in rugby fixtures. Or sometimes I actually find my limits on a mountain bike and approach them in elegant sweeps of singletrack.

A dash of rugby in a whirlwind of art can send a writer or painter on an inspirational rage and the brush strokes or words seem to materialize out of thin air. It could result in a person hammering out 15 pages as fast as the pen can fly, or forceful strokes with the planer or blows to the chisel that hone that strip to look as if it had grown into its joint with the others. A pinch of rugby lends a bit of firmness to a person's touch at just the right moment that sends a partner over the edge and into some sensual odyssey.

The correct balance runs a person along the razor edge of maximum performance, operating completely in the zone, or however you want to describe it. It makes the humanly impossible flow with ease, and all it takes is balance within our environment. It necessitates knowing our tools, the trail, ingredients, colors, partner, the playing field, or the materials with which we are working. It separates superstars from athletes, artists from chicken scratchers, craftsmen from hacks. If only I were able to bring that balance into more areas of my own life, I would not drop passes, leave tearouts in my oak gunnels, add too much peanut butter to my pasta sauce, leave sketched lines untrue, or bull my way over rocks in the bike trail.

If the idea sounds really foreign, think about it the next time you don't have a smooth thing to say to someone you're attracted to, are unable to find rhythm on the dance floor, are too intimidated by the cold rain to get out jogging in a beautiful storm, can't cast your fishing jig to the spot you need it, have a hard time lifting a box that is sometimes hefted with ease, or awkwardly paw at your partner instead of lending a tender touch. It is too much of one aspect of your duality or not enough of the other?

Many get rugby pounded into them whether they like it or not. People get kicked around enough and it hardens them or puts them at a different level than others who have been sensitized by a gentler life. They are forced to dig down to a bolder level of ruggedness in coping. The rugby needs to come out, and it does. Instead of being channeled constructively, the dam may be blown and the torrent cuts its swath. Emotional, physical, sexual, and substance abuse may be the channels of least resistance. The baggage is passed to others, and if they can't shoulder it, the cycle of harm continues.

Someone who comes from a background with substance or personal abuse may be living at a different level of survival than someone who hasn't had their physical or emotional well being accosted by such threats. The ones who are battle calloused may be able to deal with life's blows, but they may have a harder time refining themselves to relate to the emotions or less dramatic struggles of others. The best we can achieve is the strength to forge a balance between the trials and the indulgences.

As the entities we relate to can only be things we identify with, I wouldn't expect very many people to buy into the metaphor of Art and Rugby, any more than a person might adopt Photography and Masturbation. Perhaps Backpacking and Dancing would be a better fit for some. As characteristics of Art and Rugby hold specific meaning to me, I can use them to make sense of the balances and imbalances of my life. Any two entities are inappropriate for everyone who does not share this symbolism. Everyone needs to find their own balance, just as we need to be our own guide along our path. There are no guiding lights other than the intuition we as individuals have to find our own way. Art and rugby just happen to be the ends of the scale by which I measure the contours of my life's terrain. Having an idea of the composition of that terrain, I can better choose the route and strategy for the trail I blaze through it.

Disclaimer

While the previous chapter may not have much of anything to do with boats or boat building, I see Art & Rugby in every aspect of both. This philosophy has helped me define my path and find ways to navigate it. And their role in the path of my life is ultimately what the boats of this book are all about anyway.

Boat 2: Whisper

Truth doesn't need to scream. It whispers.

Creating Whisper: Setting up Shop in a Gorges City

The Ithaca Saga

Upon returning stateside, the call of the Big River grew stronger. Taking advantage of regular internet access, I began surfing the web and found the perfect boat design for the remainder of the trip that had started in Ladysmith 5 years previously. The Lincolnville Salmon Wherry from Duck Trap Woodworking was originally used around the 1850s for salmon fishing along the coast of Maine. High sided for taking heavy weather, it can carry big loads and is a beauty to behold. Perfect for the Big River. Since I don't know how to pack efficiently, my backpacking philosophy of get stronger and carry a bigger backpack was extended to this boat design. This pulling boat was big enough for all my camping gear with room to mount a bike to the bow.

I was again faced with the dilemma of a shop. I had my connections at Cayuga Wooden Boatworks out in Ithaca, NY, from working out there before my time abroad. I contacted Captain Dennis and talked with Trish, the office manager, on the phone. I asked if they needed help for the fall haul-out, pulling boats from their slips and hoisting them up on beams for dry docking through the winter. Trish told me to get out there, and we'd worry about where I'd stay once I arrived.

I bought some tools online, packed a box full of ones I already had, packed my huge backpack, and hopped a bus for Ithaca. I had plans, a shop, and now only needed a place to sleep. The floor of the shop looked cozy, and Trish brought in a hot plate, air mattress, and even a bicycle so I could run out for errands and groceries. Without her, this would not have been one of the top three places I have lived. I made myself at home in the upper loft of the shop, right next to the space where I would try piecing together this next vessel.

I worked through the seasonal haul out, dragging steel beams along piers and climbing in the rafters of the boat house to rig a crane for lifting the boats. As the weather turned (my first glorious winter stateside), I worked alongside the shipwrights in the shop.

Evenings were spent working on this new boat. I built a jig, similar in concept to the strongback that I built for my canoe. The stem, keel, and transom were applied to this and their edges beveled to receive the planks. Planks themselves were laid out and spiled from a pattern that took lines from the jig. This was tricky with all the compound curves, but what I lacked in precision I made up for with epoxy thickened with sawdust, known as dookie schmutz, to plug any gaps in my less than light-tight joinery.

I had about 5 months to work on this boat before returning to Wisconsin. This meant I didn't have the luxury of muddling through the process and taking my time as I had with Ripple. I often reminded myself of the need to take bold action, even when I didn't know what precisely to do next. At times like this I would ask myself, *What would someone do next who actually knew what they were doing?* Then I'd just impersonate that craftsman and move forward with bold strokes that were empty of confidence and security.

After glueing up and scarfing together my 1½"x10"x16' keel board, I laid out the center line. From that I was able to establish the broad arc of its outer edge. This curve was drawn at a late hour, so I awoke before work to cut it out with a circular saw. Bright and early, I started at the port bow and cut my way along the left side of the future keel toward the stern. Reaching it, I turned around and worked toward the bow on the starboard side. As I was cutting, it occurred to me how straight this line was that I followed. Turns out I was cutting the center line and not the curved edge of the piece! Without internalizing my blunder and giving myself the appropriate level of flagellation, I quickly took some scrap I had just removed from the port side and ripped a sliver just under 1/8" on the table saw. I tapered an end at roughly the diameter of my circular saw blade and made up a batch of dookie schmutz, about like soft peanut butter. I slathered up the sliver in this goo, and slid it into the erroneous saw kerf I had made in my keel. The disaster had struck and was fixed before my 8:00 start time for work, so no sweat. Besides, this boat was going to be painted anyway. Blunders like this afforded me the opportunity to develop, and

Feminine curves.

with repeated misjudgments hone, the concept of an *acceptable level of imperfection*. Less fixable mistakes were largely prevented by the boat builders Dave, Don, and Tom, who gave me plenty of guidance as I pieced together the hull, replicating, at least to some degree, the 170-year-old design. This train wreck had left the station!

Once fastened to the jig, I plotted the rabbet lines for receiving the first (garboard) planks on the keel. The result is a pair of matching curves that, if looked upon with a certain eye, could be seen to resemble a slender figure in a long dress, belonging to a dusky-voiced singer with thick curls in a smoky cocktail lounge ... if one were to look at it a certain way and use their imagination.

Checking My Course

At times I would work late into the night, to the point of sleep deprivation and exhaustion. It was hard to stop after I was in the flow. More than once, it might be two or three in the morning before I would finally make a bleary-eyed mistake that would throw my frayed nerves over the edge. I'd freak out and, feeling that the world had just ended, drop my tools on the floor, blow up my leaky air mattress, and crash out. Other times, doubt crept in. What was I doing in this place of strangers anyway? I had just been 2 years out from family and friends during my flinger in Ecuador and here I was, gone, *again*? A song by Neil Young came over the airways that really made me think twice about what I was doing. "*If you follow every dream, you might get lost.*" I considered that for quite a while:

> *I'm trying to chase down every inclining I have, aren't I? Is this too much? How can I bring it back into the Wisconsin world of who I am and where I come from? Wait a minute, this boat is everything of who I am. I'm building it myself out of wood. It's for a trip I've wanted to do since high school. It is part of a larger dream of sharing this experience with youth someday. This dream won't get me lost because I know what I'm about. This dream is a matching fit to everything I want to do with my life. If you follow every dream without knowing the essence of what you're after, you might spread yourself too thin, cross your lines in contradictory endeavors, and get lost. I'm following every dream I have right now. I'm in a spectacular place revisited, and it's tying me closer to everything else I want to do. This isn't a path that will get me lost, it is bringing me to the hearth where my soul-warming fire burns. This is the closest I have ever come to finding my … Home.*

On the nights of even the most intense and manic tantrums, this thought process brought me back into the moment and I was able to sleep well, knowing I was on the right path. Sometimes I would step out of the shop at dusk to get some fresh air and measure my path against the sunset. Inevitably it reassured me. Although solitary, I kept myself comfortable living by the warmth of my dreams.

Over the course of a few weeks, the hull took shape. In establishing the planks, I replicated a process for each one, separately on both sides of the boat, called spiling. A thin batten of wood is applied to the jig along the upper edge of the new plank. A thin pattern plank is laid in roughly the space of the new plank. A slender (scalene) triangle of hardwood is placed with the long point where the batten meets a station mold and traced on the pattern. A line established on the previous plank is marked on the pattern in the same way. The pattern is then laid upon the plywood from which I cut the planks and the triangular outlines guide the triangle placement for the marks to be transferred to the plywood. A batten is bent to the marks and the plank traced and cut. This *spiling* is the black magic from which boat planks are derived.

It takes time, a few hours. I always tried making two planks per evening, or one lap around the boat, but I was never able to do it. One night I went through the process of establishing, marking, transferring, tracing, and cutting a plank. When I lifted it from the floor to the boat it broke under its own weight due to a void in the plywood laminates. Several hours of work

Rabbet line.

Sheerplank spile.

Second plank.

Garboard plank install.

down the tubes. This event filled me with an energy that greatly expedited the breaking of the plank over my knee into many pieces that were no more than a foot long and discarding them to a neat pile on the shop floor below, and I went to bed. One of the shipwrights came in the next morning and noted, "looks like it was a bad evening to be a boat builder.".

I developed a routine for covering the basics needed for life on the floor of the shop. On Saturdays, the Ithaca Farmers Market called to me and worked well as my source for groceries. I also started running a few evenings a week. I was living in my usual austere way, but I was comfortable. I was able to enjoy the present because, well, I was living one hell of an adventure that contributed to a plan for the future. I was making progress on the boat, enjoying the good company of the crew in the shop, and loving this chapter of my story.

A strong indicator of my path would come on as the sky started turning pastel colors out the big showcase windows of the shop. My easterly perspective through this glass afforded beautiful views of the back sides of sunsets. The quieting hours as the sun approached the horizon brought on a calm easiness that assisted the transition from my employment with shop-work to shipwright. I felt at home as I got back to spiling, like rejoining with a close friend.

Just a block down from the boat works is the Boatyard Grill, the fanciest restaurant in town. I looked out the glass showcase windows in the afternoons and watched the pretty waitresses go by on their way to work. Then as night fell, the people would come by the carload. All dressed up, shuttled to the door via golf cart as the parking lots filled. These people had arrived at their place in the machine, and society was rewarding them for it. They had warm, comfortable beds to go home to and what I imagined to be comfortable lives to live at the head of the community. Here I was alone in the shop, sleeping on the floor, scraping by to afford this project.

Late at night sometimes when Dave, the head shipwright, would be gone I would have all the lights off except in the loft where I was working. I had taken the loft rail down so my boat could be seen from the street. I imagined the waitresses looking up at it as they returned to their cars at night, watching my progress and wondering what I was doing working on it so late, all alone, on a Friday or Saturday night. Even though I knew better, the thought gave me the feeling of a romantic starving artist, chasing his dream and putting off the good life so that he could realize something all his own. Boy, am I ever a glory hound. I tried not to fall into such self-absorbed back patting, but sometimes it did get lonely and those thoughts were comforting. I would crawl into the sack, alone, but it was alright. The fire of this boatbuilding dream was enough to warm my bed.

Moving the Show Back to Wisconsin

In January 2006, my dad drove out to Ithaca to pick me up, along with the hull I had created. It was planked up to the sheer; I had attached an outer gunwale; and the cutwaters and shoe were affixed to the outside of the hull. I even steam bent some oak ribs to reinforce the structure. We built a cradle for the boat in the bed of his truck and drove it back to Wisconsin after touring Ithaca and making lunch for the crew at the Boatworks. That was a good subchapter for me.

Completed hull.

Outer hull flipped.

Back in Stevens Point, I rented a room in a house sight unseen. Whisper was stored in a rickety garage with no door and no possibility of serving as a shop through the Wisconsin winter. I took some classes and worked part time. I started running more, but still had spare time. There was something more I felt the need to do. I wanted to share the meaning of all these stories and experiences somehow. I tried writing about the two boats and my Peace Corps experience. The pieces of the story were scattered, and cynicism came out in everything I tried to get into words, making for a pretty dismal manuscript. I still had a giant chip on my shoulder because we live so distantly from, and continue to destroy with our everyday lives, the resources that sustain us. What my ego would not allow me to see were the missing pieces of this puzzle. I still had some living to do before it all made sense, despite my rush to force the story's conclusion.

After a couple-month hiatus on the boat, I rented the perfect shop space from a friend, bought a homemade trailer, and my old rugby buddy Tackleberry helped me move the hull to its new home. I moved into the pantry of an actual house with a couple of fellow rugby players for $100 a month. Finally, after a marathon of late nights and long hours, Tackleberry and I drove the finished boat to the cottage for christening at the annual party.

I had one last task to finish this thing off, to carve a mast out of a balsam fir tree I had cut the year before. I debarked it, ripped its curved edges and taper off with a chainsaw, and used hewing axes to round out the resultant square piece. As I stood over the braced log with a chainsaw, wearing khaki shorts and sandals (not OSHA approved), my dad walked up.

"Ya know, If this were 3 years ago, I'd chew your ass for doing something so silly. But I gotta say, I've seen you pull through on enough things that I'm just gonna let you be."

Thanks Dad.

On July 15, 2006, Whisper was set afloat for the first time on Long Lake in Lincoln County, WI. I was a rat's nest of frayed nerves, but he floated true, rowed like a dream, and I was even able to hoist sail for a spell upon my new mast. We toured Long Lake and stopped to crash what turned out to be a huge birthday party. As my buddy Earl and I grabbed the quarter barrel from Whisper's bilge, we wondered if we should really be imposing ourselves. But since Tackleberry was already on the dance floor, we were already in it too far to turn back. We did leave, however, when the keg floated empty in its ice and we noticed the side-eye looks from a few guys.

It was an amazing christening.

We got Whisper back to Point, where he bore us on a number of fishing trips. I was working with a stucco crew lead by an old rugger alumnus for the rest of the summer of '06, slapping stucco on new homes and businesses. September came, and I was trying to save some money while taking classes toward a teaching certificate. The university wanted me to spend four to five more semesters in getting the certification. That seemed a bit much for me, especially since I only wanted to teach so I could get a boat building program going in a school. I needed to find a more streamlined approach. So, when spring semester came round, I went back to work full time and focused on an immediate dream. Teaching was something I was definitely going to pursue, but I knew there to be certification programs out there that would only require two semesters of classes. When the time was right, I would put my energies toward that end, but it would require me to keep working and student teaching all the way through the acquisition of a teaching position. And then I would be tied down to a career. Best get the rest of this dream underway now while I still can, and while I am still young.

That winter, I set to outfitting the bilge with a set of floorboards that could also be locked between the seats to secure gear should I have to leave the vessel unattended. Through this time, Whisper was tucked nicely in the shambles of a single stall garage at the rugby house, and I was able to use a wood shop on the UWSP campus for carpentry.

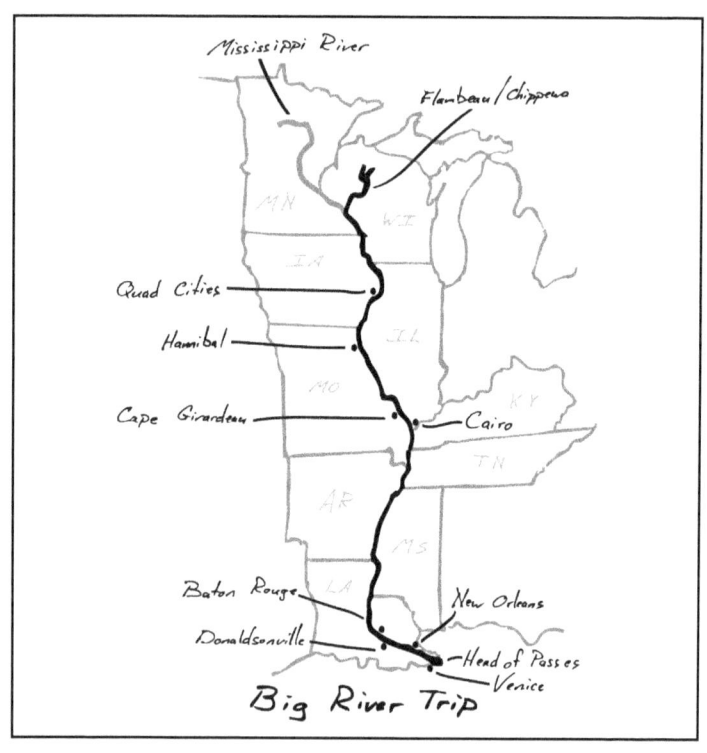

Mississippi River

Flambeau / Chippewa

MN

WI

IA

Quad Cities

IL

Hannibal

MO

KY

Cape Girardeau

Cairo

TN

AR

MS

Baton Rouge

LA

New Orleans

Donaldsonville

Head of Passes

Venice

Big River Trip

Experiencing Whisper: The Big River Trip

Preparation Pressures

I got online to check out accounts of people who paddled the Mississippi River. This was one dream that had sat on the back burner long enough. I ordered navigation charts but found they were only available for the upper portion of the river—the printer must have broken at the Army Corps of Engineers and they couldn't run off any more. I poured over my camping gear I had used on 3-day trips and tried to imagine what would be needed in the course of 3 months on the water. I broke the trip into departments in order to cover all the things I needed, then broke that list into an outline. I picked up a new stove, a solar panel that could charge a cell phone and run a small weather radio, a water tight box for my food, an old army ammunition box for my electronic junk. Dry bags, line, a new water filter, and LED navigation lights (they are not designed to be navigation lights, but being sold in red, green, and white colors, I stuck Velcro to them so they could be mounted to my boat) were all assembled.

I finished building the deck that would slip into the bilge of Whisper's forward compartment, providing a level surface for stowing my gear in addition to keeping it out of the water. Then, if I would leave Whisper for an extended time, the deck could be placed over the aft compartment and locked in place between the seats, forming secure storage for odds and ends I would leave behind. Finally, a mount for the fork of a bicycle fastened to the bow rounded things out for the Big River Trip.

When everything seemed to be assembled, I still felt lacking. I pictured myself adrift in current with barges bearing down on me, in heavy rain at night. How could I ever be prepared for such a circumstance? I read accounts of canoes passing through the locks on the river, just like any commercial vessel. The procedures did not seem overly complicated, but how could that be? This trip is over 1500 miles. How could this meager supply of gear see me through it all? The river, a culmination of all the waters of central North America, could not possibly be navigable in a craft this small, could it? I pictured myself on the river, realizing I dim-wittedly forgot toilet paper or some major piece of equipment any novice would have remembered.

So I went through a checklist. Life jackets, oars, oar-locks, lines for tying off, an anchor for mooring. Ok, I have my propulsion. Now, what of camping? Tent, sleeping pad, sleeping bag. What else is there, really? Tackleberry gave me a folding chair as a measure of luxury-came in handy too. Alright. Now what about clothes? I would need warm clothes at the start, shorts later on, and rain gear throughout. Ok, I can pack for that. What about personal stuff? I hadn't worn deodorant in 10 years so that was out, but I figured I would need a toothbrush, toothpaste, sunscreen, sunglasses, bandana, soap, shampoo, a camp towel, and since I may not bathe or shower every day, baby powder may help keep everything a little fresh. How about food? I had a good mess kit, and I picked up a stove. I would have 5 gallons of water storage plus a gallon jug to drink from, in addition to water-bottles for the bicycle I was to mount on to the bow of the boat. I had a huge food wanigan, so I eventually went to Aldi's to load up on mac & cheese, rice and pasta dishes, cans of beans, fruit, and the makings for PB&J sandwiches. Good enough.

For navigation I had my charts, and for the beginning of the trip, the indispensable Delorme Wisconsin Atlas and Gazetteer.

The Army Corps of Engineers said they would have charts for the lower parts of the river come May, but that would remain to be seen. I also had a headlamp, compass, emergency air horn, flares, weather radio, cell phone (my mom insisted I take hers since I refused to buy one of my own), digital camera, navigation lights, and a solar panel to keep everything going. Of course, there were other odds and ends: basic tools, fire starting/ wood cutting gear, book, stationary, hip waders, bike lock, camp shovel, extra fuel, bilge pump, garbage bags, and dry bags rounded out the arsenal.

The trip occupied my thoughts at work, at home, and in my sleep, but for some reason I had a hard time picturing myself on the river, thriving, and doing this thing successfully.

The other side of me was dreamy and optimistic: the river will be an extension of trips I have done already. The cool part will be when I get to the Gulf and sail along the Coast. Hell, why not go out to Key West, or even to Cuba?

That was to be the nature of the trip; I did not know when it would end, or how far I would make it. I figured I would last at least a week or so, even if I found the river un-navigable and camped out someplace for a few days.

I would at least put that much of an effort in. But maybe after 2 weeks I would have enough and call it quits. Or if I made it to my sister's place in Memphis, that might be far enough. But if I make the Gulf and it looks feasible to sail for a while, I think I just might. As is the case in so many other times, We'll have to see what happens.

Just in case, I did buy nautical charts of the Gulf coast.

Shaky Sea Legs

The original put-in was to be round St Patty's Day, before the equinox. The need to finagle a way to get back for Lew's wedding and missing an annual canoe outing with my friends persuaded me to hold off for a month. After a beautiful April day on the Wisconsin River with about 20 friends, I found myself on Sunday battling sleep deprived weariness, packing Whisper to see where all this junk was going to fit. Monday, April 30, 2007, my parents came by Point to help me pack up all my belongings from the Little Blue House and load Whisper for The Big River Trip.

This trip being an extension of the trip down the Chippewa River a few years back, I figured to put-in from the last town of that river, Durand. I talked to our friend Sparky, and he suggested putting in by his house in Caryville. What the hell, it would only be an extra 20 miles or so. Dad and I drove to Sparky's place and got dumped on by spring rains along the way. If my gear were to make it down the river, it would have to be able to withstand these showers.

When we arrived at Sparky's, I was surprised to see Lew and his buddy Eric were also there to see me off. We drove to the Chippewa River early in the evening under grey skies that threatened rain. I mounted John's relic of a mountain bike, the Sedona (complete with a rack and grocery basket) to the Whisper's fore-deck, and started backing toward the boat ramp.

"Whooooaaa!!!! Hold it! STOP!!" I heard through the rolled down window.

"What the hell could be the problem?" I thought. I was a nervous wreck already, and complications were the last thing I needed.

Well, since I was moving out from the Blue House at the same time as starting this trip, there were more things loaded in the truck than just those I would use on this excursion, like a canoe mounted on the rack in the bed of the truck. As I backed up, the ass end of the canoe swung into the bike, trying to pull it from its mount on Whisper's deck.

Off with the bike, and let's try this again. I think the only time I was ever this nervous was at Whisper's christening party. But without further mishap, we launched Whisper and I refastened the Sedona to the bow. Dad's dog, Brandi was nervous too. She knew something was up but could not decide what was going on. I boarded Whisper and tried the oars. They slid and rotated freely in their locks, but I was out of practice with them after 6 months collecting dust. Brandi swam out after me as I completed a short circle and came back to shore. Everything seemed in order.

I stood there in the water, and Dad handed me his cell phone. "Here. Call your ma."

I called Mom and fought back the small lump that was rising in my throat as I told her I was about to set out on my way. Mom's words of encouragement almost masked the concern I heard in her voice. Still worried, not particularly different from the anxiety I caused in rocking the canoe 25 years ago.

I hung up and babbled a few words about living dreams that while pragmatically foolish, make our lives full and rich with meaning. And with that, I shook hands all around and set out in a light rain under cloudy skies early in the last evening of April. Man, I hoped these conditions were not indicative of the character of this whole trip.

I love the chance to get out there, pull my own weight, and learn life skills in the process. This trip was designed around exactly that. This was, in fact, a sort of rite of passage, a dissertation on my worthiness as my own outfitter. I had a few kinks to work out if I were to pull that weight successfully. Realizing my ungainliness with the oars, my skills would have to improve substantially if this thing were going to have a chance. But with the current slow and the river wide, I attempted to relax and take in the dark beauty around me. Scattered thunderstorms passed off to the north, and heavier clouds were accumulating all around. I knew I would get wet, so I accepted the fact and had already donned my rain gear. I kicked two bald eagles off their evening roost and watched as they flew off downstream. The Chippewa River is fairly small and not dredged for navigation (thank goodness), so I had to watch for the thalweg and any shallow spots I would undoubtedly encounter. As I absorbed myself in the terrestrial surroundings, however, I lost track of the fluvial conditions. I rounded a bend in the river and found myself in small riffles of very shallow water. I jumped out of the boat and hauled Whisper to the outside of the bend where he wouldn't scape his keel on the gravel bottom. The boat lurched to the side as I swung my leg overboard, jerking the Sedona to the side and tearing the lag screws of its fork mount from the deck. The mount had lost nearly all its integrity when it got hit by that canoe. Man, I hope there aren't too many more surprises like this one. I grabbed the purple ratchet straps from my housewares department and guyed the bicycle to the gunnels. Now the fixture was rock solid. Whew. Good thing I had those straps. But what else would happen that I would not be able to fix so easily? Perhaps the weight of this trip was too much for my skills and resourcefulness to handle? I had to give myself a little pep talk to suppress the rising anxiety:

Man, things are a little rusty here… What's the problem? Everything is dry that needs to be. The bicycle is now taken care of. I've been on rivers before, including this very stretch. I know from experience and even formal coursework how to find the deepest channel and how to recognize the shoals. It's time to sharpen up, pay attention, relax, and do what you've practiced, studied, and prepared for over 10 years. You're up to this task. Just relax and live in the now. Don't worry about the Big River before you get there. Focus on where you are, and find your way through these gravel bars.

Once out of the shallows, I was vigilant to avoid them. I could predict easily enough the meandering bends in the channel where extra caution was needed, and was able to relax and sky-gaze in the interim. I experimented with different rowing strokes: blade angle, deep pull, shallow pull, grips pulled in close to midships, and sliding the oars further outboard until I slipped into an easy and comfortable rhythm. Yes, I could get used to this.

The foreboding skies gave no clue of the sinking sun. I slipped into quiet observation and bonding with my surroundings, and of course I lost track of time. It was nearly dark before I began looking for a campsite. I decided on an island with a cleared understory where I could pitch my tent. In the fast fading daylight, I grew anxious over not having shelter. Then it started raining. I took a deep breath and tried to relax. I knew what I had to do, and it was just a matter of doing it. I tried convincing myself that nothing was getting wet that shouldn't, and that I could take my time to do everything correctly since I was comfortable in my rain gear. I threw the dry bags on shore that held my camping gear, and then attended to mooring Whisper away from the rocks and sand of the shoreline.

I cannot for the life of me now remember why it was so difficult to figure out the process for mooring Whisper, but I was feeling things out as I went along. I settled in on a workable version of the system I had previously dreamed up. I ran my bow line through the last link of the 6 feet of chain I had fastened to my anchor. I let out slack between the boat and anchor, and holding the first few coils of extra line loose in my left hand, heaved the anchor and chain as far as I could into the river. So now the bow line ran from Whisper, down through the chain and anchor combo that secured it away from the shoals, then up to shore where I tied it off to a tree. The whole thing took about 10 minutes, a process that would later be refined to under a minute.

By now it was pretty much dark, except when lightning flashes illuminated my surroundings for me, which was disturbingly often. My heart was racing. *Here it's still April, and I'm trying to pitch a tent in a thunderstorm? Conditions like this can end in hypothermia, and I haven't been out for even 3 hours on a trip I'm planning to take as many months to complete!* I pitched the tent, got the rainfly over it as quickly as possible, threw my dry bag containing my sleeping bag and pad inside, and dove in. Screw the fly- and tent stakes, I would fasten them if it got windy. Right now, all I wanted was to be dry.

Of course, everything was soaked by the time it was all laid out. The sleeping pad offered some protection from the saturated tent floor, but not much. I tried sleeping with my clothes on and my rain gear close at hand. The fly was laying over the mesh tent ceiling, conducting water through and dripping on me. This lack of attention to the rain fly was a rookie mistake, the result of nervousness, laziness. I knew better, but I didn't care. This whole thing was looking rather hopeless. Lighting flashed and thunder rumbled intermittently throughout the night, preventing any sleep. Then, as I realized I was comfortable, I began to worry for Whisper. What if the river rose and the current pulled him ashore? Or if the line let loose and he drifted off, or rainwater in the bilge unsteadied him and strong current somehow tipped him over? The rain outside was amplified as it struck my tent, making the slow, steady shower sound like a gully washer. This perception fed my fears, and all at once I sprang from my tent and ran to the riverbank. There in the dark I could make out the shape of Whisper floating serenely at his mooring. If he could talk, he would have looked at me and asked, "What are you so worried about?"

Just to make sure, I bailed 2 inches of water out of the bilge and returned to my shack, this time fastening the rain fly before entering. I crawled back in the tent and zipped up my sleeping bag. The rain chose this very minute to abate. It seems to happen all too often that conditions improve at precisely the same moment I decide to help myself.

As I lay there, wet but warm in my sleeping bag in the pitch black silence at the threshold of this trip, I had to smile a little because things would have to improve from here, or else this would be a pretty short finale to 17 months of planning, building, saving, and preparation. I had been here before. Not this campsite, but at the threshold of a dream with all the glory and wonder at my fingertips, but with seemingly insurmountable odds stacked up against me. Just as at the removal of Ripple from her strongback, the phantom obstacles crept up again: This was the first night. Oh, what of all the nights ahead? How many more would be like this? Before I knew it my heart was racing and my imagination running rampant. What unforeseen walls will be thrown up along the way? Will I find campsites? What about navigating through the big cities with all the barges? Will locking through be a problem? How about security? What if I get robbed…

SHHHHHHHH. It's ok. You have done this before. You know how to camp, and you have resourcefulness to draw upon for things ahead. Others have done this before you in much smaller boats. You know the nature of fears like this, how they all pile up on each other at these times. Building Ripple, bike races, other river trips, even building Whisper have all had their moments of disparity. But that despair sprang from speculation of problems to come. You're in the same boat right now. Be patient and sit with this for a while. Face the challenges in front of you and take the others as they come along, one at a time. Everything you're facing at this instant can be dealt with. Quiet yourself and look around. Worry about your situation at hand, not the phantoms you cannot see from here.

I lay there in silence, nerves frayed from the mess I had gotten myself into. I thought of my preparations, the gear I had, and how it would be ruined by the rain. *Well, then I won't have to worry about all that crap anymore, I guess.* With that or some such notion, I fell asleep.

I awoke to a deer snorting at my tent. I looked up at the strange yellow ceiling of my rain fly-a view I would grow well accustomed to in the coming weeks. May 1st, my 30th birthday. *Huh. Let's see how Whisper is doing.* I stumbled from the tent to grey skies and trees that would have been depressing in dormant gloom had they not the first tinges of green emerging from their breaking buds. The grasses were greening up too, and the river agreeably reflected all these sentiments off its peaceful waters to any observer. I counted myself lucky to take it in, this emergence of spring.

I approached Whisper, who in his patient stillness had the same reassuring disposition he had left me with a couple of hours prior. *Huh. I guess I pack up and shove off now.*

I laid my soggy gear out on branches to get some air as I bailed the rain water Whisper had taken in the night. I packed up, retrieved and stowed the anchor, and shoved off. As I made my way slowly downstream, blue crevasses appeared in the grey ceiling that wedged the clouds apart before sweeping them over the horizon within a matter of hours. *See, this is not so bad.* I read the river more diligently and avoided the gravel bars that tried to trap me. I took a break on one rocky shore, this time mooring my boat in half the time it took me the night before. Still some kinks to work out of the system, but I was learning fast.

I saw five bald eagles playing the wind from this resting point. I looked downstream to see what vibes the far horizon was sending me. I found it to be a welcoming site, and at this moment I could care less what was beyond it. I hoped to see beyond every far horizon in good time, but I was content to take in the splendor of that moment's sojourn. As I seemed to be substantially outfitted, my success on this thing depended on me. How far would I be able enough to go?

I passed under an abandoned railway trestle that afternoon. The rails had been lifted and the route converted to a bicycle trail. A man was peddling across the bridge and stopped over the river when he saw me rowing by. He curiously greeted me.

"Hello," I responded.

"Looks like you're packed for quite a trip. How far you headed?"

"Well, I'm shooting to make it past New Orleans."

"Really? When did you start?"

"Last night."

A long pause ensued, followed by a chuckle and less than encouraging, "Good luck."

"Thanks."

I made it to Durand that day and decided I should let someone know everything was ok. Mooring Whisper opposite from the small town, I grabbed the Sedona and made my way over the Hwy 10 bridge to run my errands. I bought a candy bar and called my parents from a pay phone (I still had to set up my cell phone account), reassuring them that everything was fine. They were happy to hear from me and actually encouraging of what I was doing. They wished me a Happy Birthday in closing, and I moved on to the sporting goods store to buy a hat to keep off the sun. I wound up with a camouflage one with a Winchester logo on it. Whatever works. It was late afternoon by the time I made it back to Whisper, and I rowed another 6 easy miles before I took my time setting up camp on a small sand bar island at Ella, WI. Whisper was moored in plenty of water, secure and stable. I dug a fire pit with a berm to block the wind from the packages of broccoli and cheddar rice I prepared. At last, the sun set and left a bed of pink along the horizon that nestled blue skies overhead.

Next morning I awoke with the sun well above the treetops to the east. I was slow getting out of the sack and assembling my things. *Man, I'm gonna be sore until I'm in shape for this sort of thing.* I poked around for almost 2 hours getting my things together and waiting for the dew to dry off my rain-fly. This morning routine would also have to be refined if I were to make it south without running out of money. I had lots of learning to do, but that was a huge reason for doing this trip.

The lower Chippewa River is broad and shallow. There seem to be channels cut along the banks with braided routes between them, but they bend sharply and are almost impossible to predict. I stood on my seat occasionally to look ahead for lighter colored water or changes in the surface character that would reveal shoals, but I still had to jump out a couple times and pull Whisper to the security of the channel. I even had to row back upstream a quarter mile in one spot because the trough I was in suddenly ended, broadening out into an expanse of water only 4 inches deep. At that moment I missed Ripple. She's light and nimble enough to negotiate shallows like this, and an occasional scrape on the sand will not abrade her finish like it will the 650 pounds of Whisper grinding through the same substrate. I also missed the delicacy with which she paddles. That canoe responds with the lightest touch of the paddle to the water. I had to manhandle Whisper's oars to get this workhorse to react. My salvation would soon present itself in the weatherliness of this vessel.

I passed under Hwy 35, and soon after the railroad trestle signifying that the end of this road was near. I rounded one last bend, and there straight in front of me towered a whole line of bluffs on the far shore of the Mississippi River. The currents melded amicably enough, and when I passed the end of the Chippewa's northern bank, I gazed up at this string of points that extended all the way to the horizon, standing ever faithfully as lookouts upon the western shore. Blue skies and mild winds were celebratory of this juncture-the perfect setting for me to see a dream come true. I had done it. I built a boat and now I was rowing it on the Mississippi River. The dream has been realized. Every mile was now an extension of celebration.

On this big water, the shoals were not a concern. The shipping canal is dredged to a depth of 9 ½ feet and is marked by periodic buoys. Red on the left, port side, and green on the right, starboard. The water is far more turbid on this river than in the Chippewa, so the shallows are impossible to detect. I decided to skirt the green buoys on the western edge of the channel to make certain I would remain deep enough. I would keep an eye out for any approaching barges and keep turning to glance forward to make sure I did not smack into any buoys.

Almost on que, just as I adjusted to my new piloting strategy, I saw something rounding the far bend downstream. It was unmistakable, my first tow. The barges were strung together five deep and three abreast, all pushed upstream by a tugboat the size of a house. I had almost 15 minutes to get out of its way, plenty of time to make the 200 or so yards clear across the shipping channel if I so chose. This mass of steel stretched for over an eighth of a mile. Its 15 barges had a load capacity equal to 200 rail cars or 780 semi-trailers. The power necessary to drive all this stirred up quite the turbulence. As it drew abreast, I could see eight haystacks of dwindling size lined up behind it. When this wake spread toward the shores and hit my path, the stacks had mellowed to 3-foot swells. By this time I had a feel for Whisper's handling and welcomed these speed bumps with confidence. It would take more than that to shake this vessel. Whisper had finally flexed his muscles, just a bit.

Wabasha, Minnesota was the first town I hit, and I thought I would stretch my legs and check out a grocery store. I pulled into the marina which was still largely vacant so early in the season, and moored Whisper between two piers. I needed a sponge for soaking up the water in the bottom of the bilge, so that became my quest for the morning. That along with filling my nearly empty water jug. That water goes quick. The other 2 ½ gallon jug had not been cracked yet, but I wanted to maintain a full supply. I talked with the people at the grocery store who were interested in the trip, and called Mom and Dad to check in again. Once more, they were glad to hear from me.

I returned to Whisper and continued downstream. The afternoon breeze abated and I was left on the flat reservoir above Alma, Wisconsin in calm and peaceful conditions.

The river broadened and slowed. My rowing gradually became the only thing that propelled us forward as we approached Lock Number 4. My mind drifted into who knows what state, and I was rowing along with an even rhythm when suddenly the oar was ripped from my right hand. I jerked my head up to see a green buoy breeze by my port side, my vessel making surprising headway past it even in this calm water. Whisper was untouched, but I had struck the buoy with my port side oar, which was now floating in the water behind me. No problem, as I used the other oar to swing us round and catch the orphaned stick. That jerked me back into the now in a hurry, though. *Guess I'll have to watch where I'm going a little more.*

My second test of unknowns (the barge being the first) was upon me as I saw the water's horizon end at a line of concrete arches with two yellow markers at river left. My first lock. The directions in the navigation charts made it sound easy enough, just pull up to the sea wall, yank the rope that sounds the horn, wait for the light to turn green, and enter the lock. Then they sound the horn when it's deemed safe to exit-after the water is let out of the chamber and I am level with the lower river below the dam as the opposite lock doors open. As I drew nearer to the lock, a boat came up to me and asked if I had motor trouble.

"Wait a minute, where in the hell *is* your motor?"

We talked for a minute, and then I thanked him for stopping anyway before we went on our respective ways.

I Finally approached the lock and located the rope that was marked as the locking signal. I made my way to where it hung inside a ladder well in the sea wall. The doors were already opening and a bass boat came on through. Without my having to yank the chord, the light turned green and I was able to enter. The lockmaster was friendly enough, and not surprised to hear I was trying to run the whole way to New Orleans. "We get a handful of you guys through here every year, but you're the first I've seen this season."

"Any idea how many of them make it?"

"I don't know. I never hear from them again after they pass through."

With that, the water dropped about 5 feet in the lock, the doors opened, and the horn blasted the ok for my departure. Easy as falling off a log.

I enjoyed the current below this dam and gazed between the many islands to check out the sloughs and backwaters. I chose to stay in the main current for the sake of time and out of my

Locking montage.

fear of running aground. I talked with a fisherman who was spending a week out here for the spring run. "Walleye, bass, northern, they're all biting this time of year," he said.

Of the many misgivings I have of this trip, not taking the time for some fishing is one of them. While I was not on any schedule, I had to more or less bee-line it downstream if I were to have any chance of making the Gulf before my money ran out.

That evening I camped at Buffalo, Wisconsin on a wooded island with grassy undergrowth. Another perfect evening, and I camped early enough to set up shop for a feast of egg and bean breakfast burritos complete with salsa and cheese. I crashed early, in anticipation of a more timely start the following morning. As it was, I made 25 miles that day and about 20 on the Chippewa the day before.

Next morning dawned innocently enough. Sun was shining and pushing a gentle breeze before it. I stopped in town to make one more call to the parents to let them know everything was fine. I could feel I was slipping into a bit of a routine with my camping and stops in the towns I passed.

This was never meant to be a wilderness trip. I had gone on enough excursions to get away from people and find the wildest parts I could. I'd already done a fair job of getting out there and back, and this was merely a tour of the heartland. I wanted to get a feel for the people and places as I made my way through this cross section of Americana. The muddy water, boat traffic, towns, and industrialized shoreline I was sure to encounter gave me the feeling this was to be a tour of demographics and infrastructure more than it was of nature's splendor. With this disposition in mind, I had no problem stopping in every town along the way and staying in touch with my folks.

I returned to Whisper's tether at a public pier and resumed my way. The wind had picked up a bit, but this became quite an understatement when I hit the open water above Lock Number 5. As the islands were put behind me, so was the sun. Whitecaps sprang up, and Whisper's bow was pummeled by waves almost

4 feet. This was the treachery of the southerly winds I would become quite intimate with. I had almost 5 miles of open water before hitting the lock and the sanctuary of protected waters and, below, the relief of current. Between here and there, I was exposed to everything the wind could throw at my bow. It was time to dig down and stir up some rugby to get through this.

In the midst of trying to keep Whisper nose into the wind, I tore off my shirt and let out a loud growl. I could feel my shoulders, back, and even my legs tense up as I put everything I had into the oars. With headway being made so slowly, I would not last long at this level of effort. I felt occasional spray upon my back as yet another wave smashed into the bow and threw me off my rhythm. As I rowed, one oar would sometimes plunge deep into the crest of a wave that angled into me as the other oar jerked across the surface, barely penetrating a trough on the other side of my boat. Rhythm, thus headway, was indeed tough to gain, so I had to make every pull at the oars count. The relentless wind increased as I made the middle of this man-made lake, and I stepped it up another notch, belting out our rugby cadence at the top of my lungs.

My voice raspy now from growling in tones unachieved until this day, I kept myself going with victorious cries as yet another whitecap might pummel Whisper's bow, spray mingling with sweat upon my back on this tempestuous, cold spring day. I was winning at this aqueous scrum-down.

At last, the yellow markers of the lock drew nearer. I approached the seawall, my blood still surging from the effort and endorphin high I was experiencing. I could almost laugh at the notion of a need for a life jacket in the lock. I was 10 feet tall and bulletproof. Still, I threw on my orange relic of a PFD and locked through as the protocol demanded. I emerged in the current below, now cooled by my 20-minute rest from the locking procedure. I had noticed that the people working at the lock were all wearing winter jackets. How different our perceptions of the same conditions can be, depending upon the disposition with which we approach the situation. I put my clothes back on and gazed upon the western shore. Bluffs sprang from the bank in regularly buttressed points of naked rock, a stark spectacle against the slate colored sky—a perfect testament to this drab day.

I found myself in current once again, albeit momentarily. Soon it all but died in foreshadowing of Lock 5A just ahead. At least I was able to take cover from the wind among islands and enjoy the mid morning's progress. The skies cleared somewhat, but I could still see evidence of wind in the tree tops. I came upon Lock 5A most abruptly and was surprised to see that it only dropped the water level a foot or so.

Although windy, it was a beautiful day. I checked my chart and found a marina just below the lock. A good place for a break. As I sat eating my lunch of left over burritos, an old gentleman peddled up on his recumbent bicycle. He had lived here his whole life, and he gave me a quick history of the shipping canals.

Progressively through the 1920s, wing dams had been constructed in the river to push the current toward center channel. These dams were simply long piles of rock and rip-wrap that extended perpendicular to the shore, channeling the current into the thalweg. This kept the main channel fairly clear of debris and running deeper for the tows.

In the 1930s the Army Corps of Engineers began building the systems of lock and dams for more efficient maintenance of the channels. This was one of the government projects put on at the same time as the CCC and Roosevelt's New Deal. Locks 5 and 6 were put in as directed, but it was found that a large flood in spring could possibly still inundate the city of Winona, MN. It was decided an extra lock was needed, Lock 5A. The project cost several million dollars at the time, but today would be over 10 times that.

This man and I talked for a while, and as I shook his hand, I regretted to tell him I had forgot his name already. "Well I didn't forget yours, Dave." Then, with a smile, "It's Jack." Social graces never were my strong suit, and I did not even think to get a picture of Jack or his email address. I had a list of people I was to contact via internet from libraries in the cities I would come upon. The system worked pretty well, and I was able to send out updates of my trip every couple of days. I hesitated to put too many names on it because who really wanted to be bothered with my ramblings about this river trip? I took my leave of Jack and got back out into the wind.

The river bent just enough to the south for me to get shelter among a few islands. Once past town, it meandered to the more to the east, and oddly enough, straight into the gusty air. I was already tired from battling these conditions all day. I looked out to the channel and saw the waves were largest there, so I looked for sanctuary along the Wisconsin shore. None to be found. Instead, I ran along an arrow-straight length of railroad tracks that was built upon a moraine of man-made debris. This barren waterscape manufactured of steel and rock was no comfort to my senses or disposition. The wind tossed my vessel and I could not find a rhythm to make steady progress. It was a battle every step of the way, and my exhausted body was taking its toll on my attitude. I was pushing my limits, but there was no harbor to camp or moor along this desert of water and rip-rap. I was forced to push on through to Perot State Park, yet another 3 miles upwind. At times, particularly large waves would knock Whisper off course, threatening to push me back upstream. It was a constant effort just to keep the right heading, and I was afraid of upsetting if I went abeam to these seas. Frazzled nerves got the best of me, and I occasionally lashed out at the water, slapping it with my oar in a frenzy of a person who has reached his wits end. Still, I was inching my way forward.

I watched as my vessel crawled by individual weeds of box-elder trees. I was gazing upon this agonizingly slow progress when my boat ground to a halt and I fell backward into the bow compartment. I had run aground. My heart raced, but I realized I was not moving. I was pointed into the waves which were doing little to threaten my perch, and I seemed to be stable. *Ok. Take a deep breath, relax, and we'll get Whisper off this rock.*

I swung my right leg over the gunnel and felt a jab as I pulled my left after me. I looked to see my leg had been mildly impaled by the open horn of my starboard oarlock. The sharp pain shot through my body, and I stood there for a moment, my consciousness shocked back into clarity.

It's OK. It seems the sole of my keel took the scrape, so there should be no damage to the planking. Everything is sound within the boat, and this water I'm standing in is soothing to my dehydrated body. I can see the hills marked on the gazetteer just ahead that signal Perot State Park. Alright, let's get the troops rallied for the last push.'

With ease, I pulled Whisper off his rocky bed and reboarded. I exercised newly found patience with the waves and within 15 minutes had reached the inlet that led to a landing at Perot State Park. Whew. I made it. Before setting camp, I took a short tour of the park on the Sedona, looking for a phone. I made a few calls and stopped for a picture from a lookout over the River. Then I returned to Whisper's docking site and set up camp close-by. I was leaving first thing in the morning anyway, so I did not think this measure of security would bother anyone. With that notion, I dove in the tent and fell fast asleep. Man, that was one hell of a day. Despite the wind, I made 33 miles. I decided that if I could at all help it, I would not put myself through a day like that again. I did a fair job of sticking to that idea too—at least until I made it to Louisiana.

The next day I took my time getting ready. There was still some wind, but it was much more manageable than the day before. The biggest concern I had was nothing to do with the water at all, however. An oversight I had made in preparing for this trip was the lack of a boat cushion. The plywood thwart I sat on left a lot to be desired in the way of comfort, but I figured I'd simply harden up and everything would be fine. Then I encountered a phenomenon known as chaffing. Let's just say my hindquarters were quite tender and becoming more sensitive by the day.

I made it to La Crosse that day and rode into town. In the library there, I ran across an old rugby buddy of mine, Brady.

He was living in the area and was planning to go to Prairie Du Chein in a couple of days. We tried setting up a meeting point.

After doing my business on the internet, I went to check out the UW–La Crosse campus. There should be a locker room in their athletic facility where I could make use of a shower. I talked to the person at the desk, and he said he was not sure if it was allowed. He asked his manager to come over, who was accompanied by another staff member. I told them what I was doing, and said I was a college student at Point, but they still had their doubts. Finally, a supervisor walked over who had been listening.

I said, "Look. When the Stevens Point Basketball team comes to town, they get free use of the locker room, right?"

The guy looked down at me and asked, "Are you trying to tell me you play basketball?"

"No, but I am a rugby player. Shouldn't we be extended the same courtesy?"

The connections forged through rugby never cease. Man, that shower felt good. Ten minutes later I was a new person.

I walked over to their outdoor adventure department and tried to buy an old sleeping pad that I could use as a boat cushion. True, I had my own I could use, but I felt no urge to sleep on such a thing after defiling it all day in the sweltering heat I was sure to come by. I talked to Mike, and he invited me into their stock room. He pulled an old beat up pad off the shelf, looked at it, and then looked at me.

"You know what I'm thinking, don't you?" He asked.

"Well, at least let me give you something for it."

"Naw, just make it all the way down the river and remember where you got this thing."

Mike may never know how he saved my ass that day.

I returned to Whisper and moved on down the river, a soft rain settling on the calm waters around me. True my stuff was getting wet, but only the things that were allowed to. Everything that is supposed to stay dry did in those conditions, and I was able to relax and take my time on down the creek, soothed by this cool freshness. That shower sure didn't hurt my disposition either. I set camp in the dark on an island that had free campsites established, breaking a tent pole in the process. I just took my time and fixed it.

2 days later, May 6th, I found myself back out in the wind. This would not do, as I was entering the open waters behind Lock 7. I took refuge behind an island and looked out at the tumultuous seas. A barge happened by, rolling downstream. Not nearly as much power is needed when going with the current, and the waters behind these mammoth crafts is pretty calm in this case. Rowing like hell, I tried catching a draft in the calm waters behind the tug. I couldn't keep up. I found myself exposed once more in open water, but the waves weren't quite as bad as they were 2 days prior. An island came into view, and I decided to set up camp instead of running myself into the ground again. Six miles that day. But it was not over yet. I reached the island, moored my boat, and found the whole understory composed of vines and shrubs of poison ivy. *Screw it. I had already landed, and was not up for another day against the wind.* I busted out my machete and cleared a 30-foot circle with a walkway to it. I marked the borders of my safe zone with logs and pulled up every vine of ivy I could find. Every couple of minutes, I would break from this work and rinse off in the river, trying to rid my hands of the potent oil. Since I took the time to tell this story, yes, of course I got poison ivy. It must have been left on my hands, which spread it to various other places on my body. Let's just say it's interesting all the sensitive areas one unconsciously probes in his sleep… So now I had saddle sores from hell coupled with Poison Ivy. No cure for any of it, just to let it run its course.

Setting camp that day put me a day behind in meeting up with Brady at Prairie Du Chein, and we missed each other. I gave myself a self-guided tour of Villa Lois, a historical site with old buildings and tributes to the pioneering days. Too bad it was still closed for the season. That afternoon I passed the Wisconsin River Delta, carrying about half the waters I had ever paddled into the Mississippi. The waters of the rivers I know, the St. Croix, Namekagon, Prairie, Chippewa, Flambeau, Spirit, Eau Plaine, Pine, Plover, Kickapoo, Pine (a more southern river), and the Mighty Wisconsin were all bundled into the same waters I now traveled upon. I took it as my duty to escort them to the Gulf, living upon lands they flow through all along the way.

I camped that evening on a patch of sand at the tail tip of an island. I cooked my dinner of rice and retired early. Likewise, I awoke early, thinking dawn was cracking with all the light in my tent. I stepped outside to see a beautiful waning moon straight overhead. In the white hue that was almost blue, I could see the stillness of the river and the quietude epitomized by the black horizon of forest that encircled me. I sat there for a bit, listening to coyotes howling not all that far away. Dawn was about to break, so I began striking camp, moving easily and fluidly in the peacefulness of the setting. The sun was just below the horizon as I shoved off for the day, cutting the glass of the water's surface as I went. Ahh, the Ripple Effect is not dead after all, even on waters as large as the Mississippi and with the masculine brawn of this pulling boat.

River Hospitality

I made the Dubuque Marina right at sun-down and stopped in to see about laundry and a place to moor the next day. Best way about that, I was finding, was to have a beer at the bar. I talked to Rose and Jay, who first thought I might be up to no good and then thought I was crazy. They asked where I was headed.

"Well, I'm trying to make New Orleans."

"New Orleans, that's a hell of a trip! How long you been on the water?"

"A week and a half."

"Puh! Good luck, son."

Jay was curious about my camping and food situation. I told him about my internet contacts, my solar panel, my bike, and the hope of getting a cell phone in Davenport. The more we talked, the more accepting he became of the whole idea, until he gave me my last beer for free.

"Stop back tomorrow. Keith should be around. He likes to do what he can to help out adventure-types like yourself."

I was swarmed by mosquitoes as I set camp on a less than ideal island, but the next day I was permitted use of the laundry facilities and shower. Keith, who turned out to be the owner, was great to me.

I ran some errands and headed off in the afternoon. Dubuque is a pretty cool town with lots of small neighborhoods. I set out and realized I only had 2 gallons of water left. Shit. I checked the nautical charts, and there was one more marina in the area, on the Illinois side (enemy territory, as it were). I stopped in at this, the Crooked Prop Marina. Everyone in there wheeled around when they saw me walk in, as if to say, "Who the hell is this guy?" I talked with the people next to me, who thought I was nuts when I told them what I intended to do. TJ, the owner, was interested in the trip. He showed me some routes that would take me into some backwaters and sloughs, keeping me out of the barge traffic that was now steadily increasing.

"The main channel will get you there quicker, wherever in the hell 'there' is in the first place, but the sloughs and backwaters are where the real life is." Well put, TJ. I must have come off as quite presumptuous in my relaxed approach to the trip. People didn't know what to make of me, but it felt good to stir the pot a little.

When I left, everyone came out on the porch overlooking the slips to see me off. I overheard a conversation that was a little louder than intended:

"Think he'll make it?"

"Hell no."

I had learned a while back not to be daunted by the doubts of others. In fact, I found it encouraging. I was learning to handle the situations I was faced with on the water, my camping routine was becoming streamlined, campsites were plentiful, and most of the days were peaceful in the morning, if not the evening too. I was getting out there and enjoying myself in the process.

Three days later, May 12th, I made the Quad Cities. I stopped at the Lindsay Park Marina, thinking it to be a public place. Nope, this was as ritzy as I had seen. They let me tie off there, so I rolled with it. Still, this was not the setting like the bar where I met Mike, Dan, and Juneau the day before. Conversation did not flow so freely and nobody here knew half as much about the river as Dan, who told me about the fishing industry and the pilots whose specialty was to navigate the rapids at Le Claire. Even still, as I was leaving on my bicycle a man asked me if I wanted a ride in his car to run my errands. I thanked him for the gesture but said I needed to stretch the legs a little.

I finally got the chip I needed for my cell phone that day, so no more calling cards and pay phones. I picked up a couple of groceries and was coming back through downtown Davenport when I saw an art fair going on. Perfect. I even found a Mother's Day present for my mom.

I returned to Whisper and was stowing all my gear when the same man who offered me a ride earlier approached me again. We introduced ourselves and he was curious about my trip. Jim then invited me aboard his 35-foot dual propped Silverton for drinks and hors d'oeuvres. I looked at a couple who was walking past and listening in on the conversation. The guy looked at me, smiled, and nodded. I shrugged and said, ok. I had, after all, just showered 2 days ago and considered myself tidy enough to not be obtrusive.

I boarded the yacht and was welcomed by some of Jim's friends. A few more guests arrived and there wound up being eight or so of us in total. The people were friendly and included a high ranking attorney, an author and artist who wrote a book on the history of the area, the head cardiologist of the Quad Cities, and their respective spouses. Jim himself is an attorney turned entrepreneur. The conversation was pleasant-we talked of my trip, the river, the first bridge to cross the Mississippi (which happened to be here), and life experiences. Jim invited me to stay for a cruise and some dinner. I obliged. We motored out of the marina and into some adjoining waters on the Rock River. Conversation turned to boats, and as we powered through an abandoned lock I noted the size of the wake we were throwing.

"Yeah, you really don't want to mess with the wake from a boat this size in any small craft." Jim, after all, was very proud of his vessel he had earned through his years of hard work. I pictured in my head the waves I had handled already on this trip and just smiled. There's always a bigger fish.

As we anchored, the conversation turned to politics. Jim tossed some bread to a bunch of ducks and noted how their movements are predictable, "just like democrats'."

"That is my un-political joke for the evening."

It may have been a little head strong to respond, smiling, "Oh. Well, I won't take political offense to it then.". I couldn't resist.

Jim busted out the George Foreman grill and threw on the chicken breasts he had soaked in Italian dressing. One of the women, a social worker in the inner city (we had a great conversation after dinner), commented on how delicious the chicken sandwiches were. Jim beamed, "Yes, I am a good cook, aren't I?"

One of the other women was taken by the comment and asked, "So you made your own marinade?"

"Nope. It's Italian dressing. Got it on sale for $1.39. Great deal, huh?"

I hope Jim's notion of hard work is held to a higher standard than his requisites for culinary expertise.

After dinner we pulled anchor and started back for the marina. The conversation turned inevitably to politics, and Jim turned his back on me as he addressed his colleagues. I was, after all, a novel treat to this buffet of intellect, not to be considered for the main course.

I do not mean to sound ungrateful to Jim. He was very cordial and is a picture of success and integrity as they are defined in his mind. He even looks out for *little guys* like me. When we returned to the marina, he offered me space on his aft deck to crash for the night and told me to clean out all the snacks left in the refrigerator before I left in the morning. Before he took his leave, he even left me with four gems of knowledge that would guide me to everlasting prosperity. The only one I can seem to remember, though, is to Cultivate Favor. I am damned to be a poor bastard for the rest of my life. Shucks. But it was, in all sincerity, a great gesture of kindness and trust on Jim's part to open his place up to me. I really had a good time with that crew. If I only had remembered to snap some photos. I still had not thought to make such use of all the resources at my fingertips. Such is a symptom of the scarcity mindset, and the real reason I'm dammed to be a poor bastard the rest of my life.

I left at dawn the next day and headed on toward Muscatine, Iowa. Around lunch time I passed an island with a strip of sandy beach. A mess of boats were pulled up and people were hanging out, jet skiing, and tubing. I might have avoided the crowds if I were looking for a solitary, natural experience, but such was not the case with this trip. I pulled close and asked a group of four middle-agers if it was alright to pull up for lunch.

"Feel free. We don't own it."

I moored Whisper and began assembling the chips and guacamole/chili concoction I was to eat for lunch. One of the guys came over with a large bottle of homemade wine. We talked about the river and the trip he had gathered I was undertaking. He offered me some wine and invited me over for a beer after I was done eating. The vibe was good here.

I joined Floyd, his wife, and two of their friends, also married, for a beer. I brought some Wisconsin fare to this potluck, some snowshoe grog my dad had sent along with me (a flask three quarters full of brandy and topped off with peppermint schnapps). We exchanged libations and hung out, shooting the breeze. Floyd was a micro-engineer at an aluminum recycling plant. He and his friends are all looking forward to retiring and spending more time in the water. His wife Jane runs regularly, and at 60 still gets out on the jet ski in the summer time. Floyd's passion is fishing, and he gets on the river year round. The water below the dams rarely freezes, but it is cold.

Floyd said he would not pass the bottle around too much because he was sending it with me on my way. He busted out a bottle of red instead, and we all took pulls off that. He mixes it fairly sweet and lets it ferment until the alcohol levels kill the yeast, so it runs about 17 percent or so. Before I left, he gave that one to me too. *I only make the stuff so I can give it away.* I wrapped both bottles in carpet I had packed for random padding and stowed them as far up under the forward deck as they would fit.

Common sense finally kicked in and I got some pictures of the crew before I left. The beach is called bikini island by the locals, and the people coming out here grew to be friends over time. That makes them the Bikini Island River Rats. What a great crew.

I was finally able to release that chip on my shoulder just a bit. While it grew bigger with some of the details I dwelled on with Jim and his crew in Davenport, it all but disappeared with Floyd and the Bikini Islanders. I am not a fan of jet skis, but it was impressive to see how Jane handled one. Everyone operates by their own rules, and I would do better to stop measuring other people so often by mine. We're still in touch to this day.

Rough Water

This part of the trip was one adventure after another. I camped that evening just across from Muscatine. I was late getting in and camped on a sandbar overlooking a swamp. Those stagnant waters inspired the name of this camp: Mosquito Hell. Good thing my tent was staked in or they might have carried it away.

Next morning I crossed the river and went into town, running my usual errands of library, internet, and fresh food. Muscatine was once the clamming capital of the world, commemorated by a small monument of an old clammer on the riverfront. I returned to the cove where Whisper was hitched round 2:00 pm and noted the water. The wind was blowing a steady 25–30 mph, with additional gusting. Whitecaps raged upstream, and the waves ran most fiercely in the shipping canal. Nope, too dangerous for my blood. I went back to town and explored their button museum. I splurged on an ice cream cone and learned how buttons are stamped out of clam shells.

I returned to the harbor at 4:00. I was restless from being on land. Sitting with the idea of trying the water for a while, as with so many things in the past, made it seem doable. Despite the wind not subsiding at all, I would give it a go. This would be a test, but I was confident I was up for it.

I rowed hard out into the river from behind the piled rocks of rip-rap that had provided my sanctuary. The wind was blasting and the waves were the highest I had seen so far. I looked up and downstream; no barges in sight. I did not want to be out exposed like this for any longer than necessary, so I started out along the channel in the hopes of crossing to a sandbar just opposite me. As I entered the channel, the waves were notice-ably bigger. Five-foot whitecaps pounded my hull, trying to throw me beam to the seas. That would have meant upsetting for sure. I timed the waves and buried my oars deep into the peaks as I rode over them, as if driving a dagger up to its hilt in some God forsaken beast that refuses to die. Waves were crashing on the bow, soaking my back, but none were able to blow completely over foredeck. I was trying to hold my own.

I turned, checking the channel again, and to my dismay a tow was coming upstream. I had time before it would be upon me, but the going in these waters was very slow. I angled Whisper's nose at a sharper angle with the waves, but now their weight had more of his beam to grab on to. I was making my way to the edge of the channel, but each swell threatened to drive me completely sideways. A wave would crash, blasting my bow to the side, and as it passed, I threw everything I had into the oars to right the bow again. The mass and momentum of each surge made the water feel not particularly dissimilar to wet concrete. I struggled for about 15 minutes and exited the shipping canal, but I was at the side of the river that was more windward now. The waves continued to pummel me and my vessel until I finally caught the lee of an island where sanctuary and rest were afforded. I rowed back up stream to the island I had originally aimed for and set camp. The heat was blown from my stove, even in the vestibule of my tent, and the tent itself had to be guyed down to keep from being swept away. From inside, I could even hear the sand pelting my fabric walls. One single, solitary mile that day. Whew, but it was a dandy. I had passed the test. With that notch on my belt, I did not feel the need to go out in waters like those again.

The next day, May 15th, I was hit by a thunderstorm, so I moored Whisper and picked up clam shells in the rain. The current is stronger as one gets south, and I covered 48 miles that day. I made Burlington, Iowa on the 16th and was treated to a free lunch at Happy Joe's Pizza. Rob, (my fellow Parrothead, who appreciated my canoe as a legacy piece), had a connection with Will, the manager of the restaurant, and set everything up for me. May 17th, I went through the deepest lock on the river at Keokuk, number 19. Shortly thereafter I entered Missouri—Hoosier country.

I had found it easiest to call the lockmasters on my phone (numbers are conveniently listed in the nautical charts) to see about locking through. If there were barges ahead of me, it might be a 2-hour wait for them to break their load in half, send the parts through, and reassemble on the other side. I approached Quincy, Ill, and a particularly industrial stretch of river on May 18th. I could see three barges lined up in front of the lock, all waiting their turn. I called the lockmaster to see how long it would be, supposing I might have to row back into the upstream islands to camp for the night and come through again in the morning. He offered to let me sneak ahead of them all, but said to be ready after the tow passed upstream that was presently locking through.

I aligned myself above the lock and just to the side of the main channel. I would slip into position immediately after the tug pulled away that was preparing for departure. The tow was finally tied in and mooring lines released. The tug powered its engines and started pulling upstream, leaving behind a chaotic mess of waves and haystacks. The whistle sounded and light went green for me to enter the lock.

This would be fun. I entered the turbulence left behind by that tug and found myself bombarded by waves coming from every direction. The wake was perfectly reflected off the sea walls in the locking canal, resulting in extremely confused seas. Some waves compounded on top of each other and there may have been a couple that topped that 5-foot mark. No wind and no current, though, so I stabbed an oar into each wave as it pelted me and pulled against its massive force. This excitement got the blood flowing in a hurry, and I was all fired up by the time I was locked in the chamber. None of the guys working the lock said anything. I guess they were either unaware of what I was just accosted with, or they thought the foolishness of taking on those waves should not be rewarded with attention. I knew what I was in for as I pulled in behind the tug, and had fun with it. I was learning what Whisper was made of, and me too.

I pulled into the marina at Hannibal, Missouri that afternoon and met the foreman. He was curious about my trip and we talked a bit. He noted that I must be hungry and that there are a few joints on the main drag in town to grab a burger.

"How about something vegetarian?"

After a pause, the foreman pointed to the lawn behind him. "There's some grass over there…"

When my laughter finally subsided, I gave myself a nice little tour of the birthplace of Mark Twain's Huckleberry Finn. I rode my bike up to Lover's leap and had a picture of me snapped as I overlooked the town and river from this outcropping. I camped on a point across the river from town that night, noted in my journal as the best campsite so far. A beautiful sunset settled over the city that evening, and peaceful waters lulled me to sleep.

Fresh Perspective

I made it to Louisiana, Missouri on May 19th, and had time to stop to share a drink with two crews of river-goers along the way. Floyd's wine was a huge hit, and it hits a person hard with its sweet potency. That night I found a stretch of sand across from town and slept out under the stars, after I updated my journal and log by candle-light.

Saturday, May 20th, I could not find rhythm for the life of me. I was hung-over, tired, and dehydrated. Round 11:00 I decided to stop on a sandbar for an early lunch and hang out a bit. I already had over half the day's miles under my belt, and besides, there might be some people here to hang out with. I used the rest-room, and as I toured the island, I saw a few boats lined up on its opposite side. I pulled Whisper from his mooring and headed over there. There was one family and another crew of five guys and a gal. It seemed it would be easiest to strike up a conversation with the guys, so I went over by them. We talked about my trip, the river, and the blue collar lives of the crew. They were a few years younger than me, but I like to think we shared the same youthful cheer.

Another crew pulled up on a boat, a pair of couples and two little girls. I could not decide who the girls belonged to, since the friends were closely acquainted. One of the guys, Kurt, came over and was curious about Whisper. We talked for a while longer and everyone gathered for a picture. I busted out the white wine and we drank it all down through the course of the afternoon. They insisted I accept some of their beers, and we just hung out and talked the afternoon away.

Kurt mentioned at one point, "Whisper. I like that name. There's something about it." He looked at the bottle we had finished and said, "You know, you should write something and put in that bottle, cap it, and send it off."

I responded, "That is one hell of an idea, except we all should."

So, everyone wrote a note and stuffed it in the bottle. The plan was to take it down stream and wherever I took-out of the water, cast it in and see if anyone picks it up. Kurt, Nikki,

John, and Trisha were a great crew. Afternoon started to wane, and Nikki asked where I was camping that night.

"Well, I'd like to get a few more miles under my belt and crash on an island someplace."

"Oh no you're not. My uncle has a marina 2 miles down. You can moor there for free and join us for some chicken on the grill."

There was no arguing with that one. An hour later, I was sitting round a patio table with the crew and Nikki's Uncle Randy. They wouldn't let me pay for anything, and we feasted on grilled Chicken sandwiches, potatoes, and asparagus cooked with carrots in melted butter. We talked around the campfire until about 2:00 in the morning.

It hurt to think how much complete strangers were giving to me. People opening their homes, offering food, drinks, showers, laundry, and plenty of other things. I mentioned to Kurt how I felt guilty in accepting all these things, giving nothing in return. How was I supposed to repay all this? It felt like I was draining myself of karma tickets. Kurt responded something of the following:

"What you're doing is a pretty amazing trip. You built this boat yourself and now you're rowing it down the Mississippi River. Look how far you've come already. People see this; they see your boat, and they cannot help but be inspired. There are few people, even our age, who have the freedom or the skills to do something like this. But you are doing it. So when people offer you food or beers, it's just our way of sharing a little piece of that trip with you, helping you make it happen. We're living vicariously through you, and we're sure as hell going to do what little we can to make this thing work."

"Jeez. I never thought of it like that before."

Nikki set me up with a couch to crash on. I awoke before dawn and went out to my boat. I left a thank you note on their patio table and took my leave of the Timberlake Marina as the sun broke the horizon.

Picking up the Pace

Making my way down through the last lock on the river and the confluence with the Missouri, I rowed into St Louis. On my third attempt at going ashore, I was able to make it to high ground after sinking through the upper crust of sand and into only a foot of black tar-like Mississippi Mud. That was tolerable. The first time I encountered this stuff, hidden beneath an innocuous looking veneer of sand, one of my legs went in straight up to my crotch.

I was looking forward to my sister's place in Memphis. My camping, cooking, and shopping protocol were all pretty well established, so I was slipping into a sort of rhythm. If I averaged 40 miles per day, I would make it to Memphis in 9 days, and my arrival would coincide with a preplanned visit by my parents. It would be nice to see family again. Whew, that might be a push, but with the river so much faster below the Missouri, it might just be doable.

Rather than some temporary weekend outing where one comes back home on Sunday, dirty, worn, and in need of decent food, this trip was designed to be a comfortable one. For as long as I was to be on the River, I figured I may as well make myself at home, establish a system that works, and make this period of rolling on the River my job. It was no longer novel, it was simply 'what I do'. Now, it was time to stretch my legs.

I made 67 miles the next day, to Cape Girardeau. Strong afternoon headwinds and an evening stop in town to boot. The traffic on the river was becoming more severe. There was almost always at least one tow in sight, and now with the locks behind me, the tows were huge. The biggest I saw was six barges abreast and seven deep, almost all fully loaded. These masses are pushed by even bigger tugs, with a third diesel burner for extra drive. Fully loaded, this tow would have a capacity equivalent to 560 rail cars or 2180 semi-trailers.

I moored Whisper off a mud flat under the Hwy 146 bridge and rode the Sedona into town. It was been a bad place to camp, but I did not arrive back to the boat until after dark. Which rule would I break-a sketchy campsite, or rowing after dark? The charts showed sandbars at a bend in the river less than a mile downstream, so I packed up and went for it. I would stay in close to shore and watch like crazy for rocks. I also put on my navigation lights.

It is pretty amazing how fast a person comes up with innovations or adjustments to a system in a pinch. I eased off the shore and drifted straight away toward a rocky shoal whose riffles I did not see until it was almost too late. I barely had the strength to row Whisper backward upstream and to the starboard to get around them. Instantly I came up with the strategy of facing Whisper upstream and merely drifting at the pace of the current. This way my body was facing downstream and could much more easily row against the current or sideways to it as I approached shoals. This was still quite a nerve-racking experience, especially after 13 hours on the water plus the errands I ran.

I made it to a beautiful sandy beach, threw up the tent, and dove in for a good night's sleep. A reoccurring dream had been evolving in my slumbers that took a pretty vivid form this evening. I would find myself on the River, drifting without oars after dark. I would be out of control with barges, armed with their high powered spot lights, bearing down on me. Then I would snap out of it, that there was not really a barge, and that yes, I had oars, but that I was on shore…I must have run aground! Then I would wake up, realizing I was not in my boat at all—I had lost Whisper! At this point I would be bolt upright in my sleeping bag, heart throbbing. I'd look around my tent, unzip the door and check on Whisper. Whew, what a scare. Those dreams would be especially potent after I had drained myself rowing that day.

Next day I would take it easier. But now I faced a new challenge. I was fast approaching Cairo, Ill, where the Ohio River would join me. That is the cut-off for the upper Mississippi and the cut-off for my detailed navigational charts. I had purchased no Gazetteers of the states I would be hitting, since the way was well marked. My charts did list the cities I'd hit for the whole length of the river, and at what mile markers I could expect them. Still, it felt like uncharted territory once I left Illinois and joined with the Ohio River, entering into the Southern Mississippi River. The South. That was another question I had. Where exactly would I cross that Mason Dixon Line?

Leaving Cape Girardeau behind me, I indeed made Cairo, Illinois on that last day in May. Grey and overcast but with little wind, I loved that day's progress. I rounded the last few bends above the Ohio's union in a rain shower that dampened the riffles on the River. This left the residual swells from boats and barges naked but for a misty veneer of raindrops that peppered them. I had been without a shower for a long time and slipped out of my shorts for a period to cleanse myself in this warm downpour. In Wisconsin, the rain is cold. Here, it was comfortable. I may as well have been rowing under a showerhead set at the perfect temperature. No soap to lather myself, but I felt much cleaner as I passed under the Interstate 57 bridge. There the sky cleared and the day ripened with afternoon sunshine. The river changed, too.

Mississippi enters the Ohio River Valley from a higher elevation, and this makes for a noticeable gradient as one rounds the left-hand bend just before the meeting of the waters. High gradient equals fast current. The shores are lined with rock rip-wrap, as one would expect, and this hard bank does a good job of reflecting currents. The waters along this shore are slowed somewhat by the coarseness of the substrate. The faster water in the channel passes by and slams into the bank as the river bends around further. The result is a sort of corkscrew effect as the river pours downstream. Whirlpools and boils that I had become accustomed to thus far now reached a new level of significance. The water runs upwards of 7 miles per hour, and in my excitement, I was rowing hard to see just how fast could go. I was blowing along the shoreline, watching trees wiz by, when I saw my first monster boil of water burst from the muddy depths. It formed a pile of water that stood a full foot above the surface before it disseminated back into equilibrium with its surroundings. With every boil there seems to be a whirlpool. As with the boils, these conical holes in the surface could be heard as well as seen. I marveled at a few of them that were about 18 inches deep, and rowed on, thankful that I hadn't been subject to one. I put my back into the effort, adrenalized by a mixture of excitement, fear, and awe. Suddenly the bow was jerked hard to port and my forward progress slammed to a halt, relative to the current. I could feel water slapping Whisper's keel and garboards-a whirlpool had formed directly beneath me and yanked my entire rig 90 degrees in rotation. I gained my composure, set the oars deep, and pulled hard. No real danger, at least not with this incident in particular, but I preferred stable water.

As I passed under the Hwy 62 bridge, the last one in Illinois, I saw traffic had been stopped in the westbound lane. Not thinking anything of it, I blasted under this bridge and was amazed at the speed of the barges that were coming downstream. I could not understand how they could maintain control, and evidently that did not always happen. Just ahead at river left, I saw mile marker zero, on the point of land where the Ohio comes in from the east. I was amazed at how slow and bright that blue water was. A ragged line zig-zagged out from this point, and it was clearly seen where the Ohio's clarity became confused with the Mississippi's milk shake. Then I noticed there was no barge traffic moving. I counted eight tows staged on the riverbanks with one huge one in the middle of the river, with tugs going to and from it. I moored Whisper and talked to a guy on shore who happened to work on the barges. Turned out this tow in the river was wounded from hitting the Hwy 62 bridge as it came downstream. It was being relieved of its load and all river traffic had to wait until this was done before they could resume their way.

I took to the River again and made it another 7 miles downstream that day. Now entering uncharted waters, at least as far as I was concerned, I had a couple fears. With the joining of the

Ohio, I had seen very few sand bars. Would they peter out as the river grew and I got downstream? Would the towns listed in a table in the book of charts be accessible to me? What would the river conditions be like, would I run into other problems I hadn't anticipated? I grew nervous as the sun began its downward slide, but soon I saw a patch of sand on the horizon and camped in perfect view of one of the most spectacular sunsets on the trip. I was up to this.

Crossing the Mason Dixon

On the morning of June 1st, I rolled into the Gibraltar of the west, Columbus, Kentucky. I walked into town and was treated well by Mary who gave me a free lemonade at the local convenience store. There were old news clippings on the wall depicting Columbus' role in the Civil War, when they had a chain stretched across the river to prevent northern supplies from making it south. This was to be the capital city after the south won the war. Mary put me in touch with Tami at the local Ingram Barge office in the hopes of getting my hands on some charts of the river.

I walked to their nearby office and entered the grounds with my backpack, torn cargo shorts, and a Hawaiian shirt. A welder came out and looked at me suspiciously, asking if I had a bomb in my bag. I said no and dropped Tami's name, so he led me to the office. There, Tami referred me to Duane. Boy, if I could ever get my hands on this guy again. Duane said there were no charts I could buy, but I could take a look at his in the office there. I referenced the cities I would encounter through Memphis and took note of a couple windy spots in the river. Duane said one spot was just downstream. With the spring waters still high, I could leave the shipping canal that jogged around an island and head straight on through a more direct route that was partially obstructed by wing dams. "Water flows 3 feet deep over the largest dam, you'll make it no problem."

I had encountered this before, along the shores, where water accelerated as it poured over a wing dam and dropped 2 or 3 feet, but with no risk of running aground or even breaking its surface into a haystack or wave. With this in mind I trusted him, and an hour later entered the lesser channel that went straight past the island in question. As I approached the lower half of the island, I could hear something ahead. Water often rushes over the wing dams along the shores, but this turbulence was undoubtedly more substantial. I rowed on, too late to turn back upstream, and saw the river made a horizon before continuing on below. No rocks were visible, so I just kept my momentum and rowed on. The water dropped a bit before going over the wing dam, so I would be upon the structure before I would have a chance to read the conditions and find a V to shoot. I sat down from my perch upon my seat at the last minute and went on faith that I'd make it ok over the unseen precipice. CRASH!! I ground almost to a halt and was thrown violently off an even keel. I had smashed into a rock but continued to grind my way over the dam. In my panic, I withdrew the oars from the water and sat low in the boat. *What the hell just happened?* By now I was in the calm waters below this rip-wrap, and I looked up to see a boulder the size of a toilet above me. It was the only one in the whole dam, which stretched for almost a quarter mile from bank to bank. One damn rock in the whole river, and I hit it.

Enraged and panicked, I checked the inside of the bilge for water. There was none; the epoxy bonding the planks had held true. Surely, I cracked at least one plank, however, and only hoped that water would not breach my boat. Everything was sound, but I was in a panic over what I had done to my boat- how irresponsible of me it was to go this way-but how could I have known not to trust Duane? Had he steered me wrong on purpose, or was that drop really navigable in his mind? Still, he should know the river... I rowed on under the sun the rest of the day, although a shadow had been cast over this whole trip. Whisper had been scratched in places along the way, but this was a serious hit he had taken. Would the hull be breached? Water could seep through tiny cracks in the planking and make its way into the boat. Just as bad, the epoxy coat had assuredly been seriously breached, and now the planking would wet, possibly never to dry again: the classic dry rot sandwich.

I made it 50 miles that day and camped on a sandbar. To top things off, the bugs were out and I snapped another pole as I tried pitching my tent. Sometimes bad things just pile on top of each other. I was awakened alternately through the night by the sweeping spotlights of the tugs and my own panicked night mares of running aground or being overrun by the steel giants of the river.

June 2nd would inevitably be better. I started early since I was to meet my parents on their way to Memphis. We chose Caruthersville as the rendezvous point, another 50 miles from my last campsite. I passed through a narrow section of river where a sandbar bottlenecked the flow. A 30-barge tow was moving upstream. When abreast with me, the pilot came out of his five-story vessel. He looked me, then turned to the turbulence he was kicking up behind his tug. He looked back at me and snapped a salute before returning to his quarters.

I was making good headway and would have avoided rowing in the hot midday sun except I ran into Goodman, Billy, and Bryce who were out celebrating Bryce's 21st birthday. We traded drinks-snowshoe grog and Floyd's (now called Musky-dine) wine for Miller Lite and Boone's Farm. They said they'd seen a few guys like me, one who busted out of prison (he was apparently in on drug charges), stole a row-boat, and was headed for Mexico. They had given him beer and food to help him on his way. I rowed off the effects of the drinks and struggled to rehydrate under the midday sun as I regained my course. I met my parents just as we planned, and they took me out for pizza. A good end to a great day—Whisper had not been breached, either.

Next day I made it 67 miles again, including a prolonged stop where I talked with Dee, Luke, and company. They offered me a place to stay, but I wanted to make Memphis quickly. They sent me off with chips, venison sandwiches, and a beer. Another great crew.

I made the final 20 miles into Memphis on June 4th. I took a moment to bathe and scrub Whisper down a little before making the grand entrance into the Mud Island Marina. Roy in the office said that if a person doesn't have motor, there is no charge for mooring. Security in the evenings, too. I also had the chance to try out the security system of my deck floor locking into place over Whisper's aft compartment to secure some of my gear.

I restocked groceries and supplies in Memphis, played with my nieces, and enjoyed a few days rest with family. My mom and sister, Mary Beth, made terrific meals and I had a bathroom all to myself. I could get used to regular showers. Dad and I went down to Beale Street and tried out a few establishments. We made friends with Ms. Zeno the Louisiana Mojo Queen at Silky O'Sullivan's. She made me promise to wear a life jacket while I was on the river.

I left the Sedona with my parents to be taken back north. I figured the extra weight and wind resistance was not worth the mobility in the few towns I would be hitting in the coming weeks. Next morning, Dad and I got a late start in heading to the Marina. We missed the exit and took the next one that took us to the riverfront. Skies were dark and whitecaps were blowing upstream. I would have to get used to the idea of getting on the river… We were pointed toward Beale Street, so we decided to stop in to say hi to Ms. Zeno and the crew once more at Silky O'Sullivan's. We finally decided we should head back to Mary Beth's house around midnight. Better luck with the river tomorrow, so long as we don't miss the exit again.

On take-two of my Memphis departure, I rowed out under another stiff wind and threatening skies. I was snagged by the edges of a couple passing squalls, but the thunderstorms passed mainly to the north or south of me before the skies cleared for the evening.

Regaining the Rhythm

South of Memphis, the sandbars continued to grow as the river level dropped in its seasonal recession toward summer. Midday sun would send temperatures into the nineties and, when I could take it no longer relief would come in the form of afternoon cloudbursts. One afternoon I saw a line of boats on a sandbar, a pretty significant party going on. I pulled harder to port to check out the scene, and a few people yelled for me to stop in. So I did. I moored Whisper and had a couple guys come up to check out the boat and find out about the trip.

"How far you going?"

"Nawlins." I had previously been informed of the proper pronunciation of The Big Easy.

"Damn, boy, that's a long haul. Where you coming from?"

"Wisconsin."

"Well holy shit! You gotta be over half way there! How long you been on the water?"

And so the conversation went. Great people, but I was a bit nervous at first with so many people crowding my boat with all my gear laying out in the open. Gradually, the group thinned and the conversation migrated back toward the group's grill. I was talking to a guy a couple of years younger than me who was a commercial shipping pilot. As we spoke, he finished his can of Bud Light and tossed it over his shoulder into the river. I couldn't help myself and mentioned that I had garbage bags if he just wanted to throw his empties in my boat. In fact, I could take all his trash if he wanted. He felt bad at this and kind of apologized. I wasn't there to guilt trip anyone, so I changed the subject. Then I noticed a gal in the next boat over throwing a bottle into the river that was still half full, a stream of foam pouring out as it flipped through the air. I looked the other way up the beach and in the space of 20 seconds saw two more empties fly into the river.

I had told myself back in Iowa that this was to be a vacation, that I would enjoy the company of people rather than come down on how mindless and lazy we can be. This level of desecration was hard to swallow, though. But it was the accepted norm. No one had set a higher standard to live up to. The people were as friendly as any I had seen on the River. In fact, Hunter, the pilot, took some friends and me out on his boat to ride a buoy. Kind of like riding a bull, but here we tamed the red markers floating in the shipping channel. A good time. The party was breaking up as we pulled back into shore. I was offered use of a washing machine and a place to crash, but I declined. Still not sure why, but I wanted to be by myself for a while.

Over the next couple of weeks, I really fell into a rhythm. There was not much to see from the river, few bluffs and no mountains. Towns were set back behind levees, mainly out of sight. The days were hot, really hot for a Wisconsinite still coming off the winter temperatures, until it rained. And it did so almost every afternoon. I passed under an unknown bridge early one afternoon on a fairly nondescript stretch of the stream. There was maybe a sand bar in sight and not much other than bottomland forest on the shorelines until the river curved to the left and out of sight. I gazed downstream, in the midst of what in Ladysmith would have been the most disparate part of the day. Instead of growing anxious over my position and lack of long-term direction, however, the horizon of what I could see on the river welcomed me, warmly beckoning to explore this next bend. I was precisely where I needed to be, doing what I needed to do. The future would take care of itself. I was content to be in this moment, living the dream. What a great existence that was, beautifully impermanent because it had to be. This river wasn't my destination, but part of my path, a beautiful poem.

Evenings were terrific. I would pitch camp under the pastel of passing afternoon clouds, the rich light softening everything around and making it more welcoming. Thinking back on it, perhaps the path I was on lent itself to that warmth at that time of day... sunset. Far from instilling fear, a contentment would often wash over me at this powerful hour of the sinking sun. I was happy.

There really was not a whole lot going on south of Memphis. I stopped in at different towns, made a great friend Charlie at the library in Greenville, Mississippi, Jimmy Jones at Vicksburg, Roy and his wife at Natchez, and I kept rolling on from there. As I passed out of Arkansas on my river right and into Louisiana, the song Louisiana Saturday Night by Mel McDaniel popped in my head. Another consideration loomed about this trip. Would I sail along the coast or not? Dad was totally against the idea, and almost talked me out of considering it. I talked to him on the phone, though, and told him I could not give up the idea without chewing on it for a while. I had a good grasp of what the River would throw at me. No idea about the Gulf, though. I noted in my journal on June 14th: *I feel a bit reckless. Not as a hazard to myself, more like I'd chew up & spit out anything that'd be thrown at me.*

Dad was really sweating this decision, though. He had other issues going on, and the last thing he needed was more stress. The more I thought about the trip so far, it had the character of professionalism. I was well outfitted for the journey; I was organized in my routine of rowing and camping. Everything was documented, and I left campsites better than when I arrived. There was a standard protocol for everything. To venture out onto the Gulf, even if I would remain close to shore, would be a whole other can of worms. I would have to build a mast, experiment with a bowsprit for a jib, and re-learn what I was doing. To make that leap on this trip would be changing the whole character of the voyage, and probably not for the better. Best to end it where it would die naturally—at the end of the River. To do it now would be forcing things, and that is where a person gets into trouble. Limits need to be exceeded with greater discretion than that.

Cloudbursts and Commerce

On June 14th I was pushing again for 70 miles, my third attempt at that mark. The first two had ended at 67, the first at the Cape Girardeau stop, and the second abbreviated by Dee, Lulu, and company north of Memphis. It really looked like I might break that barrier when the afternoon storms started blowing in. No problem, I would row right through them. But today was different.

Winds whipped in bursts that snapped across the river. I looked to the west—black. *Ok, I'd best pull over for this one.* I moored Whisper just off a sandy point and tied the painter off on my reliable army shovel that was jammed into the sand. I looked again skyward. Uh-oh. Black skies with fingers of grey clouds extending down almost to the treetops along the front. The whole mass was flying to the east, and behind it the sky boiled in tones of deep blue and green, like a giant bruise aging before my eyes. *This was gonna be a good one.* I walked up to the edge of the forest and took cover by an old tree that had drifted to that resting spot. The rain came sideways, slapping my flesh more than wetting it. Lighting flashed and thunder clapped all around me, and I was overcome with excitement. I ran out onto the open sand and did a quick scan of Whisper's mooring. Check. I threw my head back and screamed at the sky: *Wheeeeewwww—Whooooo!* It was idiotic for me to be out exposed like that, but I was living this storm for all it was worth. I had gotten myself here, and if I was somehow struck down right then and there, it was with the satisfaction that I was living the biggest dream I ever had. This storm was nothing to be scared of; it was a celebration.

I looked again at Whisper's mooring lines once the storm hit. The sand had become saturated with rainwater running through it, and the solid beach I had jammed the shovel into was now becoming more like quicksand. Not good. I ran over to the lines, gathered them up, and waded out to Whisper. I grabbed the bow eyelet in my hand and crouched in the river to weather the storm alongside my vessel. I grew chilled in the rain, but the storm soon passed. I decided to take my chances with remnant lightning as I took to the water again, under skies that were calming and growing soft in the evening light. What a beautiful evening. But alas, even with the added few miles after the storm, the last sleepable site I hit came (again) at 67 miles from the day's starting point. Still, not a bad haul.

Those last few days above New Orleans were pretty interesting. The day after that storm I rolled into the industrial waters of Baton Rouge. No secure place for my boat, and now I was surrounded by mammoth ocean tankers coming and going from the Gulf and ports all over the world. I was a veritable fly in a soup bowl. With bad feelings about any prospective mooring spots, I blew through town and stopped on the outskirts only to fill my water jugs at a veterinary clinic. I moored between a shore of rip-rap and rafts of staged barges waiting for cargo. This seemed to be quite the desolate section of river. May as well get used to it, cause there would be traffic, staged barges, rip-wrap, and industrial docks for the rest of the route into New Orleans. The river channel was straightened (relatively so) and engineered to not waste shoreline with woods or sand bars. This meant campsites would be few and far between, so I had to check my stops carefully.

I returned to Whisper's mooring spot and was clamoring on the rocks to retrieve the lines when I saw a dragonfly hatching from its nymph stage. I watched as it sat there, gently flexing its new wings, waiting for them to dry. Suddenly, it beat them faster and took flight. New Life. I just have to know what scale to look for it. The river has not been stripped of all its beauty, even here.

I rowed on for a few hours and rounded a sharp bend that harbored a thin strip of beach on its inside shore. Ahh, refuge for the night. It was a bit early, but this would be the last chance I would have this evening to camp on a sand bar . A beautiful place to take shelter, at that. Next morning I snapped a picture of a waxing moon over a predawn sky that cast hues of pink across the ripples on the river. Beauty before chaos.

I struck camp, and since I hadn't been able to stop in Baton Rouge, I headed for Plaquemine, Louisiana where I would run a couple errands and update my email list at the library. This was a cool town. Now deep in the boot of Louisiana, I began seeing plants familiar from my time in Ecuador. Banana trees that bore fruit, hot pepper plants, ornamentals, palm trees, and southern conifers all told me that I definitely was not in Wisconsin anymore. This exotic flora indicated that I had not just rowed from one location to the next, but an appreciable distance. Like I covered some significant arc of the Earth's surface. It felt good to be here, perhaps a step closer to connecting my home in Wisconsin to my home in Ecuador. The two most distant corners of my world tied that much closer together. I took my time and spent a couple hours walking to and from the library. I made some calls and picked up some fried southern cuisine.

Those hours were quite an investment of a scarce resource, but if I was to live in the places I passed, then this was the only pace to travel. I launched again at about 3:00 and rowed through the heat and building clouds. I passed another sandbar—do I camp here or not? It was about 5:30, and I still wanted to log some miles on for the day. Winds weren't too bad, and if I pushed it I should be able to make the next sharp bend at Donaldsonville perhaps just after sunset. I moved on. The clouds continued to build into isolated towers of black cumulonimbus set off by the blue sky and sun shining between them. I took my time, snapped some photos, got drenched, and the clouds passed. Man, I felt good.

I leaned into the oars and noticed the wind building. Seems like it's almost easier to find motivation to row hard when there's a bit of wind pushing against a person. Well, I would get plenty of motivation because the skies darkened once again and the wisps of wind grew into a steady force marked on occasion by powerful gusts. Waves sprang to life and the current died a slow death. The sky mourned its passing by donning a cloak of black, and I got poured on for almost an hour. Barges staged at river right reflected the waves of the tow and tanker traffic, preempting any attempt of a rhythm. The day was petering out; I was about to as well. No place to camp, and I knew there would be no haven before Donaldsonville. I was pelted by wind, rain, and waves. My only company were the rusted steel walls of tankers, tugs, and barges, which weren't any fun at all. Progress was a crawl. I was going to be out after dark.

I knew what I was in for, so I set up my lights ahead of time and turned them on. How would any pilots see such pitiful lights in a jungle of other lamps, reflections, and spotlights? Would I make it to Donaldsonville, or would I be lunch meat for a tug? And those options assumed my strength would hold out. Man, what had I gotten myself into? I had indeed taken a monstrous bite out of a hog's ass, and now had to get my own ass out of it. I pressed on, the day growing darker, but winds not relenting. I needed rest, but no shelter was to be had and constant vigilance was needed to avoid tugs and ferries that were crossing between docks and tows that were being assembled.

Finally, I snapped. The fear was gone, displaced by rage. I threw my head back and screamed to the heavens: *You want me? You take me, Mother Fucker! But if it ain't my time, let me live by my own fucking means!*

Well, I wasn't struck dead. The remaining light prominated the wind over the horizon and abandoned me, . I was left alone with the manmade river traffic as my only concern. The long straight channel I had been on was drawing to an end, and Donaldsonville was at the bend—my goal. The river turned to the left, which meant I needed to be on that shore if I were to catch any hopeful sandbars on its inside curve. That meant I had one last danger in front of me, but the worst one: I had to cross the river in the dark with barges, tows, tankers, and personnel ferries to contend with. I was the subject of a video game, but stuck in slow motion.

I waited for a pause in traffic and put my beam to the current. I bee-lined it for the southern shore, and put everything I had into the oars. In the middle of the river, I looked downstream and saw a boat bearing down on me. I redoubled my efforts—man if that guy doesn't see me, I just may be done for. When he was within about 300 yards, he veered to port and gave me plenty of room as he passed. Whew. I made the other shore without incident but still had about a half mile of docks and shuttling tugs to deal with. Finally, I left the artificial lights behind me and was in the midst of hundreds of staged barges, floating silently at their giant mooring posts. The bend in the river was approaching.

Passing the final series of barges, I looked to the shore. In the blackness I could only make out the contours of the treetops; anything below them in the foreground was completely obscured. I lowered my head to the water and gazed downstream as I entered the bend. Where the hell was that sandbar? Did it exist? (My assumption of it was solely based on my reading the river. These things are not marked or even depicted on any maps.) Would I see it if it did? Would I be able to fight the current to get there if I did sight one? Shit, I didn't even know what sort of figure to look for. How deep was the water here, anyway? Would I run aground on rip-rap?

I risked a closer run to shore, adjusting my course harder to port. I lowered my head to the water again. I could see a level something just off the water about 100 yards off, but I could not make out what it was. I tried not to look directly at it, allowing the dim lighting sensors of my eye to do their thing. It was level, but with a squared end. Was it a loaded barge? No, it sloped gently from the trees. It was dry sand! Cautiously, I pulled harder to port and eased to shore, playing slightly into the current as I went. It was a steep drop from the beach into the current, thus the squared end to the sand. Just upstream, in a harbor formed partially by a mass of staged barges, was a perfect mooring place for Whisper. Salvation at last. I threw my bags ashore, moored Whisper with his lights on for the night, and pitched camp. I dove into the sleeping bag with the biggest sense of relieve I might ever have had. It was about 11:00 pm, but I made it. I was still tense and scared, but safe while Whisper was well protected. That was a warm feeling. No more risks like that, though.

What would tomorrow bring? I learned that below Baton Rouge there are no wing dams to channel the current. The river runs at least 65 feet deep for the tankers too. This means slow current. Where I had been pushing 70 miles, I now struggled through the heat of the day and impending storms to force out 45. I pushed on with La Place, LA as my goal for the day. That stretch of river…well, it sucked. Nothing but industry, cranes, steel shores, confused seas, wind, and heat.

There comes a time in every good trip when a person gets sick of the toil of the trail. The trials are being met, but less enthusiastically. The thing starts to drag on, and the end is a welcoming notion. Dehydration, lack of sleep, fatigue, sunburn, those goddamned saddle sores, that unforgiving sun, and now noise, artificial river banks, seagoing monsters, dust, and that relentlessly muddy water. I had known to expect trials, fears, tests of will and strength, and I had weathered them well. But now the shit was getting old. There was no peace here. No backwaters, no dragonflies, no eagles, deer, coyotes, or drunken river rats to keep me company. At about 1:30 pm, at the apex of the day's heat, I scribbled across a half page in my journal: *Get me the fuck off this river.*

But I couldn't bail out like I did that night at the cottage. I had grown enough since then anyway to know better, even if the option were there. I knew what to do. I slowed down, drank some water, took a breather, and set out again with a slower rhythm. I would make the river bend at La Place that afternoon, and that was all I needed to worry about at this point. There should be sand there to camp on, but I would make do with whatever I could. I knew the shoreline would be bare of barges and docks, same as all the large bends in the river.

I did make La Place, just in the nick of time. The clouds were building, but not in cumulous piles. A frontal line was moving in, another storm. Now for the question: Do I wait this storm out in Whisper, or do I scramble to get the tent set and hope I get it guyed down before the rain and winds hit? In my characteristic habit of pushing things, I scrambled. I moored Whisper between rafts of staged barges and went to work on this less than level strip of exposed sand. In the middle of setting the tent, I looked toward the sky and caught a glimpse of whisper being broadsided by a monstrous wake from a tanker. He washed into shore and was nearly dumped on his ear. I dashed to the water and grabbed a gunnel as if my life depended on it, just as the largest in the series of waves struck. I was able to keep the boat upright, but barely. Whew, that was close. I reset the mooring line as far out from shore as I could muster, and fastened a stern line that I pulled tight enough to keep the bow pointed into any more waves. All of which takes extra time.

I did get the tent up and dove in just as the showers struck. The wind howled and I couldn't see anything through my rainfly. The downpour was deafening as it plastered my shell, and I sat in the open doorway of my tent (protected by the rainfly), holding the poles of this meager shelter in the hopes that they wouldn't break. Worst of all, I couldn't see Whisper. I sat there for over 90 minutes, hoping like hell that Whisper was ok. The deep fatigue of the trip was upon me. In this moment, it overcame me. I sat there, in a storm that although severe did not pose an existential threat, and got choked up with tears brought on by the wear of the trip. Each challenge was met with less energy, and the conditions were becoming overwhelming. Finally, the winds let up but the rains kept on. I ventured out, getting instantly soaked to the bone, to bail some water from Whisper's bilge and returned to my tent, emotionally and physically spent. Despite my worries, compounded by the illusory walls thrown up in front of a dream that was about to come true, I slept deeply and soundly. New Orleans was 30 miles downstream. Those walls really weren't so illusory, though. Storms, heat, industry, and harsh waters were taking their toll. How long could I go on like this? This level of effort surely wasn't sustainable—trying to get the 60+ miles I'd grown accustomed to and averaging 45 hard earned ones below Baton Rouge. I was only moving forward on the momentum of this dream, not my own endurance.

Rising early, the goal was to set out before the sun. As I unzipped my rainfly to welcome a clear morning, I heard the familiar SNAP. A third busted tent pole. Something must be in my favor (Thanks Quad Cities Jim) for this not to have happened in the winds of just a few hours previous. I don't ask too many questions; I just try to figure out how to earn more karma tickets to keep these little miracles coming.

I threw my wet tent and sleeping bag on top of my gear aboard Whisper and hit the water. It was going to be a long day. I rowed through the most industrial waters yet as I approached New Orleans. I skirted a huge dock when I saw longshoremen standing there staring at me. Then I heard over a loudspeaker, "Row, Row, Row your boat, gently down the stream…" I returned their salutation with a wave. It was good to be acknowledged.

In all this industrial mess, where was a guy to moor? I was definitely going to check out the Big Easy, and it seemed I would have to find a marina on Lake Pontchartrain where I could crash. But first I would have to get that far. Back in Vicksburg, MS, Jimmy Jones gave me the pages of the Lower Mississippi River's nautical charts for this stretch. He ran local river tours up there and was in no need of these pages. He even told me to take the whole book of charts, but I had picked up Gazetteers of Mississippi and Louisiana and only needed details for this very last stretch. To get to Lake Pontchartrain, I would have to row all the way through the crescent-shaped river bends to the canal just east of town. Then I would lock through and row another 5 miles out to the lake, and hope there was a marina within a reachable distance.

After passing some deserted docking areas that had been destroyed by Hurricane Katrina, I came round a bend and passed under the main toll bridge. The high rises of the business district were directly to my left. Next to them was the French

Quarter and Jackson Square. That was where I wanted to be, but I had no possibility of mooring here. I rowed on to the entrance of the canal and entered.

Two shrimp boats were pulled up at the lock, and a tug with a single barge just behind them. I rowed up to the guys on the shrimp boats to get some information. White and his buddy DD each had their own vessels they claimed to have built themselves. They were accompanied by their respective sons and a yellow lab. A very laid back crew, doing what they loved, shrimping. They would work all night in the canals, harvesting their catch.

I heard over a loudspeaker behind me: "Hey, you in the rowboat. I want to have a word with you." It was the captain of the tug. *Great.* I had been in industrial waters for 4 days, and I'm sure I had pissed off more than my fair share of tug boat captains. I could only imagine what they had to say about that dumb ass rowing a boat through these waters, a risk to himself and everyone who tried to avoid running him down. I rowed over to the barge and the captain had come out and walked to its bow.

"Hey. Were you up by Vicksburg about a week ago?"

"Uh, yeah, that's about right."

"I knew it was you right when I saw you just now! I was doing a run up there, in the middle of nowhere, and I see this guy rowing a boat and he doesn't even have a motor. What in the hell is this guy doing way the hell out here, I asked myself. And now here you are again!"

Frank is this pilot's name. Super nice guy. DD had mentioned something about a current in the shipping canal in rhythm with but lagging just behind the tides on the Gulf and the Lake. I asked Frank about them, and he invited me aboard to check out the tide schedule. We went up into the air conditioned pilot house, and he showed me the controls, one independent set for each diesel burner. We talked about life on the river as a deck hand and pilot, and he went to his laptop for online tide schedules. "Looks like you'll hit the tail end of a nice push, if they let us lock through anytime soon. Lockmaster said it'd be about another hour."

Here I thought these pilots and captains were suffering in the heat just like me. Nope. They have fresh water, showers, air conditioning, sleeping quarters, cd players, a full kitchen, and wireless internet. Not too shabby. By contrast, I had to hold onto the pilot's chair to steady myself upright, was red as a lobster from the sun, hadn't showered since Memphis, and was living on PB&J, beans and rice, and dehydrated milk. Yum.

Finally, the lockmaster called frank's phone and let him know he could stage himself. Frank talked the guy into letting me lock through with all three vessels, but the powered ones were to enter the lock first. No problem by me. After they had all positioned themselves in the lock, I pulled alongside DD's boat and held his gunnel as we locked through. I said my goodbyes and we were all on our respective ways. It was about 5 miles through the canal. I passed scrap yards and beached boat corpses that had been tossed there by Hurricane Katrina. There was a bit of a head current as I shot one last narrows in the canal before coming out on the lake, but it was highly doable. I entered onto the waters of Lake Pontchartrain; my first salt water (yes, I tasted it, even back in the shipping canal) that didn't have a terrestrial horizon.

A number of sailboats with their billowing spinnakers glided a ways offshore. A local afternoon regatta. DD and White told me about a marina 4 or 5 miles to the west, so I made my way in that direction. The boats rounded a marker and joined me on that course. Now I had some competition in these light airs. I was just able to keep up with most of them, but as darkness fell, so did my energy. I could make out the lights of a restaurant that seemed impossibly far in my condition, but I assumed that was the finish line and bucked up to the task.

There was indeed a marina there, but for some reason I felt it imprudent to enter. Instead, I pulled into the dock of a restaurant that was situated on a small inlet across from the marina. Landry's Restaurant. A fine establishment, and just what I needed: a meal.

Luckily, they had outdoor seating. A waiter offered to get me out of the heat and inside, but I objected, "I don't think you understand. It would be better for everyone if I stayed out in the open air. Let's just say I haven't exactly been up on my personal hygiene the past few weeks."

It was 9:00 pm. Fifteen hours on the water that day, topping off one hell of a 5-day push. I called Mom and Dad to let them know I made it, and told them I would probably not hang in New Orleans, but head to Venice. That was the last town on the River where Dad was to meet me in 4 days and another 80 miles downstream. Tomorrow, however, was for rest and digging the Big Easy.

A day's rest. It would take that long just for my body to realize how depleted it was. Basically, I had been pushing myself since leaving Memphis 2 weeks prior. Long days on the water, storms, sun, heat, and the stress that comes with industrial traffic were eroding my strength with each passing day. This final push into New Orleans had been the real kicker. The current was slow as ever, and with the destination in sight I was forced to run an extra 10 miles in zero current to land at this restaurant after dark. Forty-nine grueling miles.

A Crescent City Respite

I feasted on conch fritters and onion rings, stuffing myself silly. I drank down water but was still dry from the 100 degree heat. Finally, I achingly took my leave and returned to Whisper. I crossed the inlet to a new section of dock that was in replacement of more Katrina damage. I threw a sleeping pad and bag on the planks and dove in, sweltering under the covers but assaulted by mosquitoes if I left any part of me exposed. For the first and only time that trip, I put on my mosquito suit and finally dozed off around midnight.

I awoke in the morning and finished my left over grease pile of onion rings. All my gear stowed neatly, I again crossed the channel to Landry's where I moored in the open, forced to put some faith in the human condition if I were to check out New Orleans. I tied Whisper between a pier and a post. It would take some finagling for someone to board him, and I hoped that the time needed to do so would dissuade any would-be thieves. It looked like a decent neighborhood, anyway.

I walked through a parkway to a main drag. Katrina had hit this part of town harder than just about any other, and there was little in the way of infrastructure. It seemed people were waiting for local businesses to return before they resettled here, and the businesses were waiting for the people to come back. So it lay stagnant, blocks of dilapidated houses with the dikes holding back water that flowed at a level higher than the surrounding land. Strange.

I hoped to catch a bus downtown and make my rounds for the day. No busses here though. Just a gas station, where upon inquiring I learned I was forced to walk 2 miles to the central cemeteries. That was the closest stop for the buses, the point where they turned around and headed back toward the business district. I walked down Canal Street, gawking at the vacant lots and houses that looked just as I had seen on the evening news. Waterlines still leveled almost with the tops of their doorways. Orange circles and Xs were spray-painted on the façade. Other lots sat vacant; the houses wiped out. Some had returned and remodeled or were living in the famed trailers still parked in the front yard. This was a fairly affluent neighborhood, too. People's lives simply washed out to sea. As a northerner, I sympathized with the plight so many people here were going through. Still, part of me reasoned that it's common sense not to build a house below sea level, much less a city.

A dull exhaustion was wearing on me. I can normally afford a day's walk without blinking twice, but this meager stretch was really taking its toll. I actually stopped and took a break under a pine tree in a broad median at one point. I reviewed my route for the day and drank some water before moving on to the central gardens where acres of above-ground tombs filled the cemeteries. Within minutes a bus came by and I was on my way to the business district. I hopped off a couple blocks from the library and took care of business before heading out into the city to see what was there. I continued southeast on Canal Street, dividing the business district from the French Quarter.

Then I saw it labeled on a lamp post: Bourbon Street. A lane where a person can get into precisely as much trouble as they want, seek out remnants of a French colonial origin, or just have fun. There are drinks, drugs, music, art, sex, Huge Ass Beers, and more. It's the kind of place a person has to live with a bit if discretion in order to last long. Just like the river. I love it.

My knowledge of New Orleans, like so many other places along this River, and the River itself, is embarrassingly scant. I learn best and most enthusiastically by doing, always too antsy to study much. I walked through the French Quarter and on to Jackson Square where I listened to an old duo play "The Streets of our City," and out to the Riverfront. There were tourist shops and art galleries, and I talked with a few people along the way.

Then I made my way to Laborios, a Cuban Restaurant in the business district where my sister in law and her friend hung out every afternoon on their NOLA visit, chatting it up with the owner with whom they maintained contact and told about my trip. Something about really great mojitos and food. I walked in and Felipe, the owner, was on the phone. This was a really nice place and I was severely under dressed. I waited uncomfortably until Felipe was off the phone and he came over, looking at me with my torn shorts and beard.

"Is there a position you are applying for?"

"No. Ahh, it was recommended to me to stop in here by my friend back in Wisconsin."

"OH! You're the guy who's paddling down the Mississippi River! Yeah, come on over, let me get you a menu…"

Between phone calls about ordering napkins and setting reservations, Felipe came over and sat down with me to catch up on Guadalupe and Felicia. A very busy person, but he still welcomed me in his place, even despite my ragged state. Then he wouldn't let me pay for my lunch or the mojito I sampled. Great guy. My sister-in-law was right about the food.

I made my way back toward the French Quarter. I wrote out a couple post cards and sent them off, thinking of heading back to my boat a bit early. I was still exhausted. I thought it might be wise to rehydrate, so I stopped in a tropical looking establishment to get a lemonade.

"Sorry, no lemonade."

"Well… ok… How about a strawberry daiquiri?"

"Whoa, that's quite a change of pace, isn't it?"

"Yeah, so much for complete innocence today."

I sat at the bar, drinking my daiquiri, and I learned that I could walk anywhere I wanted with an open drink so long as it was not in a glass container. Common sense is not dead in our legal system after all. Walking down the street, I stopped on a corner, the low angle of sunshine illuminating the building in front of me with alpenglow. Live music came from some of the bars, and barricades were put in the street to keep cars out. I looked at the street sign: Bourbon and Toulouse. What a great spot. Then I heard a band in the bar across the street, jamming out Louisiana Saturday Night. Must be a sign because that was the song that popped in my head as I crossed into Louisiana from Arkansas.

I walked in the bar and noticed bottles of Guinness in the cooler. I shouted my order to the bartender over the Cajun band. He put two bottles in front of me and took the seven dollars.

"Happy hour?"

"Yep."

"For how long?"

"Dunno. Until the beer runs out, I guess."

I watched the band leader bang on the keyboard and the crazy fiddle player make love to his violin as the singer belted out lyrics to old Cajun tunes. They were all new to me, and I loved 'em. After a few rounds I called Tommy and Tackleberry to tell them where I was. I had made it. This was indeed cause for a celebration. I walked around the block once more and returned to this place known as The Old Opera House for more Guinness. I got a chance to talk to Lisa, the singer, and the keyboard player. They were a couple of years younger than me, easy going.

With that I headed up Toulouse Street but thought it may be imprudent to have a drink on the bus. Then I saw a sign for Faye's Irish Pub just ahead and walked in. I wound up talking to LB, a judge who heard a landmark murder case from which they later made the movie *Disgraced*. Then he beat me in pool. A great bar that I was sorry to leave, but I had no choice if I were to catch the last bus out to the cemeteries.

It was about 12:30 by the time I returned to Whisper, found him untouched, and crossed the inlet to my private dock. A day's rest, but now I would get about 4-hours sleep before I headed out again.

The Big River's Final Leg

Next morning I took one of my favorite pictures of all time of dawn breaking over Whisper's bow. I rowed back through the canal, this time with the tidal current helping me along-just as planned from my reading of the tidal charts the day before. I arrived at the lock and awaited passage with another tug. While sitting there I saw a log floating about 50 feet away. Then I noticed it had nostrils. My first gator, about a 9-footer. Pretty darn cool. My energies awakened and I had a morbid urge to wrestle it. He wanted nothing to do with me as I eased closer in Whisper, and made his way amongst some pilings and out of sight. A lizard with teeth. Maybe wrestling wasn't such a good idea, but the idea got me fired up to tackle the river ahead.

While I locked through, a tender tossed me a line to moor by. As the gates were about to swing open, I heard a horn blast, so I released the line just to prepare to exit the lock, just as I had in obedience to the blasts some 1000 miles upstream.

"What the hell you doin', boy?" growled the voice of the lockmaster.

"I heard the blast, so I released the line."

"You don't let go a that line until I tell you! Yer Gonna Git Killed on the Mississippi River..."

"OH YEAH?!? WELL IT DIDN'T KILL ME IN 1600 MILES SO FAR!" I growled back.

He was silent after that. I took my leave, pleased with my handling of the situation.

The next 2 days were spent passing through no-man's land on the delta. The Coast Guard hovered over me in a helicopter at one point, and two of their boats stopped by to see how I was doing. A fire boat also came round, and one of the guys tossed me a Diet Pepsi to help me along my way. Good people. Other than that, there was nothing but dykes along the banks, helicopters ferrying people to and from oil platforms, and tankers. That evening I camped on shore in the midst of some pretty active piers. A crane was unloading a barge, its contents being transferred to a tanker. I left my navigation lights on, but was still worried my boat might be crushed by a tug driving a barge aground. I left my tent when I heard them changing barges, and the pilot of the tug must have seen me by my LED light. He shined me with his spotlight, swept over to Whisper, and back to me, as if to say "I see you, nothing to worry about." I almost slept soundly after that.

I hammered out 45 miles and 35 miles those 2 days, respectively, which landed me at Cypress Cove Marina at around 5:00 on June 24th. I had been in contact with my dad, and he was going to be there round 6:00. I hung out for a while, met Sabrina who worked the store, and a fisherman who let me shower in his room after hearing my story. That 10 minute aqueous massage was exactly what I needed. I dropped some trash in the barrel at the marina and I saw a pick-up with lumber hanging off the back pull up. I walked over, with maybe the biggest shit-eating grin ever running across my face. I grabbed two beers from his cooler before he saw me and walked over to where he was walking his dog, Brandi. They had just come one hell of a long way for me. Brandi took a minute to recognize me, being the last thing she expected to see in this strange place. Then she was all kisses. Dad and I shook hands and didn't know what to say to each other. I'd made it. So had he.

I showed him Whisper's mooring, and we met back up with the fisherman whose shower I used. We all went out for dinner, at the only restaurant left after Katrina within an hour and a half of the joint. Good stories were traded among good company, and we hung out for a while. Then Dad and I returned to the marina where we pitched camp for the night. Another short rest, cause I still had 10 miles to go the next day.

I left at dawn under grey skies, running 2 miles against the current to get back to the River. This was the only time I had been on a channel that *departed* a river rather than contributing to it. I counted down the mile markers as I passed on, until I got to a cross roads. Three channels went three different ways, but I was at the end of my road. The Head of Passes. I snapped a few pics of the featureless horizon and sat there, reveling in the anti-climactic air of the moment. Just another spot on the River, the crescendo of a dream I'd been living since I put-in almost 2 months ago in Caryville. The trip was over.

I flagged down a fishing boat coming in off the Gulf, and the guys offered to tow me back up to Venice. Nice, but with one last thing to do. I dug under the bow and retrieved Floyd's bottle of white wine, now with a dozen or so messages in it. I kissed it and heaved it into the water—to see if anyone would answer the messages.

The guys in the fishing boat were great. I explained to the captain that we would have to go slow because Whisper didn't have the support in the aft quarters to go up on plane. He smiled and nodded, wondering what the hell I was talking about. We took off and sure enough, the transom squatted in the water with the bow pointed skyward, even though I braced myself as far forward in the bilge as I could for ballast. I grabbed my GPS, perhaps the fifth time I used it on the trip, and tracked us at 14 miles per hour. Pretty darn fast for a 15-foot displacement hull. I wonder how much gas he burned to get this boat to do that?

After the tow back upstream and the short row to the Cyress Cove Marina, Dad and I went to work building the cradle in the bed of his truck that would haul Whisper back north. We still had to find some guys to help lift the thing up there, which would be no small feat in itself. Steven, the yard manager came over to see how we were doing. We told him our idea, and he offered the use of marina's giant forklift to hoist Whisper into place—Perfect! I unloaded my gear on the dock, a small pile of bags, containers, and odds and ends that saw me so well through this trip. Steven paid me a great compliment as he checked out my gear: "We get a few guys like you coming downstream every year. I gotta say, though, that you seem to be in better shape and spirits than most of them. Looks like you outfitted yourself pretty well for this trip."

Steven dropped his forks into the water off the take-out slip, and I jockeyed Whisper in position over them. Then he lifted him out of the water and backed away from the edge of the slip so we could roll him over and power wash the hull. He pulled up to the cradle that sat in Dad's truck bed, and we slid Whisper into place atop it. I lodged gunnel bocks into place over the truck cab, fastened blocks to the top rails of the cradle to lock the boat in place, and we tied the whole thing down with four ratchet straps.

"Looks like you guys have done this before." Steven said.

We had, in fact, in coming from Ithaca back to Stevens Point. Now we were about to leave Steven's cove and head back north. One last thing to do. Lew had given me bottle number 64158 of Midleton Extra Rare Irish Whiskey for being a part of his wedding party. Now was the best time I could think of to crack it. I stood by the tailgate of the truck as I uncorked the bottle, with one problem. No shot glasses. Well, no problem, either. In prost of the occasion, I growled out a couple words I'd adapted from an old Irish folk song:

> *Here's to those that are dead and gone and the friends that I love dear*
> *And here's to you, Dad, for helping this dream come true*
> *Cause Dave Mangin rowed his boat here.*

I took a hearty pull, then passed the bottle to my dad, who did the same.

Moments later, I noted in my journal: "There's a truck parked at the Cypress Cove Marina in Venice, LA, USA. It has Wisconsin license plates and a boat atop it that won't take a motor. It's about to go Home."

We made it back to New Orleans and needed a place to crash. Dad had picked up some coupons at a rest stop at the Louisiana border for accommodations in the Big Easy. We wound up on Toulouse Street, half a block from Bourbon Street and a block and a half from Faye's-smack between the bar where I listened to music and the one where I shot some pool.

We were dead tired. It was early, though, so I asked if we could just go to Faye's for one beer and a game of pool. No problem. We walked in and I saw two dogs in the bar. I asked the bartender if a third would be ok, and he said it was fine so long as she's friendly. Brandi's warm and calm demeanor were an absolute hit. We were invited to the annual picnic thrown

by the patrons of Faye's the next day, so we said we'd be there. Then we made our rounds to see what other fun was to be had, still keeping it clean. I never put Brandi on the leash again since she stuck by our side. We walked by a couple police officers, and I waited for one to say something. As we passed them, one got our attention and approached us.

"How did you get your dog to behave so well?"

And that just seemed to be the way things went. We had a blast everywhere we were, and it seemed the people around us did too. Thirteen hours after being almost too tired for a game of pool, we finally made it back to our hotel.

We did attend Faye's annual picnic the next day. A couple tied the knot as part of the celebration, and Dad won a spontaneous horseshoe tournament. Fittingly, we drained the last of Floyd's homemade wine given to me way upstream. We took the next few days to drive north. We visited a couple places along the way, including the marina where Nikki and Sergeant hosted me on my way down. This time we had provisions to treat them to a cook out. Lots of laughing and just plain fun. A terrific trip that restored my faith in people by a long shot.

Thanks for getting me home Dad.

Sharing Whisper: Central City Boat Building
A Fish out of Water

Upon returning to Wisconsin, I housed the boat in the driveway at my parents' house for about a month. One day a neighbor came over, asking about it. He told me about a friend of his who started a boat building high school in Milwaukee. I got some contact info, and paid Bill Nimke a visit. They were staffed for the following school year, but I stayed in touch. I went back to putting mud on the wall with a stucco crew that fall and winter, but I also went through an accelerated certification program for teaching secondary education. Before my classes ended, Bill hired me at the Inland Seas School of Expeditionary Learning, or ISSEL. And so, in August 2008, I moved my things and my boats to Milwaukee to try my hand in the classroom.

That teaching experience is worthy of several volumes unto itself-me, whose street smarts rival that of one of my work boots, trying to manage a classroom of students from Central Milwaukee.

I knew so little about teaching that during our week of class preparation, which had the other teachers in a flurry to get their rooms and coursework ready, I wasn't sure where to begin. And then came the reality of the attending students. Shell shock would have been a good descriptor for my demeanor on the orientation days. I was absolutely petrified. But the school year began, and I was teaching Spanish, earth science, and physical education.

Physical Education was ok. The school was set on a short stretch of the Kinnikinnic River that retained natural shoreline. The rest of it was lined with corrugated sea wall or was channeled through a concrete swale. Classes were taking kids out in our fleet of plastic canoes for water testing, wildlife surveys, and more. I took it upon myself to teach all the incoming freshmen how to paddle a canoe. We spent a month getting out on the water as much as possible. Other subject areas included bicycling, nutrition, and even a short section I came up with on how to chase your dreams. The class flowed fairly well, but there were flare ups I didn't know how to handle. One day a particularly outspoken student named Abraham, a leader among his peers, called me out: "Mr. Mangin, you're acting just like a stuck up old white man."

Of course I was. How could I possibly relate to the challenges faced by so many of these kids forced into adulthood? Some students were born into households with single or non-existent parents, drug addiction, and unemployment. Most come to school with Mountain Dew and flaming hot cheese puffs for lunch due to a lack of grocery stores in their neighborhood, with gangs, drugs, and professional sports as their perceived best hope for a better life. I had gotten an emergency teaching license, so no student teaching. And in Central Milwaukee, I was a complete outsider. My classroom management skills were essentially nonexistent.

Earth science was a bit more of a challenge, as it required more lesson planning. I knew the material but had a hard time writing a curriculum that fit with the Expeditionary Learning model. Spanish, however, was dismal. It started rough, with simple vocabulary, and the class went downhill from there. Forty percent of my students were Hispanic and could fluently swear at me in a dozen ways that I as their teacher couldn't even understand.

There was one boy, Tim, who was not outwardly aggressive, but wanted to put on a show. He walked into the class, grabbed a desk, and turned it around to talk to his friends behind him.

I struggled to get the attention of him or his crew for about a week, and then I paid a home visit to where he lived with his grandmother. We talked for a while about the challenges he faced, not having parents involved in his life and all the pressures of living in the inner city. The next day I wondered what kind of retribution Tim and his friends would try to impose on me for taking the power struggle to his home. He entered class without his usual smile and walked straight up to me. He looked me in the eye and stuck out his hand to shake mine. He thanked me for stopping at his house and meeting his family. We had few issues after that. It was my first victory in the classroom. I savored it because there would be few others.

A week later I tried the tactic out by visiting the home of another grandmother who was trying to raise twin boys on a fixed income and living in subsidized housing. They were placed in the middle of one of the roughest neighborhoods in Milwaukee. "How am I supposed to raise two boys in this neighborhood with gangs surrounding us?" Another boy didn't have a grandmother or aunt to take care of him. He lived at friends' homes and wore their clothes to school, Just getting by however he could. Kids came from all over the city, and we had opposing gangs represented at the school. Many students walked different routes or waited at different bus stops every day in order to avoid gang activity.

I was underprepared, overwhelmed, and way out of my element. Then, about mid fall semester, we had our 2-week intensive courses. Regular classes paused, and the students focused on two subject areas for the entire 10 days. It was suggested to me that I build a boat with the kids. Of course, I accepted the challenge.

We had plans for a Bevin's Skiff, put out by the Alexandria Seaport Foundation. I walked through the plywood construction process-simple enough. I set up rubrics for comprehension of the process and competency with the tools and skills the students would learn. We started the first day with making paper models of the boats in order to familiarize students with the different parts and how they would go together. That took about twice as long as I planned. When we got to laying out the centerline of the hull, nobody knew how to read a tape measure. And why would they? I had to back up and start with more basics.

By the end of the first week, we were almost 2 days behind. I finally realized that it helped to put the daily objectives on the chalkboard (yes, we had a real one) so everyone knew what we needed to accomplish in order to stay on track. But we were still lagging. Some students were focused and wanted to see this thing happen. Others felt the whole thing to be as hopeless as all the other things that went awry in their lives and did not buy in.

One student, James, was a bit of a wild card. He struggled in the classroom, more so than other students. He could sit still for about 10 minutes at a stretch without acting out with commentary, discussions with friends across the room, or walking out of class. On the second day of looking at the list of objectives and seeing that we were half as far as we needed to be, he declared "We've got a lot to do today. We better get to it. C'mon, Mr. Mangin, no more talking; let's get to work!"

And everyone followed James' lead. I divided students into groups to get more done, and some kids stayed late to finish some component they were working on. James was the last to leave every day. At the middle of the second week, we were still behind. James stayed late and I drove him and another classmate home. The next evening we worked until 11:00 pm. And he made it back in the next morning.

We finished construction on the second Friday, when the intensive was scheduled to end. But we still had to paint the boat. Students showed up on the weekend and after school to make it all happen. Finally, on the day before Thanksgiving, the school gathered behind the building on the Kinnikinnic River where James himself christened the first boat of the Inland Seas School of Expeditionary Learning. He named it Gucci because from day one any victory was decaclared as "Gucci."

After that first success, we needed a way to get more boats launched. We were known, after all, as "The Boatbuilding School.". Bill, our director, came to me and proposed an after-school program. We met with another volunteer, Jesse, who would become one of my best friends, and we devised the RAFT Program: Real Apprenticeships for Teens. The program was split into three areas that students could choose from: ecology, bicycling, and boat building. Here I was: in over my head during the day with lesson planning I wasn't able to keep up with, struggling to maintain attention in the classroom, and exhausted and frustrated in my afterhours. So why not pile one more thing on the heap, right? Another 2 hours a couple of days a week that required planning, getting materials ready, and figuring out logistics like transportation for students.

As it turned out, RAFT turned into a respite of sorts for me. It flowed the way the classroom courses were supposed to; practically driving itself. We had students from three schools including ours, and they were all locked in on the project we were undertaking: a cedar strip canoe. We milled our own strips and built our own molds for the strongback, so this thing was authentically built from scratch, in house, by the students. I was there to demonstrate and instruct. If a block plane needed tuning, I showed the kids how to adjust the depth and angle of the blade. Then I would take it apart and have the students do it. I removed more than one strip that I stapled into place in order to show how to properly seat and fasten it. I figured we would have the boat done by May. Fat chance. But the program was popular and we ran two 4-hour sessions throughout the summer.

Among this crew was a group of students from the Clara Mohammad School who joined us. They were all related in some way, mostly as cousins. Their families were from Somalia and had fled to Kenya to live in refugee camps, where most of these students were born. Their families then immigrated to the US and some were placed in Milwaukee. They could speak English for the most part, but technical comprehension was

dicey. Upon entering the country, they had no birth or medical records, so they all had the same birthday: Jan 1.

They were the most upbeat, enthusiastic group of kids I had ever seen. When I'd get stressed out over a mis-cut or a gouge in the boat hull, someone would pipe in, "Master Mangin. It's ok. Every little thing is gonna be alright."

Even with all those additional hours poured into it, the boat wasn't christened until August. But toward the end of the summer, we did Christen *Little Thing* behind the school.

Just before the start of my second year at The Inland Seas School of Expeditionary Learning, we took a group of teens from the summer program on a 3-day canoe trip, as with the young campers 7 years previous, we ventured out on the Lower Wisconsin Riverway. I chose a shorter route this time, and one that didn't take us past a nude beach. It served as a great end cap to the completion of the first canoe and rowboat the students had built. It also got them out of the city to experience some river time. Pitching tents, lounging in the warm shoals, and burning marshmallows were completely foreign concepts to this group, especially the boys coming from refugee families. For the students and me, it provided yet another opportunity for bonding and appreciating one another. Incidentally, my dad came along as a chaperone on that one too. The kids really took to the raspy voice, beat up hat, and scrappy attitude of this old marine.

The following school year we built another cedar strip canoe with the shop classes during the school day, and the RAFT program put together a stitch-and-glue plywood rowing wherry as well as wrapping up two more skiffs that were started before I began teaching. We had the four boats hit the water all on the same day, and of course it came down to the wire. While Mr. Nimke was giving a speech of introduction, we were installing oarlocks on the wherry. The fresh gunnel paint came off on the kids' fingers as they carried the vessels down to the river. But four more boats entered the fleet that day. The two Bevin's Skiffs were *Sophie*, named after the dog who was brought in by our other shop coordinator, and *KK Explorer*, named after the river behind the school where outdoor classes were held. The second cedar strip canoe was named *Patches* because I had the students fix every mistake with black walnut as a contrast to the lighter surrounding wood, a testament to the boat's creation story. Finally, *Unknown*, the rowing wherry, was named by Nick, the student who did the most work on it. He chose that name because he was unsure what the future would hold, for him or for the school and the RAFT program.

The school was forced to close its doors that summer because of loss of funding. We launched six boats in 2 years and the lessons abounded on and off the water. I still wonder who received a greater education, the students or me. Bill Nimke is still getting kids and grownups alike into the shop and on the water through a program he started called All Hands Boatworks. They've built hundreds of boats all over the city of Milwaukee, sharing passion and education through connections that span all socioeconomic and racial spectrums.

That was the end of a saga, but perhaps the beginning of something even bigger. There was a sort of completeness about the bundles of experiences surrounding my two boats. These collections of memories and character-forming stories that took place over the course of 10 years have contributed palpable richness to my life that cannot be articulated. At least, not by me. I developed skills and built two sturdy boats, one of which carried me on an epic journey inward, the other an equally significant outward voyage. And then I was fortunate enough to share some of that passion in the classroom where six more vessels were built by students from Central Milwaukee. As time put more distance between me and the building of Whisper, The Big River Trip, and the opportunity to share aspects of it in the classroom, greater perspective was gained of the experiences. That sharing brought meaning and purpose to the passions I had chased. The compilation of memories surrounding Whisper became known as The Big River Trifecta, or BRT.

Boat 3: Endeavor

Goin Down the Road Feelin Bad.

—Woodie Guthrie

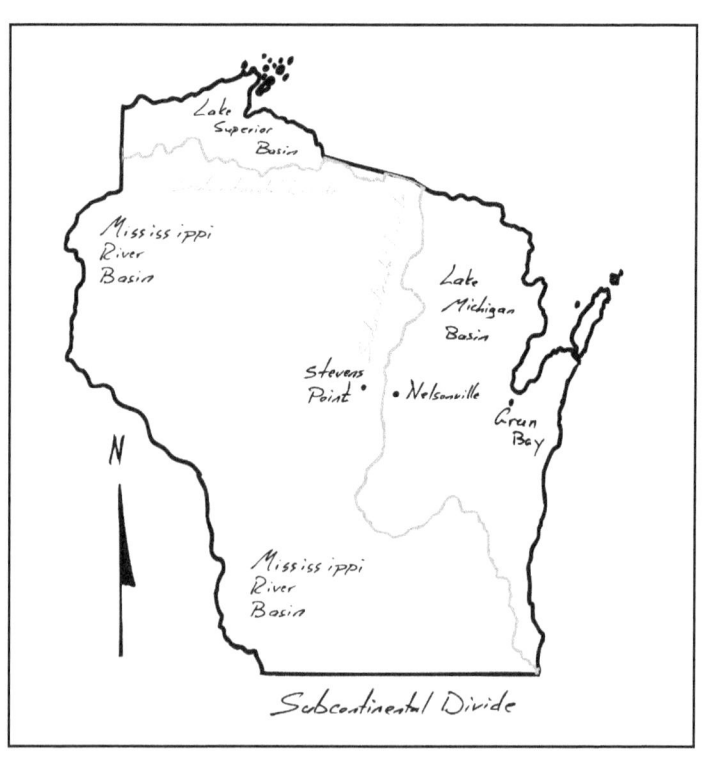

Creating Endeavor: Boats to Build

Enriched Undertakings

The building of Ripple was magical because it was my first boat and there were so many scary unknowns that had to be overcome: sourcing tools, scraping together money for materials, developing the requisite skills, and finding time and confidence to do the project. Building Whisper was rewarding as well, especially with the travel and additional learning curve involved. Although there were not as many boundaries pushed or personal firsts in building Whisper, the construction of this boat was part of a larger series of experiences in the Big River Trifecta. There seemed to be some sort of continuity and wholeness to it that I could not grasp.

Teaching at the Inland Seas charter school may have seemed separate from building and rowing Whisper. In truth, it enabled me to share what I had learned, passing on the passion of creation and also exposure to how our modern lives displace beauty, richness, and stability in nature. Providing others that exposure, that passing on, represented a potential solution to the brutality we inflict upon our natural systems. It gave me enough hope to release part of that inner cynicism and conflict. The inspiration of others through sharing of the passion and story are an indispensable part of what makes the story whole, and bigger than my isolated personal experiences. They are what makes it continue, grow, and evolve.

Another Calling

I live in Wisconsin, where, thanks to the moraines left behind by the glaciers, a ridge runs through a good portion of the state that forms a subcontinental divide. This means that roughly two-thirds of the rain and snow falling upon the state spills into rivers that feed the Mississippi and the waters that I followed into the Gulf. The balance of the precipitation that is not absorbed or evaporated runs into rivers such as the Fox, Wolf, Milwaukee, and Menomonee, all which drain into the Great Lakes Basin. After spending upwards of a few hundred years in those Sweetwater Seas, the waters make their way out the St Lawrence Seaway and to the Atlantic Ocean. This I haven't internalized because I haven't rowed or paddled those waters… yet. And that is the current intention. New trip, new boat.

Years passed between boat building projects, and my life underwent some major developments. My wife and I moved our budding family from Milwaukee back to Central Wisconsin, and I got back into the trades after burning out in the non-profit sector. As raising my kids, work, and various side projects took precedence, I was not taking much time for myself. I would get a taste of the Ripple Effect, stealing away for an occasional paddle on a local river, but as time went on, I realized I had gotten away from who I was. The best way to get reacquainted was through the means by which I originally found myself. It was past time to build another boat. What would happen if I took on the kayak project I had been considering for the past few years?

I did not know what this endeavor would entail when I started off. I figured to build a sea kayak that was suitable for the big waters of the Great Lakes and see where things led. I had been to Door County and Bayfield, WI too many times to not have a vessel that accommodates an aquatic perspective of these destinations, so tantalizingly perched on Lakes Michigan and Superior. But first I needed a shop. I took measurements, and the garage at the house was simply too small. Yes, with all the changes, I lived in a traditional abode, with a wife, two kids, and a dog in the small village of Nelsonville, with the trout-filled waters of the Tomorrow River running through it. At around 150 people, this village is about as Norman Rockwell as it gets.

As long as I was building the boat, I did not want its limitations on the water to hold me back from my wildest dreams. I went after the biggest boat that Nick Schade, a premier cedar strip kayak designer and builder of our time, made plans for. Incidentally, 25 years ago when I went online to look at boats instead of to class, Nick's website and pictures of his boats were what hooked me on the cedar strip idea. My boat would be the Expedition Single, a stretched version of his flagship Guillemot sea kayak. With an overall length of 19 feet, my 20-foot garage just would not accommodate the hull, my tools, and a workspace. Bigger boat, bigger shop. Luckily, my friends Rubina and Isaiah had a barn that might eventually suit my needs at their B&B, the Tomorrow River Homestead, also in Nelsonville. And as the name of the property would have it, the barn happened to have the Tomorrow River out its back door, whose ultimate destination was not the Gulf of Mexico, but the Atlantic Ocean.

Reflecting upon Ripple's construction and the mood of the shop that evolved over the course of that project, it occurs to me that the character of an endeavor originates as it enters the consciousness of the person who dreams it up. The person's mood, preparation, company shared, and level of fulfillment during the pursuit all contribute to the feel of the dream that is being chased. Given the feel of the barn on that April afternoon that I first visited it in 2018, this dream was cold, drafty, unlit, and in need of some serious work. For years, this barn had been used merely for storage. The major renovations Rubina and Zay embarked upon had not yet reached this outbuilding. 300-pound wooden horse stanchions stood over rotting holes in the patches of the 130- year-old timber framed floor, as best I could make out by what little light filtered through the cob webbed windows and flickered from the single fluorescent plug-in light. The loft was more readily discernable since the gaps between the siding boards let plenty of sunlight and fresh air pour through. There I had no problem making out all the bat droppings and layers of dust that accrued through the years. I also had no trouble making out the beautiful timber frame construction and the potential of that space, were one to add a couple corner windows facing the river out back. I immediately fell in love with the place, even if having a reliable entrance meant removing screws that pinned the door shut and replacing it and its rotted jambs.

Couldn't I just go buy a boat? Yes. Cheaper, sooner, with no investment of time or effort. But this is about the process. If you think of someone running after a frisbee, sprinting all out after a lofty throw that slowly floats back to Earth, the farther, more seemingly out of reach the launching of the disc, the more glorious the victory of chasing down and snatching it from the sky to save it from the ground. As such, the pursuit of this goal would make for a pretty swell memory if I could pull it off.

The challenge of converting this old storage building into a viable boat shop and experiencing the fulfillment of building a vessel here, at the exact location where the journey toward bigger waters would begin, brought an element of poetry to this story that I was about to begin living. Both my other boats had nuances to their creation stories that make them more precious. The script for this new one was already looking pretty good, based on the hurdles to even establishing the shop where construction would begin. And with any luck, this labor would result in something easy on the eye, adding a touch of style to the toil of this chase.

I looked forward to the journey of this new boat, to see how the work would progress, how the shop would feel, music that might accompany me, and things I could do to make it all the more meaningful and intimate. Would the toil, side stories, and result be as steeped in meaning as with the other two? I looked into what made the BRT so special in order to try replicating the elements.

Anatomy of a Dream

In the case of Whisper, I had moved out of state to start building a boat with a new style of construction I had to learn myself. The shipwrights at Cayuga Wooden Boatworks would offer tips on that, though. My dad and I bonded with our trips from Ithaca and New Orleans, with no shortage of material for conversation. I created the vessel that took me on the longest camping trip of my life, geographically and temporally. It was an experience of a lifetime. And then, in a whole other chapter, I got to share the new skills I had acquired with others at a Milwaukee high school. I learned new skills, created something, had an amazing experience, and then I got to share my passion and inspire others. Hmmm.

As I journalled and turned these things over in my mind, reducing their value to the essence of their purpose, I kept coming back to the same core components that made the Big River Trifecta so rewarding:

> Learn
> Create
> Experience
> Share
> Inspire

And I realized this concept is open ended. By sharing what I had learned and my passion for this type of work and travel, it inspired others. Some actually took on boat building projects of their own, and the cycle continued.

Could I apply this model to the building and use of a kayak? Well, I ordered Nick Schade's book, *Kayakcraft*, which would teach me what I needed to know about the intricacies of kayaks beyond the familiarity I had with cedar strip canoe construction. With my young family, what would the building process and paddling experience look like? I hoped to eventually paddle to the ocean, but I could never stand to be away from my kids for an extended period of time. And the sharing component—how would I do that? I could put posts on social media, but that seemed pretty thin, considering I had personally taught students to build entire boats as a result of the previous boat project. Well, one thing I was coming to embrace: You need not see the finish line before you even make it to the start. Now that I'd located the barn, it was time to establish a foundation for this venture.

It was early 2019. I was running out of projects to serve as a distraction from embarking on this endeavor. The barn needed remedial work before it could serve as an enjoyable shop space, but it would feel good to breathe another chapter into this building with previous lives of horse stabling, auto shop, storage space, and other uses untold. As for the kayak, I could buy a kit with the station molds and strips already built and milled for me, but it would feel more authentically my own if I made those things myself. Plus, I could weave a little artistry of my own into the strip patterns as I selected my own wood for them.

I figured it wise to document this process more extensively than journalling or random social media posts. I had a vision of something bigger than the kayak itself, although I was not sure precisely what. I took a bunch of concepts that were loosely orbiting the chaotic outer reaches of my mind and started a website called Art & Rugby Endeavors. This would be the platform from which to begin sharing, but I wanted there to be space for it to grow beyond me. It could serve as a platform for other people to record their stories as well. Who knows, maybe a community of people could form, sharing ideas and holding one another accountable for their respective dreams. I compiled concepts of what made an experience authentic and rewarding and tied them together in the best order I could manage. They were complicated, repetitive, and confusing, but at least all the ideas were in one place. I could refine the presentation of it all later. Most importantly, I created a blog to post updates of the building process.

The first tangible step was to fix up the barn. Entering the place, the old horse stable was too dark to see much of anything. The only light in the place hung near the horse stanchions and half of its fluorescence merely flickered. The floor was a challenge to negotiate with 2-inch gaps between the floor boards and knots, heaved planks, and rotting members. First thing was to get these 300+ pound dividers out the back door. Then fix the patches on the rotted sections of flooring. Two new doors, a window, wiring, insulation, lighting, and a ceiling-that should do it.

The thing is, I had more to be concerned about than just the barn and this project. About the time I discovered the barn, my marriage was in serious trouble. We did not have much financial security, and I needed to work extra side jobs in addition to this project. There were also local issues of groundwater contamination and park management in the community that I got involved with. Needless to say, I was spread way too thin. I promised myself to keep the barn and the kayak as the extra, to be tended to after care had been taken with other priorities. But over the course of a year or so, my relationship with my wife had alternated between nonexistent and toxic. We just could not see eye to eye. My tendency to take on every opportunity that comes my way certainly did not help matters, but it took my mind off things. Then, in early spring, 2019, after both of us had a chance to step away from the situation for a bit, we came back together and moved forward.

Priority Checks

That April, as my marriage regained some stability, I received news that rocked me to my core. My good friend Rob, whose fireside conversations inspired me to read Jimmy Buffett books and chase my dreams, who commended me on Ripple as a legacy piece, who hung on my email updates from the Big River and arranged for a lunch for me along the way, was diagnosed with stage four colon cancer that had spread to his liver. A death sentence. The doctor gave Rob about 2 years, and he would need aggressive chemo treatments to make it that far. His colon would probably be alright, but it'd be his liver that killed him. It was a foregone conclusion.

Rob is the kind of guy we could all aspire to emulate. Hilariously self-deprecating, supportive of wife and kids to his core, he focused on work and home with an eye toward the bigger picture of our experience on this planet and the effects we have on those around us. His rock-solid marriage with his sweetheart of almost three decades produced two kids, their son 10 and daughter 6 when this calamity struck. A worse prognosis could not have been foisted upon a more undeserving family.

Rob and his crew were all about living their dreams at full throttle. He had moved them to Michigan's Upper Peninsula to live at and manage an outdoor camp for a few years. They provided all sorts of people the opportunity to get out there snow shoeing, kayaking, camping, skiing, mountain biking, and fishing. Of course, he was versing his kids in those things as well. They had just moved back to their hometown of Green Bay a year before the diagnosis of symptoms he had previously chalked up to gut issues and depression.

With this new reality constantly looming in their face, Rob and his wife Teri took on a whole new perspective of life and family. Work slid to the back burner and experiences took center stage, in between checkups and chemo treatments.

Later that spring, the reality of impermanence hit me even closer to home. It became clear that my dad's congestive heart failure was getting worse. Over the course of a few weeks, he went in for tests and received increasingly dire reports. After a 3-day stint in the hospital he told the doctor and nurse: *I'm sick of this nonsense. You keep doing more tests and get bad results, and say you need to keep doing more tests. Goddammit, just let me go home for Chrissakes.* He was admitted into hospice care that day.

Over the course of the next few weeks he received visits from old friends, coworkers, neighbors, and family. He progressively became weaker and ate less and less. I spent a lot of time visiting him and my mom in Green Bay but needed to get back to work and my own family as well. Finally, on July 12th, I got a call at 7:30 in the morning from my sister. I heard in a quiet voice, spoken over a huge lump, *He's gone, Dave*. I rose from where I was sitting on my porch and went for a walk to digest this.

It was a sad time, but perhaps bitter sweet. He had been slowing down for years, and simply was not able to do the things that made him the scrappy old Marine that he always had been. Tackleberry summed it up best: *Well, he sure as hell outlived his warranty!* I found myself remembering the adventures he had with my brothers and me: mountain biking, skiing, cross country bicycle trips, and of course all of my boat building ventures. Now I would be chasing this dream on my own, but perhaps for both of us. Although who knows, maybe rather than driving out to some far-off destination to retrieve me I could now have him as a co-pilot. At least there would be fewer arguments than on our cross-country road trips!

I harnessed the adventuresome spirit of these two dying men and doubled down on the barn. My wife gave me space to work through my emotions there, and somehow new lights, doors, and ceiling all were installed with relative ease. This project just felt good in my soul, even the parts where I was itching from fiberglass or cleaning out a century's worth of dust, droppings, and cobwebs from a rotted window opening.

I finished the laundry list of projects and even replaced the old oil burning furnace with a wood stove. I would certainly be in here through the winter months, and wood glue needs to be 60 degrees to dry properly. Ripple still has a couple white streaks where the glue dried in the cold conditions of Lew's garage, although that is now just a warm reminder of that creation story and another lesson I learned along the way. For this new boat, perhaps growth would be evidenced as I avoided repeating the old mistakes and new, less severe, lapses in awareness or skill imparted their respective signatures of character. I wanted to get this as right as I could.

Art & Rugby

The days started cooling and it was high time to get this thing underway. Plans arrived from Nick Schade. I plastered the paper patterns to some plywood to cut out the station molds. I also began building a box beam that I would use for my strongback. With priorities of work and family, plus an ever-present urge to be outdoors, the work took a lot of determination to begin. I was spending extra time I didn't have to initiate this new project. How could I possibly fit this into my schedule? Shop time was spotty and progress slow, buth at least it had begun. And getting started is the hardest part.

The weeks slipped by, the strongback not really taking shape, and my thoughts turned to yet another distraction: my friend. With his illness and treatments, Rob had already cut back hours at work and was spending more time with his family when I wrote him a letter. I knew he had started a boat through a weeklong class 6 years previous that had been collecting dust in his garage ever since. He valued things that would get his family out in the wild, and that could be passed down generationally. Being a person who finished what he started, I knew this unfinished project ate at him. The barn was just about ready for occupation, so I suggested that if he had any inclination to resume work on the boat that we should make it happen. I could come to Green Bay once a week, or he could bring the boat to the barn if that worked better. Rather than a period of waiting and seeing between medical tests, maybe this could be a period of living and doing. He went for it. Now, more than ever, was the time to make things happen and tie up loose ends.

At about the same time a social media acquaintance, Bill, who I had never met in person posted about a duck boat he had inherited from a neighbor. It apparently was water-tight but needed some work. I sent him a message that if he needed any assistance, I had a shop where he could work on the boat and that I might be able to provide some direction, if needed. Surprisingly, he got back to me and accepted.

As the sun-washed days accelerated their descent into the longer shadows of late autumn, Art & Rugby Endeavors received their first two clients on the same evening. The situation was uncanny. Rob, one of my oldest family friends, came in with a brand new boat to be finished off. Bill and Marissa, friends whom I had was meeting for the first time, came in with their old relic of a duck boat in need of an overhaul. Both boats were designed for the same use, with decked ends and a broad cockpit for decoys, a dog, and gear.

Introductions were made as uncertainty mingled with the cobwebs that hung in the air. Rob had just a few coats of epoxy to brush on, some paint to apply, and trim to install. But his time was short, energy limited, and distance to the barn great. Bill and Marissa, well, they had a long road ahead. I looked at the disintegrated stems and multiple layers of flaking lead paint and wondered if they would have the approach it would take to see this project through. (Looking back, I obviously didn't know at the time who I was dealing with). Only one thing to do, and that was to get started.

After a bit of small talk, I got Rob sanding his previous coat of epoxy. Bill and Marissa started building a tent over their patient to trap the lead dust from the five layers of paint they were to remove. Bill took to this task like a puppy on the scent of a rabbit in a foreign wood. He may not have been versed in boat building techniques, but given direction, he got after it with unbridled enthusiasm. He learned quickly, picking up skills on the fly. Lots of rugby with this one, whose art is in some cases painted in broad strokes, often with a sawsall. And Marissa, Bill's quiet partner, would dive into the task at hand while keeping an eye on the general flow of things. She gracefully accepted the role of patiently pointing out when things started to go awry. They instantly were counted as friends.

Rob and Bill paid for the shop space they used. I tried to refuse Rob's contribution, but he won out, being even more stubborn than me. Admittedly, I needed the money. The rent and renovations had worn my funds thin, and I still needed to purchase supplies for the kayak, not to mention pay the bills to keep the shop open.

I was open to other uses for the shop. Rented time and space for projects was one avenue. I hoped to do some teaching in small groups too. It turned out that Rubina was planning to host a community building retreat on the homestead and asked if I wanted to partner for the event with some woodworking programming. Of course I would.

On a Saturday in October, a group of strangers entered the barn and built wooden caddies together. The participants forged heartwarming creation stories as they learned the use of some basic power tools and were able to return home with an attractive piece. Rubina hosted sessions that produced canned goods and embroidery by which to remember the weekend. It was a huge success that reacquainted me with the warm feeling of sharing my passion. In this script of Creating, Experiencing, and Sharing, the order in which they happen can evidently be nonlinear, and the components of Learning and Inspiration happen all along the way. Capitalizing on opportunities as they arise is just part of the magic of things unfolding organically.

Tuesday nights became Shop Night. After trading news of the previous week, Bill and Marissa would don masks and other PPE before disappearing into their tent to labor away at sanding and scraping. Rob would be there to make more headway on his boat. We all got to know each other in new ways through exchanged stories and perspectives. A culture was developing that warmed the shop in a way as deep and penetrating as the heat and light from the wood stove. Add to that the ambiance created by the soft bulbs in the vanity lights located throughout the shop, (creatively installed by a previous owner of the property) and this place of dust, noise, and booming personalities was taking on a rich character. Rob introduced a vital staple to the shop culture: The Poor Man's Amplifier, consisting of a mini speaker placed inside a metal bucket from which I could blast some balance of Jimmy Buffett, bluegrass, and the Grateful Dead.

The tools that made this shop come together were acquired from many sources and over the course of generations. I purchased a few myself, but many came from my dad. Others were obtained indirectly from family friends Cliff and Thomas, both who had passed on from different chapters of my life. An old high school friend's father was getting on in years and following my posts on social media. He donated his entire shop to the cause, which created perfect duplicity of key components for hosting groups. Now I had doubles of table saws, routers, bandsaws, and sanders to help streamline production amid a group. As tribute to friends past and present, a wall of memories displayed pictures of my dad and Thomas, as well as other aspects of my past that contributed to the concept of what played out in this space.

There was another section of wall, above a long rack of bar clamps, which was fast becoming crowded with quotes that

were blurted out at different times in the shop. In addition to the one liners scribbled on scraps of shiplap pine, notes of lessons learned and mementos of times with friends and clients made the wall a clutter of fresh, rich, memories.

More projects rolled in. Furniture undergoing reconstruction, a headboard for a bed, Quick one-off borrowing of tools, and multi-phase ongoing endeavors. A couple of buddies, Shane and The Reverend Eddie Danger, came in and built a marionette stage over the course of a few days. Other times, friends would stop in to just sit in a camp chair, watch the mice, and talk about life over a libation from Central Waters (the brewery was only 5 miles away). This shop was taking on a life of its own. It was about more than just the boats.

As Winter drew in, a friend contacted me about hosting another workshop, just for women. Done. On a cold day in February 2020, a group of six women who had never met came into a chilly shop surrounded by loud and potentially dangerous machinery. As I am slow to start, we awkwardly gave our introductions, and I described the drink tray and stand that we would be making as a means to learn the safety and use of almost every tool in the shop.

Before you knew it, people were advising each other on aspects of laying things out, telling jokes, and bonding over this new learning adventure. Taking breaks to warm hands by the fire and trade stories, the musty environs only enhanced the experience undertaken by these hearty souls. While not everyone was able to follow through on completion of the project, we all left as friends and the barn was an even richer place as a result.

But I still had barely begun mounting my station molds to the strongback. I could not have cared less. If this whole thing was about the process, then I was making the most of it. Forward progress was, in fact, still being made. The programming and teaching was taking on a larger role than anticipated, but it felt so good that I just trusted the flow of it. This place was something I could pour my heart into that enriched me at a soul level in return. And with the clientele I had, it barely put a dent in my bank account. My kids loved hanging out there too, and their patience with projects grew along with their skills. It took almost a year of exposure, but my daughter warmed up to the scroll saw to cut out and paint variations on her favorite shape-hearts. My son explored the use of a few more tools and fed his addiction to ballistics. If it launched something, he wanted to build it.

Then COVID hit. The programming shut down immediately after the Women in Woodworking finished their drink trays. Bill and Marissa kept away at intervals as new developments of the pandemic came about. Rob stayed away for a while. At least I was able to pour more time into the kayak, now at the phase of stripping.

I slipped into a solitary rhythm with the shop. The woodstove fire would melt the work day from my consciousness as I'd warm my hands by its radiating steel. Anticipation of the next steps on the boat would displace the fatigue in my body. Settling into my camp chair and gazing at the firelight coaxed my mental state as the mercury came out of hiding in the base of the thermometer. The raw austerity of the place was the heart of its charm. It was akin to the untamed souls I rolled with on the rugby pitch and forged lifelong bonds.

Very few areas of my life have manifested themselves in such graceful blend of art & rugby. Designer cabinets, custom lighting, and lacquered floors would have detracted from the character of the space. Basking in its authenticity, my hands warming by the fire, I would be overcome with the peace I occasionally enjoy at sunset when my internal whispers are heeded. The same soul-feeding sensation came on as in the boat shop in Ithaca, knowing that my toil was worthwhile in its own right and propelling me toward something bigger. It is at these moments that my indirection of adolescence is assuaged. I am on the right path.

Soon strips were bent into place, and wrestling with the reluctant bends in the stern hull occupied my focus as the oblong hole in the bottom of the boat shrunk in ¾" increments. As this form took shape, my ambition was encouraged and the project took on a life of its own. Work on the boat now became a matter of course . . . until April.

The snow thawed and it was time to be outside. The irresistible lure of new life pulled me out for fresh air and warming, lengthening days. My kayak sat abandoned for nearly 6 months as I turned to more time with my family and the outdoors.

Finally, in October 2020, I got back to it with a vengeance. Bill and Marissa returned after bear and deer hunting seasons were over. The paint finally removed, most of it anyway, they were now tearing into the extensively rotted portions of the boat. This was easy for the stems at each end, whose rotted oak pieces could be pulled out by the handful. The plywood sides and frames were largely intact, retaining the character of the original vessel. The dissection continued until the ends of the boat were gaping holes. The sight of it unsettled me, like the gore and dysfunction of a knee splayed open on an operating table.

At last, after over a year of toil, they were able to start adding new parts. We got into it with the compound-angled stems, the most technical pieces. How do you pattern a piece that is defined by a void and whose adjoining boards are rotted to jagged nubs and splayed apart? We drew centerlines and baselines as references and to derive angles. The pattern we made was fit by trial and error. With time, we homed in on the proper taper, angle, and thickness. Then we added an inner stem to which we fit the planks, and on the leading edge, a cutwater. The result was a 3-inch thick mass of white oak and epoxy. Robust enough to take any hits from unseen stumps it might encounter as it is rowed out in the predawn, they'll enable this boat to get its captain, their dog, and their decoys out to the best duck hunting sloughs. As winter progressed, it was on to replacing plywood decking and a couple framing members before the cockpit coaming and trim.

Rob returned as well. Lew even came up one evening to check out the barn and help with some sanding before Rob's final coat of resin. As his boat was ready for paint, Rob brought his son in, making the project multi-generational. But it was not without cost. I could see the fatigue on Rob's face despite resting up earlier in the day. He fought through the nausea and timed his visits to alternate from chemo treatments. He was on his second strategy for treatment, the first having predictably waned from its original efficacy. This array of treatments would produce encouraging results as well, but as the courses go, its results would fade too. At that point they would search for experimental and alternative treatments that might prove effective against all odds. It was a long battle with a foregone conclusion. But Rob was determined to make every opportunity with his family and friends count. He never stopped showing up to finish what he started.

I finally closed in my hull. I flipped the boat in order to start stripping the topside about the time the year switched over to 2021. The deck was approached a bit differently because I had two accent strips to lay out first, which had sort of stumbled their way into this vessel. A visit to a familiar lumber yard produced cedar and basswood for contrasting effects on this boat. As I was shuffling through piles of rough sawn lumber with Pete, the owner, I saw a strip of auburn wood that had no business among the stacks of species native to Wisconsin. Pete said it was just a cut-off from a larger slab that likely came from Africa and that I could have it if

I wanted. It came to pass that the stark contrast of the strips milled from this idiosyncratic piece formed the heart and soul of the boat's character.

Through the meditative stripping process I began to draw parallels between the stripping pattern and the course of my life. The design took shape and the artistry of this vessel started revealing itself. It was a lot to manage, but I felt like I was finding more balance. Life was entering equilibrium, or so I thought.

Getting Down to Personal Matters

As my boat started taking shape my marriage completely fell apart.

My wife and I had been seeing a counselor to get to the root of some lingering effects of the first rough spot of our relationship. As we dove in, the sessions got intense and emotions flared.

Finally, on St Patrick's Day, the last straw snapped and I needed to take emotional and physical space in the only place I could, the barn. I purchased a cot, a mouse-proof food caddy, water jugs, and rudimentary dishes. I set up a camp stove beneath the memory wall and began sleeping by the fire at night, doing my homework on the dark emotional places I once vowed to leave behind, which were again becoming too familiar. It became apparent that this mutually agreed upon 2-week break would not be enough. While I could camp out in the barn as long as necessary, my kids and I needed our time together. I needed someplace amenable to hosting them that was cheap enough for me to continue pursuing the kayak and the tripping that was to go along with it. One thing was certain. It could not be a decision between my kids and the boat. But the boat was my path, and straying from it was what brought about chronic stress and anger. And my kids. I would let nothing come between them and me. How could I stay close to both?

I spoke with Rubina and Isaiah. I would work for free if they provided the materials not already on hand or that I could salvage from my work as a residential contractor. It was a go. I would build a studio in the loft of the barn. So now I had another project to be the object of this new level of angst. How fortunate, since I did not need to be pouring that desperation, guilt, anger, and grief into the kayak. Things at the house did not improve, but I would go there twice a week to make dinner for the kids and put them to bed. We got into the routine of spending every other weekend together and making that time count as much as possible. Was my family really breaking apart? Of all the things I poured my heart into and worked like hell to have succeed, this was far and away the most important. And here I was fucking it up. Guilt, pain, and stress soared to new heights and I focused as much of it as I could on the studio. One evening in early spring we were in the boat shop working on Bill and Marissa's duck boat. I mentioned that if this thing really went south, I was going to finish my kayak, take out a good life insurance policy, and have some real fun with it.

My work performance suffered. The added work of the studio and the emotional toll of everything was making it hard to focus on the cabin I was remodeling. It was difficult to capture details, and there seemed to be a general sense of brain fog. I was building out a finished basement, often working solo with time to dwell in the family situation I helped create. The relief of not being in a triggering environment had somewhat worn off and it was time to face the impact this move was having on others-my kids. There were times, usually between moments of focused activity as I walked to grab a tool or put something away, that I would be incapacitated with grief over what I was doing to the two young souls I had helped bring into the world. I would stop whatever I was doing, unable to really move. It seems it was my truck (previously my dad's) I would often lean against while the wave of sadness, guilt, and despair would wash over me. A surge of emotion would heave up from my chest, but it would never make it to the surface. Buckets of tears just screaming to pour out over this whole situation never came. As the wave would wash over and leave me, I would remember that I was on the clock and move on, trying to resume whatever task was at hand.

A constant through this were Tuesday nights in the barn. Rob was making the trip but at less frequent intervals to work on his boat while Bill and Marissa kicked things into high gear. Cockpit coaming was steam bent and installed in March. Trim was applied, and then it was on to painting. On a warm afternoon in April, after a final coat of varnish on the hull that revealed hints of the heritage of paint coats, Marissa declared: "I think we have a boat."

On April 3, 2021, Ducky Schmutz was christened in the backwaters of the Wisconsin River, the exact spot where Ripple had been christened about 21 years prior. It was fitting for this boat, since this is the body of water where she would spend many hours with Bill, Marissa, and Jango the hunting dog. Time has now passed since that christening, and the memories, philosophies, and laughs shared with Bill and Marissa only grow richer.

From this moment, my studio took center focus. I would work on it until well after midnight some nights, building walls or fashioning window boxes to insert into the holes a good friend helped saw out in the corner. The hull of the boat was almost stripped, but running electric and fashioning a ceiling framed with timbers donated by Tackleberry took precedence. In 2 months I had a livable space-insulated, drywalled, and painted. My marital separation was a done deal, and I was contributing to the statistics of alimony and child support. I was to make this my home, the starting point of my future. My Launch Pad, as I called it.

The windows afforded a view of the river bottom with glimpses of the water through the trees. No neighbors could be seen, even though the property is in the center of town. No running water so Rubina provided a composting toilet and I showered at work. Meals were simple, and I purchased an air fryer to support the culinary arts. My friend John donated a bed; the dining room table I built for my son's birth served as a kitchen and pantry; and a bookshelf I had built 15 years ago was my library.

I once again had all the elements of my simplistic lifestyle, but I was missing one thing, a dining/reading/writing surface that I had come to call a *Bodhisattva Table* through its many iterations over the years. The first one I built I was standing upon when my previously unknown friend Tom recruited me for the rugby team. The second accompanied me to the riverside trailer park near Ladysmith as I stared down the sunset fear. Others were made or used in Ithaca, Ecuador, and beyond. I spent a few evenings building this latest one of rough sawn oak that I bought froma good friend.

My dresser was not sufficient, so I built a huge floor to ceiling wardrobe that I dubbed Hagrid. As time went on, I added more things: a wash station, shelves, and different storage strategies for various cookware items. My favorite part was the ceiling. Built of white pine shiplap boards from the Menominee Reservation laid atop Tackleberry's beams, the grain and natural patterns of the wood and knots are soothing to behold while lying in bed. I inserted lights above the respective corners serving as my dressing area, pantry, and study.

It was a ton of work crammed into a small amount of time, but I had a whole lot of emotional strife that I was more than happy to pour into it. This studio was more me than anywhere I have lived in my life. It did not afford much space for lounging, but was just what it needed to be—a place to grab a bite to eat and crash, but primarily a staging place for day trips and adventures with my kids. In its essence, it really was the Launch Pad.

Still, the family I co-created was failing, one of my best was friends dying, and I had no idea where I would land. I was living in a barn. Because of the child support and alimony I was paying, there was no way I could afford an apartment or house. At least I was close to my kids and saw them on an almost daily basis.

Nelsonville to Fremont

Turbulent Times

The studio was more or less finished in mid-May. The warm weather, longer days, and actual greenery of the outdoors made the boat shop less enticing. Time to get on the water. As the model of *Learn, Create, Experience, Share,* and *Inspire* is non-linear, I decided to begin the *Experience* portion of this odyssey before the boat was finished.

I found a weekend in mid-June that fit well. Being that I was already out of the rhythm of working on the kayak, I decided to take some time for myself on a weekend the kids were with their mother. After a bath in the Tomorrow River behind the barn, I put in with my old Royalex canoe to paddle through the soft evening light with the sun making its way toward the horizon. This being the magical hour, I was kept company by deer, herons, ducks, a man and his elderly father smoking cigars together on the riverbank, a fly fisherman, and a peaceful river that I could nearly jump across. The damsel flies were out, flitting among the shoreline grasses. Their iridescent bodies and flashing black wings making them appear as fairies. I witnessed the end of one as it became dinner for a cedar waxwing that darted out from its perch for a quick snack. The landscape is close and intimate within this narrow river valley. It could be the time of day, but everything within eye shot seems graspable. Farms, marshes, and forest passed by as I made my way through the familiar waters.

Shortly after a portage around the Amherst dam, I took out in total darkness about 7 miles downstream from the barn where I had dropped my truck. I left my canoe at the take-out since I would be continuing downstream in the morning. I had paddled this route before, most of it several times. But this was the official beginning of my venture downstream from the headwaters to chase the current as far as was practical.

Next morning I drove past Amherst where my boat was stashed and headed for the city of Waupaca. I did not know how long this stretch of river would take, and I didn't care. I figured it to be about 20 miles by the river, and I was prepared to paddle into darkness. I parked right downtown where the river runs behind the main street stores and businesses. I removed my bike from the rack of my truck and headed up to the main street level. There I discovered a hoard of vendors setting up booths and art displays for the annual Strawberry Festival. Part of slowing down and taking in the flavor of the places I paddle through is to stop and dig the local happenings, so I took a moment to talk to vendors about chef's knives and hand tied fishing lures.

A bit later than was comfortable, I got on the back roads and made time in order to get some training in, take in the countryside, and enjoy this perfect morning. I heard my phone ring. Uncharacteristically, I looked to see who it was. My friend John, wondering what I was doing that day. Already under the influence of endorphins, I suggested he and his girlfriend Yaz swing by my boat shed to grab a couple kayaks and meet me on the river. Surprisingly, they agreed.

I returned to Amherst where my canoe sat unmolested in its resting place from the previous evening. I locked my bike, prepped my canoe, and was ready in minutes to put in for a long day on the water. It was already about 10:30 in the morning, but my day had so far been satisfactorily productive. I had a quick video chat with my kids to wish them good morning and a reluctant goodbye. Then I shoved off.

As I eased along down the river, its volume growing and width broadening, I expected to ease into River Time and for my thoughts to drift with the current while I descended into the easy calm of the Ripple Effect.

It didn't happen. I was worried about meeting John. Where and when to rendezvous? Would he and Yaz do all right with my gear? Would they find the spot? What if I kept them waiting? It was irritating to not let go of the temporal dimension that runs my world outside the river. I was also attached to my phone, with updates on my progress and trying to plan a meeting point. Stressed over a reasonable meeting time, I found myself paddling hard and hurrying downstream. Perhaps this was more trouble than it was even worth? It was my own fault; I just could not relax.

The route was not totally spoiled, however. I had paddled maybe a third of this stretch of river before, different sections at different times. It was nice to tie the experiences together and watch the river grow as other waters joined it. I recognized the place where I shredded the bow of my cedar strip canoe breaking through ice on a warm February day. I passed under the numerous Highway 10 bridges and enjoyed first-hand the scenery normally witnessed from the road at 70 mph. I paused for a dip at the nexus of Spring Creek and the Tomorrow River, a splendid little cranny, crucial in Native American history-mostly lost at this point. Glacial erratics accented one stretch, followed by a few riffles as the river lost elevation a little more suddenly near the bible camp. From there the river calmed and wound through some flatlands to a place just across the Waupaca county border called Cobbtown, where the name of the river switches from the Tomorrow to the Waupaca. With that as our meeting place, it was also a turning point of sorts for the day's journey.

Although we decided on a time and location, I was half an hour late in getting there. John and Yaz were ready to go, so we got straight to putting in. As I steadied my dad's old boat for Yaz to board, I learned that it was her first time paddling a kayak. She picked it up quickly, and we made our way through the farms and forests as we meandered downstream.

There are a number of different approaches to natural experiences, especially in Wisconsin. One is to immerse oneself and take in the splendor of nature as a near religious experience and silently commune with the surroundings. Another, more common approach that is especially Wisconsin-esque is to treat it like a party. Today started as the former, but quickly deteriorated to the latter. John brought some beers and a flask of whiskey for provisions. We dug into the libations and a cool, crisp, malted beverage went down smoothly. So I had another. And another. Then the flask was broken out and we passed that around the crew a few times.

We were soon awash in buzzed conversation and the beauty of the landscape, with edges eased and sensitivities dulled. I used to treat every outing like this as a party. There is a flow to the experience, and a rather audacious vibe is established. Over the years, and especially after living in Ladysmith, I had drifted away from the party atmosphere. I held more of a reverence for the experience and closeness to the rich surroundings. It became more akin to being in church than at a bar. Today, with my company, everything going on in my life, and considering my inability to naturally fall into River Time, I embraced the bar scene.

As the afternoon wore on, it became obvious we had a few hours yet to go. Alcohol finally facilitated my release of temporal anxiety, and I adopted the mantra *Time is of no consequence. The party's right here.* The alcohol was running low, however, which meant the party was quite vulnerable. I ran the numbers and learned we would run out of beer well before reaching our destination. We would be forced to paddle through a killed buzz and possibly the beginnings of a hangover.

We reached a renowned covered bridge at the outskirts of Waupaca. Still well over an hour left on the water, with one portage around a dam. We pulled to the side of the river and took a breather. I knew we were close to a strip mall district, and in the name of riding the vibe, we did the most unnatural and unwholesome thing I could think of. We walked out to the main drag and perused the liquor department of a gas station. Having outfitted ourselves with the elixirs necessary to carry us through the rest of the trip, yet not defiling ourselves to a satisfactory level, we stopped in at a fast-food restaurant to order tacos.

We walked back to the river and rode out the rest of the day along the trajectory that had been established. We paddled, talked, drifted, and let our cares flow on downstream without us. The current slowed and stagnated at the mill pond. There was a bit of work as we amassed the carnage of empty containers and food wrappers from the bottom of the boats and toted them with everything else over a dike and down the steep rip rap to put in below the dam's spillway. But all without incident. The circumstances mandated a level of functionality I had grown accustomed to 25 years previously and had practiced scores of times.

Below the dam, heading toward the heart of town, the river changed character. It flowed faster over a relatively steep grade, around rocks and through riffles. I lead the way between the obstacles and felt a foreshadowing of something I was missing. The river flowed on, though, and my cares were nowhere to be seen. Then, as the river rounded a bend and the main street bridge could be seen ahead, I saw it. And my obscured memory came back with face palming obviousness and horrifying clarity: The horizon on the water, just in front of the bridge, is a waterfall. And it was too late to get to shore before going over it.

The drop isn't huge. About 4–5 feet, but still with the potential to severely damage a person, or possibly worse. I put aside the regret of what I was dragging my friends into for half a moment as I drifted toward the precipice. In the line of the ledge I was about to go over, there was a small notch, and through some stroke of luck I was positioned perfectly to slide right into it. I rode the current slightly askew to the main drop of this rock outcropping as I went over. It softened the vertical plunge just enough for the bow of the canoe to nose dive under water and then rebound up without getting stuck or taking on too much water. I did scrape some rocks, but my forward momentum carried me out of the tumbling whitewater at the base of the drop. I came out of it with about 3 inches of water in the boat but still with the open side up.

Immediately, my thoughts shot back to my friends. I turned around to see Yaz approach the drop. "PLEASE DON'T DIE. PLEASE DON'T DIE.". The words pounded in my head as she took it straight on, dipped her bow, came up just askew of vertical and couldn't quite recover before tipping into the calm waters below the falls. Wet but unscathed. Whew. My biggest fear went unrealized. Yaz was ok. Then John approached. He had drunk a bit more than me and I figured was relaxed enough to not get too beat up by this thing. But still… I felt awful to have put my friends in this position. He went over on the same line as Yaz. His dipping bow flooded his cockpit. As he came up, the sloshing weight of the water around his lap made it too difficult to balance and he dumped it. With a spray skirt both would have made it through.

In the end, clothes were quite damp, and we had to scurry about to catch all the things adrift from the boat cockpits. But spirits were high—for John and Yaz, anyway. I was pissed and ashamed of myself to have forgotten about the Waupaca falls and endangered my friends. All were smiles, though, as we loaded the boats on my truck. It was dark now, and we picked up John's truck and headed out for an old fashioned to toast the end of a truly eventful day.

I'm not sure if a smile or scowl prevails at my recollection of this reckless defilement, but no one got hurt, everyone had a good time, and we made an interesting memory. But is this really the tone I want to set for this Endeavor? It was a messed up outing in the midst of a messed up time in my life. This was not the character with which I wanted to continue my route downstream. The party is a blast, the camaraderie amazing, and memory an embarrassingly rich one, but I wanted the way in which I got to the rest of the river and the waters leading downhill to be characterized by the subtleties of the surroundings, not imposed by my own debauchery.

In the end, I could not have made too bad of an impression with John and his soon to be fiancée. Yaz's family came out from California for her and John's wedding, and Yaz asked another friend and me to take them out on the water the day before the ceremony for a *truly authentic Wisconsin experience.* There were brats, beer, curds, sun, and boats on the backwaters of the Wisconsin River near Stevens Point (the same put-in used for the christenings of Ripple and Ducky Schmutz.). No waterfalls, just lots of food, swimming, and smiles. Sure was good to be able to redeem myself at least a little.

The first leg of many was now under my belt, and the character of the odyssey was being established. I didn't like it one bit. As is the case so many times, my head was at the root of the problem. I was seeking out things to worry about for most of the day and hurriedly forced my way downstream. The second half was a revisit to a whole chapter of my life where social sobriety was the exception. If this route to the end of the waters was to be anything more than a self-inflicted measure of solitary confinement or just another soul-defiling booze cruise that does as much outward damage as it does inward, then some adjustments would be necessary.

Finding River Time

WAUPACA — FREEMONT, WI

7/17–7/18/21

A few weeks after the initial leg that landed me in Waupaca, my schedule opened up again, this time in the middle of July. I had made no further progress on my kayak on account of having a blast with my kids and trying to fit as much quality time as I could into the fleeting Wisconsin summer. I also took a moment to apply some strips of Kevlar to the stems of Ripple, along with a couple coats of epoxy, to patch the scrapes incurred from that incident of breaking through ice a few Februarys earlier.

But suddenly, with no major plans for the weekend, I found myself on a gloriously beautiful Saturday morning with gear packed, kids with their mom, food stowed, and on my way back to Waupaca to drop my canoe and provisions. My put-in was downtown, near the waterfall that keynoted the previous leg.

I eased my truck down the steep entrance to the riverside park nestled behind the downtown businesses. You would be able to hear the falls from the put-in if not for the cacophony of the foundry just a block away. A few people were walking through or helping their toddler on the playground equipment. There was also a cook-out of sorts with a group of bikers in their leather and bandanas hanging out in the pavilion reliving the glory days of big hair bands. When a song by Poison came on, I had half a mind to join them! But this was a day for the river.

I unloaded my canoe, paddles, life jacket, water jug, and line from my truck and brought it to the river. I rolled my canoe atop the gear and locked it to a tree with the cable running through my life jacket. The paddles and other things could be easily taken, but according to the broken window theory, things that look tidy are more likely to be left alone. And this set-up just kind of looked secure. Still, I was prepared for an overnight, so what of my backpack with my tent and other more valuable items? People were coming and going and I would be gone for 2 hours running the shuttle. I realized that leaving my gear out would be a systematic risk throughout this endeavor that would eventually bite me if I tested the odds enough times. Deciding not to tempt the karma of leaving my valuables under the canoe, I headed to a nearby book store, the Book Cellar. I told John, the store clerk, what I was up to and that I needed a place to stash my pack for a bit. He gladly offered a storage room for me to secure my gear, taking interest in this little trek.

My bag stowed and gear secure, I drove to an outpost called Gill's Landing at the confluence of the Waupaca (Still the Tomorrow River; I'm remiss that it changes its name at the Waupaca County border) and Wolf Rivers. I had seen this little municipality of sorts on maps and it looked like a version of my kind of place. On the waterfront and close to sloughs to explore, this was an outpost at the end of the road—literally. I was excited to see what was there besides the boat landing that the map showed. After passing through the village of Weyau-wega, about halfway to this secluded destination, the tone of the landscape changes just a bit as you drop into the Wolf River bottomlands. Swamp and marsh replace farm fields; houses are smaller as residences are juxtaposed with more recreational dwellings of the area's working-class. Judging by the tidy yards, modest but well-kept homes, fishing boats, and river-oriented lawn trinkets, the people here are down to earth and connected with the water.

I came to the end of the road and the huge parking lot that serves the public boat launch as well as what seems to be iconic tavern, itself called Gill's Landing. Come the right timing in spring, this 2-acre asphalt plain would be packed with the trucks and trailers of people chasing the annual walleye run.

I approached the bar. Door was open but not a soul inside, not even a bartender. Dimly lit and appropriately behind the times of today's sports bars, I scanned the aging interior with satisfactory approval. This was the kind of establishment where I had spent many hours with my dad—a bit crusty, but rife with the character of do-it-yourself fixes and handiwork. It is not glossed over by homogenous big box finishes that are representative of how things are supposed to be done nowadays. I hit up the rest room, taking care not to unnecessarily touch anything. Yep, the sinus clearing vapors coming off the urinal pucks had the familiar artificial aroma that was just right. This was my kind of hole in the wall, at least ideal for the sort of revelry my friends and I stirred up an age ago. But where is everyone? Walking past the pool table and stepping up a level to the bar I found the back deck. There the party was in full swing. Kids playing under a sprinkler in an old volleyball court, people coming and going from their moored boats for drinks, music and laughter accenting the scene. I asked who appeared to be a manager about parking my truck overnight—no problem. The bar opens at noon the next day for me to mingle with the scene.

With that mischievous notion in my head, I checked the back-road route in my Gazetteer, grabbed my bike, locked the truck, and hit the road under a warm sun and before a significant tailwind. It was a beautiful ride back to Waupaca; the breeze encouraged my pace the entire way. My mom called during a pitstop, and I could hear concern in her voice as I told her about my activity for the day—yes, I have sunscreen and a lifejacket, and the water is hardly ever over my shoulders with no motor boats until the end. That call and another stop for fresh cheese curds at Star Dairy on my way back through Weyauwega (Wega) made my cruise up to Waupaca a pleasant one.

I retrieved my pack from the Book Cellar, taking a moment to talk with a second John, the owner. Turns out John-the-owner lived for a few years in a house in Nelsonville just on the other side of the park from where the kids' house is now. I left him and John-the-clerk some curds I picked up from Star Dairy and was on my way. Encounters like that one are one of the gems of a trip like this. A bit of forced interdependence stimulates the exchange of stories, common bonds are found, and karma tickets earned. Next stop was T-Dubs restaurant to lock my bike on their patio. No matter since COVID has them closed, and the owner's son Sarge is an old rugby buddy. I was finally ready to hit the water. This is supposed to be a day on the river, after all. But because of the necessary preparations, I had made two new friends at the Book Cellar, checked out a new haunt I never would have stumbled across on my own, logged a few miles on my bike, and got to stop for fresh cheese curds. It had already been a great day before even getting to the main event.

Approaching the river, I paused to take in the sight of Ripple. I had burned the midnight oil just a bit to make it happen, but my cedar stripper now sported new skid plates, several coats of epoxy, and a single coat of varnish that were all wrapped up the previous week. It felt good to place her on the watery cushion for the first time in 3 years, reinforced for encounters with rocks and logs. I was finally experiencing this endeavor as was intended, in a boat of my own creation. The bottom had once been painted black up to the 4" waterline, but that was sanded off as I installed the putrid looking Kevlar skid plates for added protection against shock and abrasion. It was like going out in public in underclothes without the bottom paint, but again, opportunities need to be capitalized upon. Imperfect and now is better than a refined product that never hits the water. Bottom paint could wait.

The urban portion of the Waupaca River is about as straight as a twisted spaghetti noodle. It winds past a wastewater treatment plant, some industrial buildings, and through a golf course before completing its gauntlet of riparian defilement. From there its bends relax a bit in the shade of towering pines as it grows wilder. Rounding one bend, it comes to a point as the Crystal River unassumingly converges, increasing the volume of the Waupaca (I still want to call it the Tomorrow) by a third.

There's something about the meeting of different rivers. Each watershed has its own character and history. Every river derives personality from interactions with its respective landscape. As they join, personalities mingle, as if stories are exchanged, and the gathering builds in this party, all the way to the ocean.

Leaving Waupaca, the river bends mellow out and more pines, grassland, and farms marked the passage through the heart of rural Wisconsin under the softening evening sun. The day was made easy by the accelerated current, flushing several inches of rain that had fallen on the region a few days prior. I was pretty well at ease, except for two things that haunted me—time and the party going on at Gill's Landing.

My plan was originally to sleep on an island just above the Wega mill pond, but I was making really good time. I checked my progress against the map and the clock—I might make Gills Landing yet tonight—surely the beer would be tasty and conversation easy after a day on the road and water. I appreciated the surroundings but still could not allow myself to totally be where I was—I couldn't help hurrying to get to someplace I currently wasn't.

Speeding along, I paused for a moment as I entered the lake grass of Wega's mill pond, somewhat akin to a scene from the *African Queen.* I took a moment while I still had current to indulge in the delectable nourishment of spring rolls from 13 Chairs in Amherst—a quintessential collaboration of Art & Rugby in their own right. Come to think of it, that was my turning point of the paddle. I was no longer in a hurry. I would make Gill's Landing without issue and had time to enjoy the twilight.

I made the passage across the flowage by following the wake of a pontoon boat and took out at the downtown boat landing. I was impressed with the handicap put-in on the downstream side of the dam, which made launching a cinch for anyone.

Upon returning to the water my world immediately changed. The sun lowered and the light eased back. I was still virtually downtown but trees towered on both banks and the wild was coming back to life after the day's siesta. A bald eagle spooked a sandhill crane just downstream, and both came flying up the channel. Soon afterward I heard a screaming match between a mating pair of eagles. The male flew off, but the female sat high and proud on a branch directly over the river as I paddled under her. Deep holes and large rocks held the promise of smallmouth bass. A commotion on the grassy shore startled me as I paddled past a river otter diving for deeper, darker water. Farther down, a muskrat and then a beaver followed the same course. Encounters with deer became standard, but an owl flying away into the forest was especially noteworthy in its silent haste. All this action had me wrapped up in the moment, relishing the surprises that seemed to be around every bend in this golden hour. The sun set with the first quarter moon approaching its peak, the world slowly closing in around me. With no lights to spoil the dim, my eyes adjusted as the evening wore on and night was welcomed like a friend. As the Waupaca dropped into the open bottomlands of the Wolf River marsh, the starry abyss split open beyond the strip of sky between the tall trees and steep riverbanks like the opening of a celestial zipper. Just as it was almost too dark to see the river's course, I entered more human development. The small cabins and man-made sloughs of Gill's Landing slipped by and I found new water.

The Wolf River. The red navigational lights of a railroad trestle just upstream, a few passing boats, and riverside cabin lights illuminated my path. I rounded the bend into this broad river with my destination just a few rods downstream. The drop into the low wetlands and marsh of this fluvial plane was a precursor to the character of this stretch of river. I now beheld it in its entirety. These waters flowing from the north tell a different story than those of the Waupaca, but all are now combined in their collective voyage toward the ocean. The river is far larger, and rather than small streams joining our party, we had entered into a gathering much larger than our own, like a group of friends entering a festival. Looking back, I suppose I was lucky to hit this confluence in hours of darkness when the subtlety of this change was not drowned out by the roar of boat motors or the impositions of human development.

I made it to Gill's Landing Bar just as the place was closing up. Perfect. I shot the breeze and bought a round for the waitstaff, the only ones there. We enjoyed good conversation before they went on to Wega where there was more action. Saved from my own defilement since the party had gone. Whew, what a blessing.

I threw my sleeping bag out on the dock and was subject to the contest between mosquitoes, body aches, penetrating dew formation, and passing trains to see which one could most effectively keep me from sleep. I at least got a few hours rest before my return to the Launch Pad the next morning. Funny how when camping like that, even somewhat long term, sleep deprivation is not nearly the issue it is in the modern world. If I am tired the next day, I simply paddle slower.

Next morning I rose drowsily to load gear on my truck that had been awaiting me. My destination for the weekend had been achieved early, so this would be an easy Sunday. I got everything packed on the truck, the canoe tied down, and was on my way back to Waupaca, anticipating a day compiling trip notes, napping, and updating my blog when the realization sank in: *I was going to spend the day behind a computer when I could be on the River instead.*

That would not stand.

I returned to the downtown park to grab my bike from where it rested safe and sound. But instead of continuing west, home to Nelsonville, I headed straight back to Gill's Landing to drop some gear and once more run a shuttle. With Ripple at a mooring, stocked with a cooler and water aboard, I checked the map and headed to Fremont, the next town downstream. I had to double check the map once I parked my truck there because I could not believe it: about 7 miles by river, and I had to put about 12 miles on the bike to find a back road route to Gill's Landing. It was a rare instance of the river being shorter than the shuttle. This was because during the widening of Highway 10 to four lanes, they chopped up many of the backroads.

I took my time riding and enjoyed the morning. I had never been on any of these roads before and the flavor of the land/land use had some new notes to it. I got lost in thoughts of the uprooted nature of my life and lack of a path. I was indeed groundless, swimming. I decided it did not matter, that I'd live the most authentic version of myself possible and see what happens. The notion of swimming was a good metaphor. I was not floundering or even treading water. My living situation was highly temporary, but my studio was beautiful and effectively served its purpose of keeping me close to the things that mattered most: my kids and my dreams. That realization was a bit of a breakthrough, that I did not need to have a long-term course or bearing, that I could just BE for a while and it was ok. I was sure digging it so far-extra time on the river, pleasant ride through new territory, and no pressure from my greatest adversary: time.

I returned once again to Gill's Landing still before anyone was around. I locked my bike and hit the water with clockwork efficiency. In no time at all I was ready to get underway, that is, to drift. It was time to take advantage of the calm wind, warm sun, and broad water to just slow down and do some catching up. I wrote extensively in my journal but took a moment to swim/bathe at a sandbar. For the first time since taking to the river in earnest these past few weeks, I was at last living on River Time.

Power boats were coming along more frequently as the morning drew to midday. They were after the morning's fish at first, then to swim and just be on the water. I checked the map and saw I was not far from Fremont. And as I got closer the boats got bigger, faster, and louder. House boats came and went from Partridge Lake just north of town, and from there the riverbank was lined with docks, seawall, and manicured lawns. Goodbye to the intimate, wild headwaters. From here human development would be the norm for the next 200 miles or so, and with bigger water there was need for a different boat. Time to get that kayak completed.

Arriving at the truck, I loaded up and made my fifth trip back to Gill's Landing just in time to join the party. The bar was mostly full and empty tables becoming scarce as I pulled up a stool. The remnant effects of last night's minor indulgence were an excuse to enjoy a bloody mary with a chaser as I updated my journal and reflected at the bar. It took a while, however, as the same staff I met the night before were all there again and conversation resumed. I'm afraid I made some good friends on this stretch.

The anonymous camaraderie of strangers was a welcome opportunity to step into different shoes than the ones I was wearing back in Nelsonville. The upheaval brought on with the ending of my marriage had been a lot to manage. We were amicable and working through the process pro-se, each with our own reasons for divorce, but the worst of it was facing my kids as a part-time dad, having failed them in providing the foundation of a solid family. Despite their flexibility and resilience, I could feel their heaviness upon entering their world just a few days a week. The plan was set for them to stay in the house, their home, with their mother who cares for them most of the time. I stayed as close to them as I could as I built the studio in the barn. A product of transmuted anger and pain, it was authentically me and I loved it, but goddamn I miss my kids when I'm not living in their home. A few evenings a week and every other weekend. Those are the terms that worked best for me to be a father.

I was trying to balance work, time with my kids, and making the most positive choices I could in any given moment. It manifested in the pursuit of every healthy expression of myself I could conceive to live my best life and provide for my kids. We will see where this all leads, but I want to model an authentic life that sets them up for thriving in the face of challenges they will encounter in their own lives. With the host of socio-environmental-economic calamities afoot, perhaps the resilience gained through all this will serve them well.

Breathe In Breathe Out Move On

After the run to Fremont, my odd weekends without kids began filling up with additional work on my studio. Afterall, I had to start thinking about what winter there would look like. I needed to finalize insulation and install a wood stove next to my bodhisattva table.

And as the fall approached, a wood stove was added, but only after doing extensive roof repair work, predicated by some arborist work on a tree that was the culprit of lifted roofing shingles and rotting sheeting. Then came insulating the ceiling. I could not use a blower for the cellulose as it required two people, so I brought a couple bales up atop the ceiling that had been covered in plastic and taped in integration with the rest of my air sealing package. I grabbed a wire whip that attaches to my drill and went at the bales of cellulose. The resultant cloud of dust was so fine and thick I could barely see my hands to keep them safe from the whirling drill. Turns out I had up to an 1/8" film of cellulose dust throughout the rest of the barn in addition to the 14" of fluff in the target area. At least I was ready for the winter.

And winter came in early October when Rob texted that he was being put into hospice. I was in the dark loft of the barn, peppering re-purposed plywood with pneumatic nails to provide exterior sheeting on my studio when this news came in. It was the last phase for him, the inevitable conclusion to his story, and this just happened to be the moment it was coming down. After reading the news, I pocketed my phone and went back to blasting a line of nails down a stud hidden behind the plywood. Then it hit me. Rob was dying. This was it. My friend, this awesome father and supportive husband was at the end of his rope. I dropped the nail gun to the floor and began sobbing into my hands. The wellhead of tears that had been building for months over this situation and the shattering of my kids' home finally came pouring out. Anyone on the road at the edge of the property could have heard me wailing as the emotion finally burst the walls of composure I was never even trying to have there.

These two tragedies in my life brought some hard truths to bear. Here Rob was fighting for his life and doing everything he possibly could to get just a few more experiences and memories and days with his kids while I, from one aspect, was walking out on my own. The whole thing was more than I could bear. Finally purging from my person, the shower of tears and howls of despair faded and then stopped. I picked up my nail gun and resumed nailing, still thinking of Rob and our respective situations.

I was not walking out on my family. Deep down I knew that. For years I had been unable to show up for my kids in the way they deserved. My chronic stress had distilled into anger that was scary at times, to them and their mother. Since the separation, however, I focused on them every time I saw them and was able show up and connect better than ever before. I was a better part-time dad than was I able to be as a full time one. But still, the tragedy of Rob and his young family. How could this be happening? All I could do was channel the emotion into work, my abode, and eventually my kayak in order to take care of my things and keep moving forward. Except for one loose end: Rob's boat.

I texted Rob to see if there was anything I could do to shoulder some of the pain or the burden of what he was facing. He responded with a single request:

"I know you're busy and have a ton on your plate, but if you could possibly find time this winter, maybe after your kayak is done, to wrap up the last details of my boat and preset it to my family before spring, then they can have it to paddle around and spend time on the water."

The hell if he wouldn't be around to see his family enjoy his legacy piece. It seems to me that conversation was on a Wednesday. I took an evening to get a coat of varnish on its hull, and then brought the boat to the cottage for our annual wood cutting weekend. On that Saturday evening, my son, Lew, and I added another coat of varnish. I brought it back to the barn for the fourth and final coat and took a day off work to add trim. That Tuesday I called to see if Rob would be around and up for a visitor. When I pulled in with the boat that evening, he was busy organizing gear in the basement. He was literally preparing the house for when he knew he would no longer be there to take care of things for his family. When he realized I had his boat and that it was finished, he was absolutely beside himself. It was too late in the day for a christening, but that would come.

On October 17, 2021, a gorgeous Sunday, family and friends gathered a few blocks from Rob's house with boats and snacks to christen TBD in the waters of the East River. Rob and his son climbed aboard and paddled around. It floated level and held a straight course. His daughter paddled her own kayak, and his wife Teri was in Ripple with me. Others had boats of their own, including Lew and other close friends. We left the river bank close to the home of his family, and Rob lead a tour of the waters he had known as a kid growing up in the neighborhood on the opposite shore. A beautiful tribute to the past and present of a life extremely well lived, being cut way too short. It was the last outing Rob would have with his family, as he passed only a couple of weeks after. I do not know how he mustered the strength to make it through that day's activity, but he was all smiles and jocularity the whole time. Just good ole Rob, exactly as anyone would ever remember him. He had his boat, his legacy, a product of many hours of labor by several sets of hands, that he could pass down to his children and through following generations. The example he set as a father, friend, and human helps me be a better person.

Doubling and Falling Down

DOUBLING

It was fall now, beginning of boat building season. If there is one thing I took from Rob and my dad, it is that life is too short not to get after the dreams that tease you. When loved ones pass, a portion of my mourning process is to embrace some of the character they embodied, to adopt some of their light. With Rob and my dad, I took it almost as a responsibility to chase after dreams they would value. Hard work and an adventuresome spirit that they both personified seemed to come through me and my labors.

I had the cockpit to strip and wrap in laminations of ash for the coaming. There was a whole lot of fairing and filling of gaps with dookie schmutz, and more fiberglassing than I care to recall. The glowing fires in the wood stove, soft hues of the ridiculous vanity lights, and musical themes of Jimmy Buffett, reggae, and my female rocker station on Pandora set the mood. The hull and deck were separated like two halves of an eggshell in order to remove the strongback, and then more fairing and fiberglassing. With great trepidation, I cut the hatches into the deck (putting two huge holes in a perfectly good boat) and went through the motions to glue the two halves of the boat together.

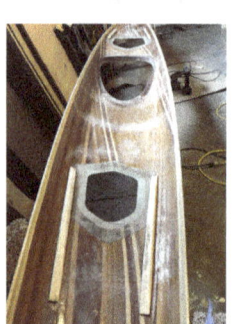

FALLING

While my work day melting into the glowing fire of the shop procured the same feeling as the warm sunsets of Ithaca's Winter during Whisper's gestation, there were contrasting indicators that I was not in such a great spot. One evening in particular sums up the hollow nature of so much of my days. It started with the fire in my studio wood-stove…rather, it didn't start. Smoke plumed from every orifice as I tried to ignite the tinder and the soft flame of matches and paper died a subtle death. Hmmmm-chimney must be plugged. The 4-inch stove pipe on this miniature heater culminated in a slotted chimney cap that could easily clog with soot. To clear it, I had to get up on a steep barn roof on a cold February night with 6" of snow to facilitate either my foothold or my sliding off the pitch.

The barn roof is out of reach of my 16-foot extension ladder, so I had fallen into the routine of standing the ladder on a lean-to shed roof I built off the barn wall. This afforded me an extra 8 feet of height from which I could easily reach the eve of the barn. The metal shed roof was cluttered with frozen pine needles and the aforementioned snow. Where I usually tied the legs off to the wall, I figured this frozen litter would afford purchase of the ladder legs, even if it were off pitch and could dislodge from the sheer surface of the metal.

I also had taken to an extensive process of throwing a line over the roof of the barn and dragging a climbing rope after it, the far end fastened to my truck or a fence post. This way I could rig a safety harness in order to securely work on the roof. Not tonight. I'd first test the grip of the roof without it. The ladder might slip; my personal footing might give way—I was too lazy to take the appropriate precautions. Moreso, I just didn't care enough to. My divorce had finalized a month previous, I missed my kids, and I was on a road through emptiness with a detached approach to a strange environment called online dating. And for cripes sakes, cleaning the chimney would take only a few seconds, versus almost an hour of getting everything set up. *Let's just get this thing done and go to bed.*

I leaned a small ladder upon the shed roof. I carried up the extension ladder, being careful to compress but not dislodge the frozen debris on the shed roof. The bigger ladder upright, I pulled the rope to extend and lean it into place against the barn roof.

The first step was a ginger one, and I gained confidence as I ascended. At the upper eve, I very carefully set my foot in the snow that covered the asphalt shingles. Nope, no grip. Ok, I'd need to set up the harness, at least. And with these additional trips up and down the big ladder, I'd probably tie it off as well.

Too late. Just as I got my foot back on the ladder, the sensation of acceleration overcame me. It is amazing how much things slow down when you know you're in serious trouble. The feet had broken loose and were sliding down the shed roof. I was headed down, but what was the best path? I could jump off the ladder whose trajectory in this series of events I tried figuring ahead of time (I really had given it a bit of thought) but couldn't quite foresee, or I could ride it out. My weight still on my left leg, I'd only have time to propel myself to the right, where loose rocks left over from foundation work and railroad tie steps would facilitate the painful halt of my downward plummet. Too uneven. All I could do was hold on and ride it out, probably crushing a leg or an arm in the process.

There was a hard thud as the top of the ladder slid under the eve and slammed into the barn wall. Now things really picked up and I couldn't keep the events straight as they unfolded. Evidently, my fingers clenched the fiberglass ladder as we slid down the wall, the ladder feet rocketing off the shed roof and over the top of a chunk of plywood covering some firewood. I smacked into the shed roof, losing my grip on the ladder. We shot backwards off the shed roof and onto the woodpile where something solid caught a ladder rung, slamming it to a halt. My momentum flung my torso backward like a bull rider clinging with his spurs. Time regained normal flow and I regained awareness of my surroundings now that they weren't passing in a dark blur.

I was laying back on the ladder, my leg jammed through one of the rungs. Pausing to consider the damage, I figured the minimum of a broken wrist, and as I realized the positioning of my leg, well, that was sure to be busted too. I wiggled my fingers. Minimal soreness. My leg was pinched, but I could move my toes, my ankle. Wow-how the hell could it be that nothing broke?!? I figured adrenaline obscured the pain, but with time it never came. A bit of soreness, but how I could careen from such a height and come out virtually unscathed entailed more luck than I cared to imagine. A line came to mind I've heard many times directed at me from my brother John. *What a dumb-ass.*

No one I wanted to tell the story to, no one to complain to, no one for comfort. I pulled myself from the ladder and unassumingly prepared the safety lines. Afterall, I still had to unclog the chimney before I could get a fire going and finally go to bed. I still find it noteworthy how out of such numbness toward my personal well-being, my nerves were not even all that frayed. In that moment I was too ambivalent to care.

I had fallen down, almost to the bottom. From there, things picked up.

BACK TO DOUBLING

Winter wore into Spring, and Spring stalled out, as if waiting for me to finish the boat. I completed the end pour of epoxy to secure the stems at the ends of the hull. This was accomplished by standing the boat (I could finally call it that!!!) on end at the foot of the stairs and reaching to the roof of the barn loft. I lowered a cup of epoxy through the boat's cockpit and into the far reaches of the hull. Then I pulled a string taped to the base of the cup in order to dump the mixture into the end of the vessel. Tedious, but I was getting closer.

As a deadline, I wanted to christen this thing by May 1st, to take the best advantage of spring paddling that I still could. Nothing like an impossible goal to guilt a person into a flurry of productivity. Of course, I didn't make the date. Heck, I originally hoped the construction would take a year and a half or so. Then I had hopes for 2 years. It turned out to be closer to three, but who's really counting? Ripple was to be a summer project that wound up taking 10 months. Whisper was a 5-month project that stretched to 10 months as well. In my boat building ventures, there seems to be a doubling effect between planning and executing. It matters not. As long as the process is enjoyable, nobody really loses.

All through April, however, pretty much after the hull was glued together into a cohesive unit, I was nervous. And my imagination provided no shortage of things for me to worry about. Would the fiberglass seams fair out? Would the finish be cloudy? Was I scuffing the surface enough between coats for good adhesion? Would the varnish coat be dusty? Leaky hatches? Would it float true? Enough fiberglass coats? Would it be too heavy? Basically, the nearer the launch date loomed, the more obstacles my mind would throw up to prevent completion of this boat. It had been 4 years in the making, encompassing all the memories and connections within the walls of this barn.

Once finished, I knew I would get on the water, but what else loomed beyond the horizon of this dream? I would miss the peaceful calm I had slipped into as I settled into my evening's toil in applying strips. I would miss the cozy, rugged functionality of this shop in active use. What would paddling be like? The big water I hoped to venture onto? Would I have the same fulfillment with the next chapter? The closer I came to the eventuality of this dream becoming reality, the scarier the unknowns became on the far side of its horizon. The work on the kayak, however, had been engrained into my routine so much at this point that progress on it was almost a matter of habit.

After a number of weeks of various fiberglassing exploits, it was finally time to move onto varnishing and finish work. The unseasonably cold weather would not hold on forever (we had more days of snow in April than through the whole winter), and I was urgent to finally finish this thing. I ordered cleats for bungee lashings, foot braces, and a seat. Upon arriving, however, the seat was bigger than expected and would not fit well with a spray skirt. I had notified my mom of a christening date, so there was no going back on it. There was no time for another seat to arrive. I looked into carving my own seat from closed cell foam, but that would involve a special order as well. I looked around the shop for something that I could use. At last I cast eyes upon an archery target I had laying around. I bought it for my son, but in all fairness, it was too hard of foam for his bow, so he used my target anyway. And I did ask him, kind of, after I had cut it down to size and carved the profile of my buttocks into it with an angle grinder, when he asked if that was the target I had bought him for his bow and arrow. And he's ok with it, really… So after carving a full moon with an angle grinder into a block of foam initially destined to be the recipient of flung arrows, I applied Velcro strips to the back, and correspondingly into the bottom of the kayak. As it turned out, that full moon was slightly less than perfect. There is a slight imperfection in the hard foam that creates a small pressure point on my right cheek. I still to this day have not ground it out. But with that, this kayak was ready for christening.

At last, on May 11, 2022, as planned (for the third or fifth time), Tackleberry, Bill, Lew, my mom, Rubina, and several other friends came by the barn to watch the kids and me carry the boat to the river to the theme of Sugar Magnolia. I stammered over some words, probably about chasing dreams and Art & Rugby, and we had a toast of good Irish Whiskey as I christened Endeavor high in the watershed of the Tomorrow River on a gloriously warm evening. Endeavor sat lightly upon their cushion of water, like a dragster idling at the start line ready for takeoff. I very shakily climbed aboard, being awkward in bracing my paddle with one end on shore and the other across the cockpit. (I had seen it in books but hadn't actually tried it in person.) Such were the shortcomings of my kayaking prowess. Nick Shade's final instructions in his book say to place the boat on the water and paddle away from shore. That is what I did. In the 100 yard symbolic float to my takeout at Ruby Coffee, I already felt the speed with which this vessel would fly through the water. I couldn't wait to truly test it.

An amazing day at an amazing time of year to snatch a dream into reality before it slipped over the horizon of *someday*. This journey had been a 4-year pursuit. Now that it was ended, I well-knew that a shift in focus was at hand, but what would fill the void left where the intense focus on this work had been? Would I simply take more time to relax? What about considering more permanent housing where I could better host my kids? And the prospect of a new partner? Just as Endeavor took to the water, changing in form from a project to a vessel, my life was about to shift, yet again, in a way far greater than I could have imagined.

Approaching a Horizon

That year, from roughly March 2021 to February 2022 was a place I do not care to dwell. My marriage collapsed and was legally terminated, I lost one of my best friends, and I faced the prospect of yanking the rug of family and home from under the feet of my kids. People deal with that kind of grief in different ways. I had my personal lodging and boat to focus in on, but there was still a hell of a void. Rob's passing—a huge loss in itself, had me facing head on the starkest of realities of what I was choosing to impose upon my kids. Deep in my gut I knew I was doing what I needed to, even if an array of things at the surface were telling me in equally varied ways what an asshole I was. But I was already showing up as a more engaged father in my limited time with them. And my anger, albeit replaced by guilt, had virtually disappeared.

In some respects, I got back in touch with myself. The studio reacquainted me with who I was. But in the years of tending to family, work, and adult responsibilities, that decade or so since I had really homed in on who I was as a person, I had developed as an individual in ways I had yet to discover. That is, I had grown in my absence from being in tune with myself. Because of this, I found it difficult to recognize my path beyond the building of my studio and Endeavor. It was scary.

Yes, there was a lot of paddling to do, but as was evident from the leg between Amherst and Waupaca the previous summer, I was not making the best choices when given an abundance of time alone with options for mischief. As the horizon of Endeavor's christening loomed closer, the mystery of what lay beyond had become a threatening prospect. I was in for a big transition, with no idea where I would land on its far side.

In nature, it is rare to have major transitions without any warning. The seasons, weather, aging, day to night, approaching rapids on a river, all arrive with indicators that a change is coming. Yes, there are instances where this is not the case, but when applied to my situation, there were signs of what was on the other side of this boat building project. Back in

March 2022, as I was trying to sprint down the home stretch of Endeavor's finishing touches, an old college friend, Bridget, changed her profile picture on social media. As it came up on my feed I reached out as a friendly gesture and to catch up. Following graduate school, she had moved to Denver to work in their Museum of Nature and Science, which was about the last we were in touch, almost 15 years previous. Turns out she had moved back to Wisconsin and was living in Madison.

Women I chatted with online were interestingly either in the same sort of personal recovery that I was or stalled out in some type of self-induced repression. As I chatted with Bridget, it became evident that she was not a recovering soul; she was flourishing with a house, a good job, and no shortage of energy for athletic and outdoor pursuits.

In late April, I went to Madison to do a run with my brother and other family members. I visited Bridget and we went out to eat. After that reunion, we kept in touch as Endeavor was completed and christened. Conversations grew longer and more frequent, and we started spending more time together. As summer came on, trips to Madison (or her visits from there) replaced quality time previously spent with epoxy, cedar, and visions of big water.

Experiencing Endeavor:
Chasing Tomorrow Beyond Death's Door

Getting Acquainted, and Caught Up

Endeavor lived atop my truck for the first couple days after the christening. I took my kids out to a lake so we could all venture out in Ripple and Endeavor, my first and latest boats. My daughter even got to christen the kayak in her own way as she put the first scratch in the hull by easing it to a stop on a rock. I was relieved that I was not the one to put the first water-borne blemish in this vessel, being responsible for enough of them throughout the construction process. In another outing I got out on the Wisconsin River for an evening's jaunt.

The rest of May was spent catching up on details I had neglected in the previous 6 months or so of boat building. But in the short outings I was able to get out on, I was learning Endeavor's personality. They are hands down the fastest boat I ever paddled. Endeavor simply sings across the water, even in the waves and small chop of the Wisconsin River. There was one thing I was unsure of, however. I would paddle along, getting to cruise at a good clip. When I would stop paddling to glide, the boat would bend into an arc. They didn't seem to prefer one direction over another, but the boat definitely strayed immediately off course unless paddled continuously. I would learn firsthand about this weather helm later on, a concept I had only read about previously. I would find once again that experience has a way of really driving lessons home.

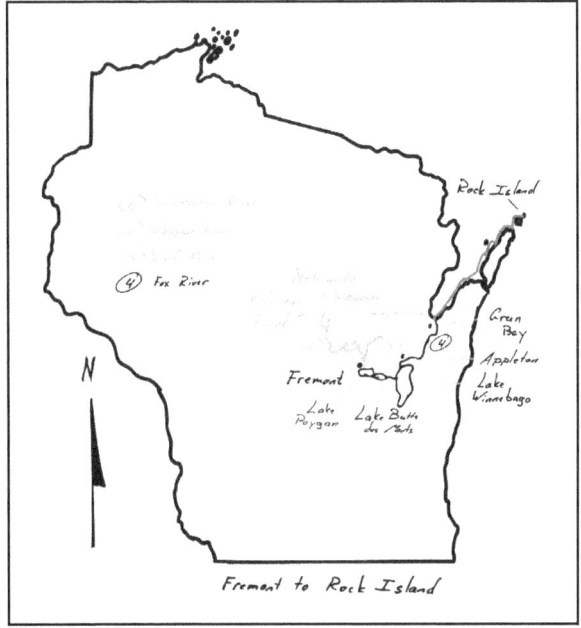

So now it was getting into June and I was drawn to get on the water and pick up where I had left off the summer before—chasing the waters of the Tomorrow River. The next leg was to venture down the Wolf River, through a series of open water lakes, and join with the Fox River to head north toward the Bay of Green Bay. I found 2 days of paddling at my disposal, but how far did I figure I could make it? Time was always pressing, and I wanted to fly through the industrialized river sections of the Fox Cities to reach the Bay as quickly as I could. Looking at the map and weather, I had to envision paddling, wind, stops, sleeping, and the coordination of portaging around or passing through 16 locks. I chose the ambitious goal of Kaukauna, Wisconsin as the takeout for my next jaunt, below the last lock in the most concentrated series of drops. This marked the northern end of the string of lock and dams as the Fox River coursed through the cluster of municipalities known as the Fox Cities and was subject to all that the progress of man is imposing upon it.

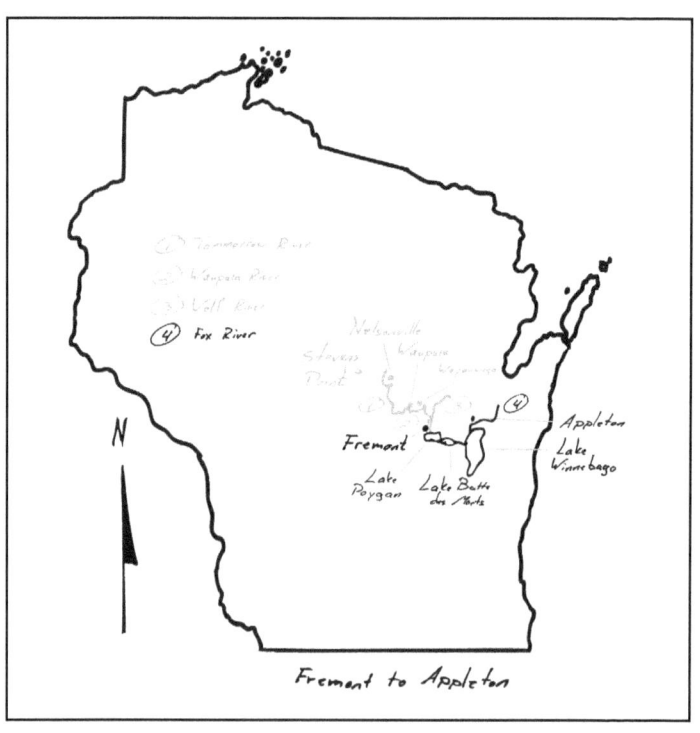

Fremont to Appleton

Endeavor's Inauguration

FREMONT — APPLETON, WI

6/3-4/22

The first thing was to organize a shuttle. I would drop my boat and gear at a public dock in Fremont, drive to my hopeful takeout in Kaukauna, and after parking my truck, bike back to Fremont to get on the water. Easy peasy, about a 33 mile ride.

I moored my boat between two public piers on the Wolf River in Fremont, trusting my gear would be there when I returned. There were people around and getting to my boat would be hassle enough for any would-be thieves, so I figured I was safe. I drove to Kaukauna and found a parking lot close to the last lock in town.

I had water for the ride but did not bother with food because it would be under 2 hours with places to grab a bar along the way, if needed. I boosted myself with a cup of coffee and a scone from Kaukauna Coffee & Tea and hit the road. I knew there would be a headwind, but I was not expecting 20 mph with gusts up to 40… Regrettably, this was only about my second time on a bike this season for anything that might be considered training. Going was slow, and I pushed it in order to maximize river time and miles. I bonked about 7 miles outside of Fremont and limped my way in, burned up from my calorie deficit. Yikes, this was going to be quite a day. But at least the shuttle was behind me and I got to see some new back roads from the bike.

Now to secure my bicycle. I knocked on the door of Anchor Point Rentals & Retail in Fremont, and Allie helped me out by introducing me to Bob (with one O). BobwithoneO is in his mid-sixties, one of the owners of the riverfront property he's developing and was working by himself cutting and laying paving brick for an outdoor patio. Kinda rare to see an owner at that level engaging so heartily in such an extensive project. BobwithoneO and I got to talking, and we wound up trading Jimmy Buffett stories, of all things. He let me keep my bike in his building, secure under lock and key. Awesome guy. This happenstance indicated that I was on the right path.

After grabbing lunch at a riverfront bar and rehydrating a bit, I finally took to the water at about 2:00 pm. A couple hours later than expected, but what the heck—I'm on River Time. Sunny skies, strong current, and a tail wind. These idyllic conditions were unprecedented. I could not believe the speed I was able to maintain!

An hour in, I had to make a pit stop and discovered the original Anchor Point Marina. The guys there were interested in the boat and my trip. After trading a few stories, I asked about a strap for my glasses in case they got dropped in the water. I was also looking for a strap for my hat in case it got blown off on the bigger waters of the lakes downstream. No lanyard for the hat, but my glasses got a new tether. We talked about my route-they confirmed my doubt of making it to Oshkosh yet that day. I was given a more detailed map and shown a cut onto Lake Poygan that would take about 4–5 miles off my trip. I contributed to their party fund before getting back on the water. Again, great people.

As the river descended into the flats of Lakes Poygan, Winneconne, and Butte des Mortes, the shoreline opened up even more to grassland and big skies. I have paddled through a lot of woods, and any open area is generally farmland perched above the bank, out of sight. Marshland such as this is a bit new to me, and its broad sky a novel change.

I passed a few fishermen and, following the directions of the guys at the marina, saw the landmark cottages that sat adjacent to the cuts off the river. I pulled into the second one and made my way a half mile or so along a rock bar out onto Lake Poygan. My pace slowed in the absence of the current, but holy smokes was fast compared to a canoe. Upon reaching the open waters of Poygan the kayak really proved their salt.

Heavy winds kicked up waves. I figured the largest ones almost 3 feet, but who knows. Everything looks big when seated below the waterline. From the perspective of an open hulled canoe, these waves would have been unnavigable. Plus, the freeboard. All that surface area sticking above the water would have offered downstream as my only possible direction of travel. I knew my sea kayak was supposed to handle water like this, but sometimes you just don't trust until you verify. It was quite unnerving at first, but I got used to the water washing over the deck and riding the bubbling foam of this following sea. My bearing was almost perfectly straight downwind, and I got a hell of a ride out of it. I battled the tendency of my hull to self-correct when waves came askew, but it was all manageable. A combination of rolling with the waves and steady strokes kept me solid in the water. I was still a novice in a kayak, but this was totally doable, given my canoeing experience. I made for the slot that welcomed me into Lake Winneconne and then entered the lee of a grassy shoal. The waves slowed a bit there, and I was able to feel them catch the hull and drive me along. It was scary as I felt my stern rise like someone hoisting the chair I was sitting upon and driving me forward… But hey… wait a minute… I WAS SURFING!! The waves on the open water had been too fast and my hull too slender to grab much of a free ride. In these slower waves, however, the brief moments of driving forward with seemingly unnatural acceleration were breathtaking.

The route on Winneconne was of similar distance to the stretch on Poygan. After consulting my chart and shaking the cramps out of my hands (I was apparently still a bit dehydrated from that ride) I set my heading for a point on the far horizon. Fatigue was creeping in, but the exhilaration of the ride bolstered my energy. These open water jaunts got long, and there was not much in the way of significant landmarks to provide scale in gauging distance. The charts and my phone are all I get, and they were stowed as I made these passages (another lesson in packing-clear bags for charts that can strap to my deck). I finally rounded Harper's Point and found more protected waters where the lake narrows back into the Wolf River and the city of Winneconne. I tied up to the pier at the Feather and Fin, took a moment to spill my gear upon the dock, and laid back on the boards still in my life jacket and spray skirt, exhausted.

A band had started and the patio was filling up with people just past middle age who were there to take in the music of their (our) generation. I grabbed my pack (wallet, phone, snacks, etc.) and headed for the outdoor bar. Ryan there hooked me up with water and a menu. Sawyer found an outlet for me to charge my phone, and we were able to talk a bit between their clearing tables and mixing drinks. Ryan paddles quite regularly and offered some tips for the rest of my run to Oshkosh.

"Have a headlamp handy, and mind the wind since Butte Des Morts can get pretty choppy. If needed, stay close to shore. If your energy holds out, you'll make it."

After finishing my Reuben and fries, I wound through the crowd of guys recalling tales of their glory years and back to my boat. It felt good knowing that my glory days had yet to pass me by.

I passed under the bridge of Winneconne and along the developed shoreline of steel, concrete and rock. The wind and sun had dropped a bit by the time I made Butte Des Morts, the latter descending lower at my back. This open-water run would be as long as my treks on Poygan and Winneconne combined. Waves were just off my stern quarter, so I had to muscle things to maintain my heading, at least until I made it around the rock wall that directs the Fox River as it joins the mix. And upon rounding that rock barrier, I was in the waters of the Fox River System. My third watershed of this sectional voyage.

The Interstate 41 bridge marked the far end of the lake and my entrance to Oshkosh. It was visible from way too far away: a white strip on the horizon, yet tauntingly close. The sun dropped from sight behind me, the wind cashed out, moths hatched, and I paddled on away from the sunset. I was on open water again with little to reference for my forward progress. That bridge sort of marked the finish line for the day's toil, but it just did not seem to get any closer as I labored away. The lack of persceptible progress was agonizing.

On rivers I commonly paddle, there are at most 100 yards or so of open water between bends. Preferred lakes are small enough to not allow outboard motors. Appreciable distance is measured in minutes or even seconds before a new scene comes into view around a bend or on the far side of a point. Living in anticipation of what is to come is met with more or less immediate gratification. I was finding that bigger water is quite different. It is best to just settle into the moment and not worry when that bridge will get closer. Just enjoy where I am while I'm there. Hmmm. Living in the present. What a novel concept.

It was dark by the time I made it under that #$%&! bridge. Sometime when you are heading south through Oshkosh on a windy day, look out at that water and see how rough it gets. Pretty gnarly! Glad it had tamed itself down for me.

I was too tired to care where I slept that night. I found a pier, tied up, threw down a yoga mat and mattress pad, and crashed out in a wet sleeping bag (another lesson in kayak packing: sleeping bag gets its own dry bag, even when stowed with a well-secured hatch).

Prior to this trip, I was completely uninformed on how much water I could cover in a day. I supposed I had a fast boat and that I could do pretty well. I used that vague metric against what I knew I could do in a canoe, and I thought Oshkosh was achievable in a day from Fremont. Thing was, I had spent myself considerably on the bike ride and was over 2 hours later in hitting the water than expected. Having not yet set up a tracking app on my phone I was unaware of the distance I covered, but according to some reckoning with the old Gazetteer, It seemed to have been about 25 miles. I was exhausted, but made the goal I had in mind. It felt good-my reckoning was just about spot on. Tomorrow would bring a short jaunt through Oshkosh and then Lake Winnebago, the largest inland lake in the state. As part of the work for the day, I was to paddle about a third of its length. I had never paddled it, but I knew this water could be sketchy in a canoe. I sure was glad to have Endeavor.

I was up at 5:30 but didn't get everything stowed to hit the water till about 6:30. My packing after a night's sojourn was a bit rusty. That is apparently when the fishermen get out too because I was escorted by a fleet of fishing boats heading out to Winnebago for the day. No wake allowed, so I was able to keep up with the vessels doing about 5 mph.

Referencing my map, the run on Lake Winnebago from Oshkosh to Menasha was as long as yesterday's runs of Lakes Poygan, Winneconne, and Butte Des Mortes combined. A doubling pattern seemed to be developing again. How boring would it get, paddling for hours along the same shoreline, staring at the same landscape when I am accustomed to the intimacy and diversity of trout streams and rapids? Hell, I wondered what that northern shore of Winnebago would look like from so far south.

I approached the open waters of Winnebago, the far shore roughly 10 miles away. I bobbed on the boat wakes as I rounded Brays Point and beheld the horizon of my destination … all water. Man, that was beautiful. And maybe a bit daunting. It also held an allure to capture the land beyond it, which was precisely my mission.

The water was calm but for the boat wakes. Gorgeous weather, with a cloudy front overhead, splitting the sky into two halves and the sun rising along the margin. I found myself at the interface of this as well, with cloudy skies and metallic water to the south. To the north were clear skies and jovial reflections off the morning chop. I was paddling north into the sun. I let myself believe that this meteorological feature was the universe poetically indicating something to me, yet another indicator that I was on the right path.

I bobbed around, then paddled away from the fishermen clustered at the mouth of the river. Houses came into view and disappeared along the shoreline, some modest, some ridiculous. My mind settled into the long trip ahead. I jumped the mouth of South and North Asylum Bays, heading for Island Park. I took a break there and resumed the soft water at about 9:30. Winnebago was clear compared to the turbid river I had come from. It was refreshing to see the bottom and encouraging to watch it race by as I entered the shoals along the points. The wind was picking up from the south, waves too, creating following seas like they sing about in a Crosby, Stills, Nash, and Young song. Upon what fate this marvelous fortune of benevolent elements rested is a mystery to me, and so uncannily encouraging it made me suspicious. I still had no problem jumping from point to point, across Cowling Bay and the broader Mansur Bay. At Wheeler Point, though, I pulled ashore and donned my spray skirt. The final jump to Menasha was the longest and most exposed.

Wind was south, now about 10 mph, sun overhead, and rollers building. Again, I am so used to a headwind on the Mississippi River that it feels like cheating to be able to ride it for a change. Waves tickled Endeavor's hull as they washed beneath us, encouraging us toward our destination... well, Menasha. The waves were not quite as big as the previous day, and I was able to ride them longer. As the entrance to Menasha drew near, the swells were big enough to douse my bow and wash over the deck again. I gave an effort with the paddle and picked up speed, when suddenly the boat was moving itself and I had to merely steer for a moment as the hull caught the surf. Whew, a bigger wave too-that was probably the fastest I ever went in a boat I was paddling. Sheer exhilaration!

I paddled into Menasha, the first of the Fox cities, if you don't count Oshkosh. Long before setting out on this journey, I was expectant of the urban development-channelization, contamination, and industrial exploitation of the river on this stretch. With the work and coordination involved with passing through or portaging around the locks, I even considered skipping it. I have come to call the expanses of industry like this *the hinterlands*, as they lie between the areas where we live and where we recreate. I do not wish to turn a blind eye to any part of what makes them what they are, no matter how it reflects upon the effects of my existence here. I have long held that a society can be judged by its treatment of women and rivers. Let's just say we don't always stack up very well by that metric.

There are 13 dams on the Fox River between Menasha and Kaukauna, with three more downstream between Kaukauna and DePere before the river flows uninhibited into Green Bay. Initially built for cargo, recreational vessels are the most common users of the system today. The first at Menasha is closed permanently in an attempt to stop the spread of invasive species into Lake Winnebago. (The zebra mussel and several others, originating in the salt waters of the Atlantic, have already made the jump via our shipping channels.) Not finding anyone at this lock, as was expected, I portaged. Two trips with my gear and my boat, with no comfortable way to carry Endeavor.

Next, I paddled through a broad stretch of river that was backed up into a flowage. At its head were the dam and associated lock, and again there was no one to be seen. So I portaged again, this time over jagged loose rocks piled in a steep embankment. Sore from the previous day's labor and now tired from today's progress, these ungainly trips further took their toll on my body and mental disposition. As it turned out, there was nobody at any of the locks I encountered to allow me to pass through via water, so I was forced to portage all of them. And each one seemingly more treacherous than the previous. Five arduous portages in total got me to College Avenue in Appleton, but it came at a cost. Endeavor had a few scratches. My nerves were frayed from several near falls on the loose rocks of the portages. The afternoon was already on the wane. And here I expected to lock through most of these barriers. I had been hoping to have my mom meet me in Kaukauna at about this time so I could take her out to dinner. Instead, we rendezvoused at this, my early takeout at College Ave where I would moor my kayak and gear while my mom and I picked up my truck. I was bushed. And discouraged. It was time to reconnoiter and pick up this trip again in the future, if ambition to paddle this man-forsaken river corridor of steel, concrete, and debris ever summoned me to do so.

But there is still a bit more to the story. As I was tying Endeavor off at the takeout, a woman walked by with refreshments for a riverboat cruise. She stopped and asked if she could snap a pic of Endeavor. Sure. I was a bit more abrupt than I would have been, but I was exhausted and quite frustrated to not pass through any locks despite having paid my online dues and was assured of the service. At least, that was the expectation set by the internet. On top of the fatigue, shortened trip, and treacherous portages, I located a number of new scratches as a casualty of the rocks comprising the artificial shoreline. That wear by active use may be what I built it for, but I can think of far more desirable places to incur scars that tell the story of this boat's life.

The woman from the river tour and I talked for a bit, Anje is her name, with River Tyme Tours. She felt bad about the ambiguous lock scheduling and lack of correspondence from the people managing them. She said there was a book of charts put together for navigating the riverway, and they were trying to draw in more people to do this sort of trip.

With positive sentiments we parted ways. Anje had to get ready for her tour, as Captain Dave was ready to welcome passengers aboard. My mom and I went to get my truck. After that shuttle, I said good-bye and mega thanks to my mom and loaded Endeavor and all my gear onto my truck. There were some notes I wanted to make while still fresh in my head, so I went next door to a brew pub for an Arnold Palmer and refill of water as refreshment while journalling. When I returned to my truck, there was a book of charts for the Fox River on my seat. In a turn of good tidings, Captain Dave recognized my boat and slipped me the charts.

Everyone I encountered on this trip, and now at least one person I never met, was interested in it and helpful in some way. By most measures I was pretty well prepared, but there were some things left up to chance either intentionally, out of an inability to control, or by the nature of my hasty planning/ prep. It did occur to me that with a loose schedule this way leaves room for a bit of magic or catastrophe. The trick is to be intentional and at least prepare against the worst that might befall. In this case, the variables I left open became some of the best parts of the trip—new friends, lessons learned, and a good story in the memory bank. The influence of people, while increasingly catastrophic to the health of the river, was one of the most rewarding aspects of this first venture onto bigger and urbanized water.

Novel as the human influence was on this leg, the next would be even more industrialized, with another 11 locks to negotiate before I made it to the waters of Green Bay and the Great Lakes. It was disheartening to think of portaging that many times, and given that the condition of the river would only deteriorate as I progressed downstream, even depressing. Maybe I would skip the next leg and just start again in Green Bay. Nope. I entertained that notion for about a minute before knowing I needed to continue on where I left off. But hey, a guy's got to look at all the options, right? At least, that's what my dad would say.

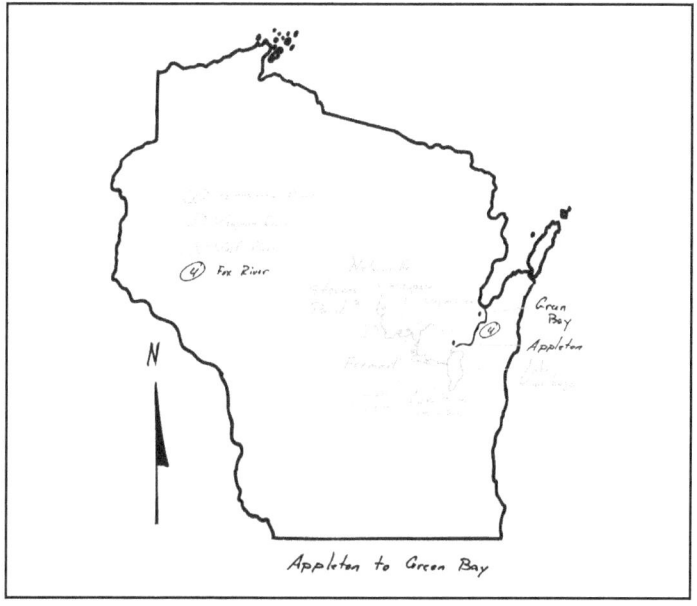

Paddling the Hinterlands

APPLETON — GREEN BAY

7/16–17/2022

Industrialized river, questionable overnights, stowing my bike, overnight parking, locking through dams, boat traffic, contaminated water, and algal blooms all held areas of worry for me. On a couple fronts, this was the best and worst leg of the trip. After portaging around five dams on the last leg that got me to the heart of Appleton, I knew I could portage the rest if absolutely need be. But because Anje of River Tyme Tours was so diligently communicative, I was able to call the head lockmaster directly to get schedules and updates on locking conditions. After that variable, most all others could be overcome, so I imagined.

I left Nelsonville at 5:30 am on Saturday, 7/16, to head toward the Fox Cities. I stopped at the put-in in Appleton to dock Endeavor and all my paddling gear. I bee-lined it for Green Bay where I would park my truck at my mom's house.

After hanging a bit with some family, I hopped on the bike and pedaled my tail off for Appleton- 33 miles upstream, but south, as the Fox River is one of just a couple of rivers in the Northern Hemisphere that flows north. This begs the question: Did I peddle *down* (south) or *up* (stream) to Appleton? No wind and steadily lifting fog made for a breeze of a ride, so regardless of the direction, I rode it *weather-or-not*.

Once I got to Kaukauna, the northernmost of the cluster of municipalities, I traced my way along the river by brail, being unfamiliar with the streets and not caring enough to check a bike route on my phone. I found some great bike paths and made zero wrong turns. That novelty was indicator, or miracle, number one.

At the put-in, I stopped in at Tempest Coffee and asked about a place to secure my bike. The barista introduced me to Tyler, the owner, who suggested I keep my bike in his office area. Being an avid cyclist himself, he sympathized with the plight of locking my bike. It's people like that who bring magic to these trips. Miracle 2. I changed out of my bicycling costume and headed for Endeavor to begin the main course of the day. As I did, who do I run into but Anje, prepping for a day on the water at a festival just downstream. We departed after catching up a bit, and she immediately texted an old family friend who was working with her at the festival, so we could meet up.

With that all set, I got underway for a couple of miles when I saw two people paddling kayaks which I could tell from a distance were not typical roll-molded plastic. I paddled over and struck up a conversation with Bob, who has a number of ultra-fast boats. The two he and his wife were paddling were respectively Kevlar and carbon fiber construction. Lighter and faster than mine, but with perhaps a touch less character. A few minutes after leaving them, I ran into my friend Keri, the encounter facilitated by Anje. Again, great people. So, within 2 hours of starting the trip, I ran into five new and old friends. This was off to a good start.

Then the locks started. Everyone running the locks was friendly and interested in the route I was doing. Turns out most of them knew I was coming before I even arrived at each successive lock. I was able to pass through easily with no waiting. I found out later that Anje talked to the director of the riverway navigation system, and he called a couple of lock masters to have them prep for my arrival. I met Bill at the second lock, who I had been in touch with a couple times about conditions and scheduling. As the locking chambers drain or fill, there is time to trade stories and wittiness, keeping things fun. It took me 5 hours to cover 11 miles through eight locks.

The village of Combined Locks was the most interesting. Two locking chambers sit adjacent to one another, so you lock from one chamber directly into another chamber. Just as the name of the village suggests. Each chamber rises or drops about 12.5 feet, for a total of 25 feet up or down. As I paddled into the upper chamber, I could tell there was a horizon beyond the gate. It looked foreboding. I paddled up to it, feeling like I was approaching the edge of a cliff. Incidentally, the lockmaster here is an old rugger, and after talking we figured out he was a referee for a couple of years at the annual tournament, Arctic Fest, that my old team hosted.

It was almost 5:00 when I finally left Kaukauna and could at last go to shore to pee. I had only covered 11 miles, with an estimated 17 to go. Would I make it to De Pere, home of the last lock on the river before it closed for the day at 8:00? It would be about 12 miles, with a portage, a food stop, and a lock to go through in just over 3 hours. Time to kick it in gear. I eyed my charts and started paddling. Half an hour to the next lock where I needed to portage, another half hour to Wrightstown, and 2 hours and two locks beyond that.

The portage I encountered was not easy. The take-out was rocky, but not too bad. The put-in was not marked, so I went down a muddy path (Fox Valley Clay makes mud like you may never encounter elsewhere) and bushwhacked through some invasive buckthorn to get to the rocky shoreline whose stagnant water was iridescent green with algae and more akin to sludge than a river. Then I negotiated half submerged branches of boxelder once I got all my gear together and stowed once more.

Back on the river, I resumed company with herons, eagles, kingfishers, and an osprey. This stretch was big and quiet-little boat traffic. Houses/mansions were smattered here and there along the shore, and the broad stretch of river left room to view a bit of the ridges and landscape beyond. This was no longer the intimate water of the Tomorrow River, although its waters are in here somewhere. This river is different, beautiful in its collective character-comprised of all the streams and tributaries that pour into it. Soon Wrightstown came into view and I docked there. Whew, I was getting tired. I grabbed fries and a wrap at the Nauti River Inn-decent food and more friendly people-and headed on my way.

Still about an hour to De Pere, as best as I could estimate, and one more lock to go through. The lockmaster at Rapid Croche was too friendly and we talked longer than I should have. My steam was running out and paddling form suffering (I have bad posture to begin with) as I shot downstream through ever-broadening river bends. More civilization cropped up along the banks, and soon it was one huge house after another, complete with lawns, docks, and seawall—the sterilization of the shoreline. I found myself counting the lots to successive landmarks, a sign that I was not tuned in to the moment. At this point, I just focused on making it to Green Bay. The De Pere bridge came into view, but still probably 3 miles downstream. I paddled for about 2 days to get to it and snapped some pics of the dam immediately on the other side. Then I noticed the time: 8:01. I was late? I raced for the lock, 200 yards down a canal, and the lock master was just taking in the flag for the night. He emerged from his hut and I asked if I could lock through, not knowing if I had another portage in me. "Uh, yeah, we don't close until 9:00." Whew-what a relief! It is hilarious how many of the tragedies we suffer that never come to fruition. Turns out it was only the locks in the upper Fox Cities that closed at 8:00.

A few people gathered on a pedestrian bridge to watch the lock do its work, all by gravity and elbow grease. The Fox River locking system is one of the last in the country to run by human power. People pull levers, wrestle wheels, and turn cranks to get water levels equalized and the gates to open and close. Water, gravity, and a muscle move thousands of tons of water and freight. Well, that was the case back in the day. Now freight is replaced by pleasure boats.

I exited the lock, heading toward a setting sun, and phoned my mom to start making arrangements to rendezvous in Green Bay. That last stretch, about 1.5 hours, was the most brutal, apart from the portage. My shoulders were in knots, legs antsy, and back sore. I stopped at Voyager Park to put on my navigation lights, stretch just a touch, and get back at it. I passed familiar haunts from my childhood in the dwindling daylight. The trail between Green Bay and Voyager Park in De Pere that my dad and I rode on our new mountain bikes when it was still railroad tracks back in the 80s, different fishing holes and a creek I used to dam up, a bench I helped install in memory of a neighbor boy who passed away entirely too early, and at last, the railroad trestle where I spent countless hours fishing and staring at the paper mill directly across the river. Were it still light, I would have stopped and checked in on the spot where I first tasted bitter cynicism from looking at the mill. But I kept paddling, more memories of my childhood springing up as I went. More piers, more sterilized shoreline, and at last the lights of downtown. I passed City Pier and under Main Street, and after emerging from under the bridge was immediately met by the blinding flashlight of my mom shining at me. We picked that spot to meet because there was parking and I remembered boat docks along the shore from years previous. Except the docks were gone. So, I had to do the final take-out on course rocks, in the dark. But whatever. I resembled the Hunch Back of Notre Dame as I exited the boat and tossed gear onto the shore. I was unsteady in hauling Endeavor from their watery berth and over the chaotic surface of rocks to get up the bank. Once the boat was on the truck, I started to relax into the evening and my accomplishment for the day.

3.5 hours of shut-eye the night before (was too excited to sleep)

33 miles riding

29 miles paddling

10 locks

1 portage

11 hours in the boat

On our trips out to Colorado mountain biking, my dad would talk about how good it feels to dive into a sleeping bag, exhausted from whatever new adventure he'd lived that day. I find that with the ultimate release of tension and toil, I find myself cackling as I lay down for the night, exhausted, happy, accomplished. On this night, as I indulged in the soft pillow and the bed of my parents' house, I laughed with exhaustion and smiled victoriously. I had, at last, paddled home to Green Bay in this vessel I built myself.

GREEN BAY – GREEN BAY

7/17/22

I awoke at about 6:00, too excited to get on the water to sleep any longer. I drove downtown and dropped my paddling gear at City Pier. Then I drove to the South Bay Marina at the mouth (the northern end) of the Fox River. I hopped on my bike and time trialed it back to the pier. I lucked out with no red lights, and held a 20 mph average for those couple of miles. This on an old Bianchi that my dad used to ride. (My bike was still secured at Tempest Coffee in Appleton).

My bike lock left with my bike, I used a logging chain to secure the Bianchi. No worries about anyone stealing that thing! I left my shoes with the bike too and approached Endeavor, docked and waiting patiently. There was algae in the cove formed by the floating dock and corrugated iron sea wall, reminding me of the condition of the river (not that algae is necessarily human caused, but we create lots of conditions for it to thrive with nutrification and stagnation of currents). I paddled out into the river, under Main Street Bridge and past the hotel where I took out the night previous.

The riverbank is industrial or commercial as far as the eye can see, with rock riprap as the closest thing one can find to natural shoreline. Scraggly box elders scrape out a living and lean over the water at the margins of the commercial lots. Inlets near bridge abutments create eddies in the current where garbage, Styrofoam bb's, and dead reeds form a mat on the water's surface. A giant pile of road salt (or something) sits on the west bank, and the old James River paper plant (now owned by some foreign entity) occupies the other, marking the point where the East River enters the Fox—the river's last tributary.

With the bigger water at the end of this river, the human exploits take on a larger scale as well. Paddling on, a cargo ship was docked at river left. I marveled at the immensity of its endless wall of steel. Beyond, the Leo Frigo Bridge looms over the water, the hum of its traffic mingling with and getting lost in the buzz of the city. From directly below, the archways of concrete seem to make a cathedral-esque tunnel that spans the river and the shoreline beyond. Reminds me of the Great and Powerful, not to mention egomaniacal, Oz.

At last with the final bridge behind me, The Bay is evident in a watery horizon beyond the river's mouth. I glance to my right and see a sliver of water extending inland. Like the last Truffula Tree, a single crevasse of wild sits quietly in an otherwise impenetrable landscape of concrete and steel. Multiple species of waterfowl occupy in this inlet, and although curious to explore it, I want to make it to the big water.

I paddle on under a warming sun, past the boat launch, and finally the opening to the marina. I stick my nose out into the Bay, paddling perhaps a couple hundred yards into it. It is tantalizingly tempting. As I linger at its threshold, a tease beckons me to plunge deeper toward its horizon and to explore the lands and islands beyond what I can see. My aqueous nerve was thus tickled, not massaged to satiation.

I loomed for a moment at its grand entryway, captivated by what was before me, longing to yeild to my urge to go farther. With regret, I turned my back to that flat line of water and pointed toward the marina and my truck. The broad horizons would have to wait for another day.

This all started in the village where I am co-raising my children, behind the barn where I came to live and build the vessel that carried me along the way. The water there was young, cold, clear, and swift. Trout had many hiding places, and its intimate bends and undercuts provided habitats for all sorts of wildlife. It ended in the city where I lived my juvenile years, on the river where I spent many hours fishing. Along its banks I dammed a stream with sticks and built forts into hillsides. This journey connected my dwelling places of past and present into a more solid bundle of *Home*. Through paddling the river and bicycling the back roads, I got to better know and understand the landscape as it transitioned from where I live to where I grew up. I had connected the waters between the homes of different parts of my life.

I witnessed the development of a trout stream to that of a full-fledged river, gathering waters from about a quarter of the state to offer them in contribution to the greatest lake system in the world. I lived out how the land and river are utilized for recreation and industry. Because of the impositions of Man, the water quality degraded as the volume of the river grew, same as with every river in the country. By the time I reached the mouth of the Fox River, I avoided contact with the water if I could help it. I had seen too much of what we do to the waters to turn a blind eye to the toll our progress has taken on them. Same old story, but a fresh reminder. And in this tale, we are not the protagonists.

Some things are prettier than others to face, but it is all part of the world we live in now. My experience is true. Not twisted by some special interest group and fed to me through some type of media. The conclusions and interpretations of this experience, and others like it when I can pry my nose away from the grindstone, are true. But even in the telling of their story here, some things are left out and many went unnoticed that would have been significant to someone else on this journey. The meaning you may have derived from planning, paddling, portaging, shuttling, and interacting with the people, places, river, and boat would have been entirely different than what I am taking away from all this. And for you to go out and live your true experiences upon the earth and directly with other people is to find your truth. And to share it is to enrich everyone it touches with the artistry of your personal interpretation.

As we share common experiences, rather than argue from our respective echo chambers within the silo of media that tells us who we are and what we are supposed to do, we come together with common understanding. We see things in a new light as others share their meaning with us. If we can bear to hear someone's interpretation of an experience that is slightly different than our own and accept and respect it, that is when we start to heal our society. If these experiences happen through interactions with the earth and we realize our effects on this planet and its communities, then we adjust our living systems to be less harmful. And that is how we begin to heal our planet.

It was midsummer as I wrapped up the voyage to Green Bay. Time with my kids was of paramount importance, and experiences with Bridget were becoming more engrained into my life. It was a lot to balance, along with work and annual get-togethers with family and friends that I could not bring myself to miss. While this journey was important, I did not want it to consume me… at least not completely. There were still openings in the dreaded schedule for more paddling that summer. I was unsure how far up the Door County Peninsula I would make it paddling the east shore of Green Bay, but I figured I had another outing or two left in me for the year.

The truth is, I did not have it in me to stay off the water. Every time my kids and I drove over the Leo Frigo Bridge (They know it as the Lambeau Bridge) on a visit to see my mom in Green Bay, I would look out upon the city and up the river at the waters I had paddled. That view would hold my attention for a brief moment before I was drawn to look out the other side window at the waters of Green Bay and the multiple points of land poking out into its right hand fringe. That water called to me. Pleading, teasing, enticing. I was certainly going to take advantage of any opportunity that arose to get back out there. I could not wait to cover that territory, effectively reaching over the horizon to grab the land and water that lay beyond and pull it close—making it home.

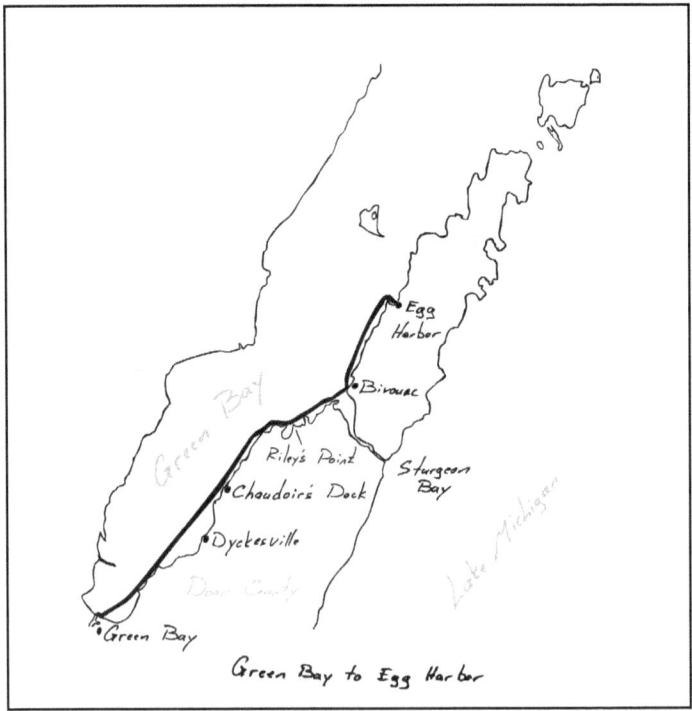

Green Bay to Egg Harbor

Bright Skies and Broad Horizons

GREEN BAY – EGG HARBOR, WI

7/30–31/2022

I arrived in Green Bay on Friday for a weekend of paddling. Before heading to stay at my mom's house, I drove down to the mouth of the Fox River. There was a glimpse of something I had caught on my previous leg that I wanted to investigate further. Under grey skies of early evening, I nestled Endeavor onto a cushion of water at the public boat launch. It felt prudent to linger at the threshold of the abyss, so to speak, drinking in the last of the riparian captivity in expectation of the liberation into big water.

I was drawn to explore the solitary natural inlet on the river just downstream of the Leo Frigo Bridge. The noise of traffic, muffled through the structure of the bridge and the 200 or so feet of elevation that separated it from the water, still set the mood with a constant drone of rubber meeting concrete. I approached the inlet, conspicuous in its greenery against the otherwise hardened industrial landscape. I was the intruder here and the cormorants, sitting guard in the bleached branches of a dead cottonwood, were suspicious. Entering the calm, murky shallows, chunks of broken concrete sporadically littered the bottom. Some sat just below the surface, no current or lapping waves to signal their threat to Endeavor's hull. I moved easily, departing the river and entering this few acres of marsh that had escaped development into coal piles, paper mills, petroleum staging tanks, electric transfer stations, and a waste treatment plant. Egrets, cormorants, pelicans, herons, and ducks clung to their claim of this last sliver of amphibious greenery. I did a small loop, held at bay from delving into the cattails by a broad mud flat. Just as well, I made my retreat without unduly provoking the wildlife the dwelt there.

At the river's end, lingered at the threshold of the Bay before visiting my mom for the evening. A whole new approach to paddling and the water awaited. I had no idea the imprint it would leave on my being. I couldn't wait to find out.

It was finally time to enter into the expansive waters of Green Bay. This segment started at the mouth of the Fox River, at the dawn of a picture-perfect morning. Calm winds were to give rise to a southerly breeze, cool temperatures to gradually warm, and a whole new chapter of unexplored waterscape open to me. I asked my mom once more for some help with the shuttle. She drove Endeavor and me to the put-in and was to meet me wherever I might take out the next day. Add this to the long list of debts to my mom, so tolerant and supportive despite all the worry. I did not feel I was missing too much by not biking the shuttle. I have ridden along the lower stretches of Green Bay dozens of times, having grown up here. I knew this landscape. Now to acquaint myself with its waterscape.

I left at 6:00 am, heading north onto broad water with the sun on my starboard bow. Endeavor's hull sliced through the flat surface under clear skies. The green water around me obscured the blades of my paddle as I drew them through the water, but I anticipated it clearing as I travelled north. According to plan, I set my course for the farthest point I could see rather than hugging the shoreline. This grew to be habitual as I would hop from point to point on up the peninsula of Door County.

I went on for 20 minutes or so, until the aches crept in of cold muscles being put to work. I grew restless and paused my efforts. My gaze wandered from the flat horizon of tree tops on the west bank, across the pale brightness of the sky as it approached the water line to the north, to the picturesque hillside of the east. A ridge parallels the shore there, the Niagra Escarpment. I had peddled up, down, and along either its head or its foot so many times. It was amazing to take it in from this distal perspective. I turned to see from whence I came. There was the Leo Frigo Bridge, and the city. And there it was: a ribbon of black smoke, the signature of industry, cloaking the city in a veil of sin, invisible from within, obnoxious from without.

I had always known it was there, in one form or another, but sometimes I would forget, taking all that concrete, steel, and disturbance as the rule of my existence rather than the exception.

It is the signature of mankind upon this Earth, flash-in-the pan progress whose light is dimming this very generation. I spent most of my life in sharp cynicism over this paradigm but am now concluding that the only way to change it is to accept and embrace it. Then improve upon it. So, this day I would not indulge in the usual feeding the guilt of my contributions to this cycle, paying my penance through self-induced struggle so as not to fully engage in the system. That has not been working for the last 35 years. I need to look ahead rather than behind for solutions. But for this moment I would try to be present to enjoy a long paddle into clear water.

As I chose that positive mindset, inspired ideas and opportunities arose. The fates enjoy a happy tale and provide happenstances to encourage such a story line. Thoughts crept in of different ways to share this story and encourage others to connect more intimately with the landscapes in which we recreate. It struck me again that there is value in seeking out and exploring the hinterlands in order to enlighten ourselves to what happens in the industrial complexes that support our standard of living.

I paddled on, the city ever so slowly receding and that far point approaching. The treetops of another point beyond formed as glimmering specs on the horizon. Individual ink blots at first and slowly combining to a thin line, they emerged from behind Earth's curvature. Similarly but in reverse, features dissipated behind. My experience has been that time slows down in natural environments, something I need in the most dire way. At least to a degree, I could finally chill out and be present in the moment.

I eventually made that first point, figuring it was about 5 miles and an hour from my start. Checking my time and distance, it was over 9 miles and almost 2 hours. Time was warped in this new environment. I love it.

I went ashore for a brief pause, grabbed a bite, and jotted a few notes. Having loosened my legs, I picked my way along the dune of zebra mussel shells and eased Endeavor back onto their watery berth. My feet were relieved to be rid of the sharp substrate made by thousands of these corpses washed upon the shore. This exotic species hitch-hiked its way here on the hulls of ships and feeds on algae and plankton. It altered the ecosystem of the Bay so that the population of yellow perch plummeted in the 1990s. The perch count is now recovering, but in my youth the cities of ice fishermen driving out onto the frozen bay in the wintertime disappeared and are only now re-emerging as part of local folklore. Clearer waters resulted from the mussels feeding as a symptom of this progression. Ironically, water clarity was not a good thing in this case.

I leap frogged past the Village of Dykesville to the opposite side of the broad, shallow bay that protects it. Chaudoir's Dock is set in a marina near this point and I had arranged with an old high school friend, Chad, to meet there. He arrived shortly after me in his pontoon boat, prepped for a day of fishing. After catching up a bit he invited me to stop over at his place on Riley's Point, just a few miles up the shoreline. We set the meeting time at his place and parted ways for a few more hours so I could make the journey. I was looking forward to revisiting his cottage, this high-school stomping ground.

I paddled along the shore for a longer stretch, and it was nice to have the closer company of trees and shoreline. The latter had begun rising from the water as limestone cliffs, a telltale sign of my advance along the bay and up the Door County Peninsula (This geologic feature, previously noted as the Niagra Escarpment, extends north, comprising Door County and Upper Michigan's Garden Peninsula, before arching to the East, under it's namesake falls, and finally returning to its subterranean berth below the soils of New York State.) Cottages popped up among the bastion of foliage guarding the shore, another another sign of Door County. Finally, small waves encouraged my crossing of Little Sturgeon Bay to Riley's Point, where Chad's family cabin sat among a few dozen others with a beautiful westerly view.

Having never approached it by water before, I was not sure I would be able to pick the place out from his neighbors. He said it was the one with the leaning willow tree, but I was pretty skeptical of that descriptor. I rounded the point and paddled toward the middle of Little Sturgeon Bay. I aimed for where I thought his place might sit, from my memory of at least 15 years previous-the last time I had been there. I kept a close eye on the houses and vegetation. Then, sure enough, there was a lopsided tree-it was a reliable landmark after all.

I pulled in just before he arrived, followed his instructions to grab a beer, and met up with him and his parents whom I had not seen in way too long. Man, you gotta love people who stay awesome through different ages. We fried fish and retold some of our favorite stories, but I needed to keep moving.

Before I left, we talked about places I might bivouac for the night. Chad recommended a spot just north of Sturgeon Bay, a closed down tavern. I thought it would be better to make more headway with whatever light I had left in the day and get farther up the peninsula. I would certainly consider this old establishment though.

Directly at hand, I got back on the water to discover that the wind had shifted to the east and kicked up some waves as I crossed Sand Bay. These cross waves sweep my stern down-wind, pushing my bow upwind in that phenomenon called weather helm. It is designed into sail boats in order to keep the bow pointed into the waves as the watery mounds become substantial. In sailing, you adjust your rudder a few degrees to overcome this. In my rudderless kayak, my upwind shoulder gets sore from doing the bulk of the paddling. After a long shallow crossing of Sand Bay, I made the point at Idlewild, the entrance to Sturgeon Bay.

The road out to this point sports small cottages on either side that all get water access, the point is so narrow. I have driven through this neighborhood of properties, and it strikes me as the kind of place where neighbors know each other and get together for things like Whiskey Wednesday. Still the flavor of working class people unashamed to hang out in a friend's garage, an indicator I am not too far up the peninsula.

Beyond Idlewild, Sturgeon Bay jabs almost all the way through the Door County Peninsula, and a canal at the southeastern end finishes the slice. Ships and all sorts of boats can cut through from Lake Michigan, obviating the need to round the northern point of the Peninsula, a passage ominously called Death's Door. The point I was passing at Idlewild still sports a reminiscent light house that guided these boats looking to harbor in the city of Sturgeon Bay or cut through the peninsula, although it is now mostly obsolete and hidden in the cedars.

I glided past the point and the cover of the land. Wind whipped up from the throat of Sturgeon Bay, churning the waters as it came. The choppiness produced significant weather helm that worked my right shoulder, but Endeavor rolled with the waves and seemed to even relish being tickled and washed by them. It was slow progress with my body feeling the efforts of the day, but the big crossing at Sturgeon Bay was pleasantly uneventful. Boat traffic had diminished for the evening and the larger waves were novel instead of a nuisance or hazard.

I had made the jump from Southern to Northern Door County. This transition was more cultural than geographic. South of here the working-class cottages and homes are largely weekend getaways for residents of Green Bay and the Fox Cities. There is not a ton of distinction between the weekenders and the locals from the farming communities of the area. The back roads and establishments all reflect this character. To the north, the shoreline is largely dotted with vacation homes and rentals. Tourism is more the norm with restaurants, shopping outlets, and art galleries. The farming community is still there, and some make a good income by marketing the authenticity of their goods made in-house. The activity still largely shuts down in the fall, allowing business owners to spend winter in a more comfortable latitude. The seasonality of this economy likely takes its toll on the working folks who are here year-round, however.

I made the landmark of Quarry Dock at the top of Sturgeon Bay just as the sun hit the horizon. I took advantage of protected waters and the gorgeous lighting to get some more pics of the trip. Then I pulled into the stone breakwaters of the old saloon recommended by my old friend. There was a familiar warmth in that moment amid the metallic sheen of the water as it reflected the sunset. The strength of its reassurance was more powerful than I had remembered. Perhaps I had been too busy for much of the previous decade to recognize the calm that can occur in this moment of the day. Or maybe its effects are enhanced in such a beautiful setting. I didn't question it. I just took solace in the fact that I was on the right path.

Once again, I had been skeptical early on, but Chad's advice proved better than my optimism in my day's progress. He always had solid judgement, ever since high school. I'd definitely crash here, closing my day out at 43 miles. I laid my wet clothes out to dry, spread out a therma-rest, and slept under the stars.

I pleasantly awoke to calm waters in my little bay the next morning. Man, it felt good to be doing this. Living the dream in every sense of the word. Taking in the water, my project for the day, I could see that the surface in my protected bay was deceptively calm. Waves could already be seen offshore. I was learning to be wary of such ascending seas, as I call them. I donned my life jacket and spray skirt for the morning leg. I rode waves another 12 miles north, all the way into Egg Harbor, much as I had on Lake Poygan. As I approached my destination, a series of small islands a couple of miles off disrupted the waves a bit, and I was able to relax, these smaller swells a pleasure to paddle and a blessing to have pushing me along.

The water here was of the clarity that I associate with Door County. I could see the end of my paddle as well as the rocky bottom in water up to 10 feet deep. Knowing clarity is not a metric for health of this ecosystem, my conscience was nonetheless assuaged that we hadn't destroyed all the waters just yet.

I rounded the southern rim of Egg Harbor where an estate sat with its own lagoon and private marina. The big money. As I paddled around this compound, I saw a couple surveying their grounds from the golf cart they were driving. We paused and chatted, the man asking where I paddled from and the name of my boat. I detected a hint of something through the southern drawl from the lord of this campus. Maybe I had something that he did not. I made a vessel with my hands and was engaging with it to experience a part of the world in a way that an all-inclusive ticket cannot afford. I was doing something real.

As promised, my mom met me in Egg Harbor with the truck to ferry my return to the city of my origin. Since she never lets me buy lunch, I insisted on stopping at a greenhouse on the way back to Green Bay so I could buy her a plant. I bid her thank you and good-bye after a lingering visit in Green Bay and headed back to Nelsonville. Driving back over the Leo Frigo Bridge as I left town, I looked out over the Bay of Green Bay and some of what I had freshly paddled. How amazing to know that I pulled my own way, much farther than I could even see, beyond the horizon that was so far off from the lofty vista of this bridge. That view would never be the same. It really did feel like I had reached my arm over that horizon, grabbed the world beyond, and pulled it close.

Again, my aquatic impulse was teased more than tamed by this jaunt of nearly 50 miles over big water and broad horizons. I could not wait to get back for the next leg, whenever that might be. The summer schedule was piled high, with warm weekends on the wane.

My competitive nature warmed me to the challenge of seeing how far I could paddle in one day. I sort of did that on this previous leg, although I could have started earlier, paddled later, and sought more distance on the second day. I would not have changed anything from that day, however. It was amazing to have my mom invested, reunite with Chad and his family, and to have an idyllic bivouac site.

It was prudent to launch out of the river on a long stretch of the legs, to blast from the contaminated river into cleaner, wilder waters. I made substantial progress, almost half way up the peninsula, which made reaching the tip of Door County seem a whole lot more attainable. But from the perspective of river time, I was no longer in a hurry to get through any particular part of this journey. Like I was already at the destination and I could take my time and linger a bit more with any chance I had to continue on up the peninsula. I was finally relaxed enough to steep myself in the beauty of the surroundings.

In other developments, Bridget and I were getting more serious. Weekends and now even weeknights were spent together, involving early morning commutes by one or the other of us to or from Madison. Time together was becoming more crucial. The thing is, she fully supported my attraction, (perhaps addiction?) to the water. She also had a sweet spot for Door County, having grown up in DePere, just south of Green Bay. So, we started looking at weekends to get back up there together. Having put in for notifications of open campsites, Bridget got notice of an opening the last weekend in August.

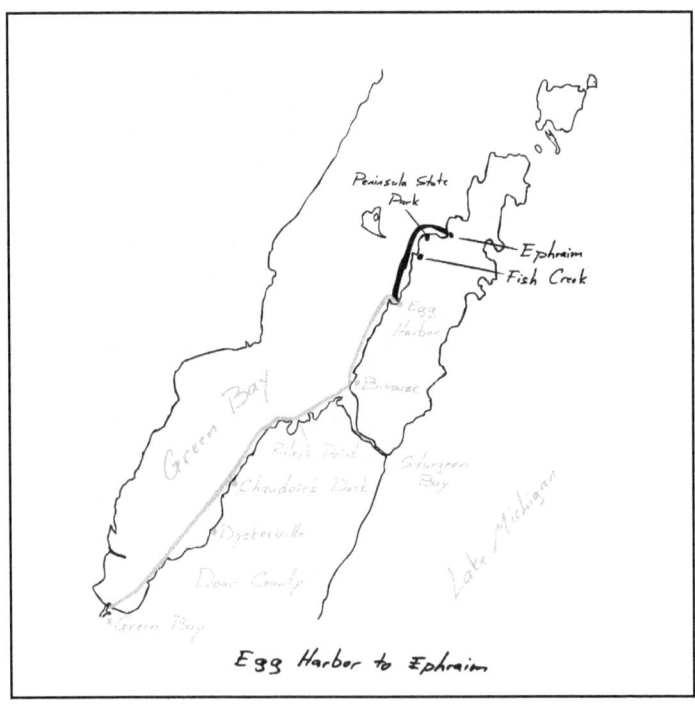

Peninsula State Park

Ephraim

Fish Creek

Egg Harbor

B. vouac

Green Bay

Bailey Point

Chaudoirs Dock

Sturgeon Bay

Dyckesville

Lake Michigan

Door County

Green Bay

Egg Harbor to Ephraim

Companion Paddling

We met in DePere on Friday evening, where Bridget dropped her car at her parents' house. We stopped in to see my mom on our way through Green Bay and headed up to Peninsula State Park as the sunlight punched out for the workweek. We pitched camp in the dark and snuggled in for a few hours rest before the adventures of the next day.

I arose early on Saturday and drove with Endeavor from the park, through the town of Fish Creek, and down to the village of Egg Harbor to put in at my previous takeout on Village Beach. Winds were out of the south at 5, but were to increase to 15 mph throughout the day under bright skies. The mercury started in the 60s and was to rise to about 80. Another gorgeous day for advancing north.

This was a comparatively short jaunt, just shy of 10 miles. I say that hesitantly because the wind was at my back. Should these distances be attempted into the wind, it is hard to say how much longer they would take. I have yet to experience a long day in the kayak and into the wind. Now by bicycle or canoe, I know this struggle well, and all the mental games that go with it. I am sure it is a similar story with the kayak—limited progress, adjusted expectations, psychological hurdles of rhythm disruption and disgruntling fatigue. In the case of this stretch, however, the fates once again with me, I rode the seasonal southerly breeze north for just over 2 hours. The consistency of such benevolent conditions is unheard of in my experience. I could swear that in so many other cases I was born to suffer at the breath of the headwind.

Rock faces had become the norm along the shoreline, with most of the homes sitting atop a sheer face that extended between 5 and 50 feet above the water. I was in bigger waves, perhaps some of the largest I had experienced. My inexperience still made it hard for me to measure their size, that and being so close to the water. What I first thought were 3–4 feet on Lake Poygan earlier this summer were certainly a bit smaller. Now these were perhaps 2–3.5 feet, some with the beginnings of white caps upon their crests. I was secure in Endeavor, rolling with the waves and paddling with solid strokes for stability and propulsion.

I had made it to clear water and the cliffs of northern Door County, where sand and limestone replace the mud and industrial shoreline farther south and on the river. The neat and natural delineation of the escarpment are draws for a lot of people. Most, even we tourists ourselves, complain that Door County is overrun with people. The popularity of this destination is understandable. With all the water, rock features, points, islands, and topography, this is a very picturesque area. Reflective of this, sailing, fishing, golf, camping, and biking are just a few past times enjoyed. Hell, some even paddle! There also happens to be a concentration of potters and artists. Perhaps it is the natural beauty of the area that draws them in and inspires. The most common activity for people in Door County, however, is shopping. With so many activities to engage in, the memorabilia is the tie that binds us all together.

It comes at a cost. Some people with the resources to do so want to get as close to the main attractions as possible without actually engaging in them. Houses and mansions and resorts (with pools) pop up along the bluffs overlooking the lake. People do not need to get out on the trail when they can step onto a concrete balcony with a metal rail to see the sun set over the bay. In this separation from the elements, it is easy to forget what we are missing. The feel of soil and forest detritus under bare feet. The rhythm of waves slapping the hull, wind filling a sail, or the beauty of the landscape when a view of it is achieved via the silent means of wind, foot, or paddle. With such dissonance we cannot fathom the challenges of paddling these routes that Native Americans have used for thousands of years. As these natural interactions are lost, so is our intimacy with the Earth. And with that familiarity goes an urgency to protect it and an awareness that our souls are starved without it.

I cleared a point that marked the entrance to another harbor, with the village of Fish Creek at its base. The masts of the sailboats at their moorings mingled with the shops and houses that crept up the bluff. I kept the scene at a distance, cutting straight across the opening, yet again shooting for the farthest point I could see on the peninsula. I take each following swell on its own, driven forward by the face of a wave and alternately lulled as the back side of the swell raises the bow and passes beneath me. The stern is sometimes swept to a side, and intimacy with the vessel accommodates my simultaneous response. I played with different types of strokes, digging in with bold and forceful pulls and forward leaning posture, contrasted by dabbling the tips of the blades and rolling at a more rapid cadence. At some point, I should really consider getting some instruction in the finer points of this art. As a beginner, though, it is fun for me sometimes just to play and revel in my own experiential learning.

The point I was heading for was within Peninsula State Park. Gaining it, I realized it served as the perch for the Eagle Bluff Light House. I paused briefly to snap a picture of the sun-shrouded landmark. This was a bit of a task, removing my paddle from the water, thus relinquishing my most effective means of stabilization. I was left to roll with the waves, relying on my hips to synchronize with the surface of the water and my sense of balance to tell me what level feels like. Have I mentioned my deficit of rhythm? I made it a quick photo op and got back underway while the open side of my boat still faced upward.

I made my way farther up the coast and past a smattering of tiny islands off my port side. Despite their being the better part of a mile away, they blocked the waves considerably. It is interesting how easily the undulations in the water were disrupted by obstacles in their path. The shoreline gradually turned away from the wind, further sheltering me as I approached my destination for the morning: Welker's Point.

At last, on nearly flat water, I made the day's destination. Just a couple of hours, but the tale of my morning's jaunt was a beautiful one. I left Endeavor on the rocky shoreline and found a route up the clay and rock embankment to the forest 10 feet above. I walked through the picnic area, across the park's main road, and into the campground where our base for the weekend had been established. Bridget was not waiting around for me. She had planned a great hike of her own and was checking it out. One of my favorite things about us is that we are both independently minded enough to chase our passions separate from one another. But it is better when we share them together.

After nosing about the campsite for a spell (A volume or two could be written about nosing around a campsite. There is no end to the level of organization one can achieve in the cooler, meticulousness in splitting and stacking kindling, and re-arranging the tent in order to make things just right. Perhaps more on that another time.) Bridget returned and we went together to the take-out to grab my gear and vessel. After sharing a hike that took us into the afternoon, I rode my bike down to Egg Harbor to grab the truck before we enjoyed an evening in the villages.

It felt great to get on the bike. As I wove in and out of cars stuck in the incessant traffic of Fish Creek, I wondered if I wasn't missing something that all these people were onto. They did their shopping at galleries and designer stores, then ate at niche restaurants. Here I was on a 25-year old bike searching out the back roads and establishing a new essence of this area based on an aquatic perspective. In the end, I decided I wasn't missing much by skipping the shops, not today. I will purchase my memorabilia later.

Next morning I returned Bridget's favor to me of schlepping gear. I staged Endeavor and a second kayak I had along on this venture (inherited from my dad who was consequently with us in spirit) on the rocky beach of Welker's Point where I left off the day before. I drove to the north end of the park and into the town of Ephraim that sat at the throat of Eagle Harbor. Jumping on the bike, I rode the few miles back to the campsite to reunite with Bridget.

We put in at about 7:00 am, wary of strong winds that were growing from the southeast. We should be protected by the mainland, while the lake side of the peninsula was buffeted by large waves and was under a beach warning. We started out innocently enough on flat water and even paddled to Horseshoe Island to check out the cove where sailboats love to moor for an evening's sojourn. Wind was picking up as we left those shores, but we were privy to a family of bald eagles out for a Sunday soar. And so the harbor that served as our destination was aptly named.

We headed straight for Eagle Bluff, which would afford some protection from the wind and spectacular views. Skirting the shoreline, we entered Eagle Harbor proper and set a heading for the beach where the truck was staged. With tame waves we enjoyed our slow, aquatic stroll into town. Once the boats were lashed to the truck, we walked to a  café for a breakfast I won't soon forget. What a delightful morning in Ephraim. About 3.5 miles, and every moment of them glorious. As Bridget mentioned a few times, "There's just something about paddling up to a destination!"

I had the peninsula three quarters of the way behind me. It felt amazing to paddle this route after looking upon these waters from shore for so much of my life. I was finally immersing in them, in just about the most thorough and intimate way possible. This exploratory venture could not end just yet. But September was mostly shot and October would be questionable for paddling. I consulted the map-I had done over 40 miles in one day, so perhaps I could replicate that and make

Dave Mangin

it to the islands off the tip of Door County and the end of Wisconsin? Maybe? There was the wildcard of Death's Door to negotiate. This haunting corridor is the passage between the tip of Door County and Washington Island, the largest of the archipelago. Wind and currents stir up big waves that get funneled between land masses. A careful survey of conditions would be needed before exposing myself to the first effects of open Lake Michigan. Of course, there were other factors too. The southerly winds of summer would be changing soon, so who knows what the weather might bring. Would there even be any campsites available if we were able to pry ourselves free for a weekend? The rest of the season was up in the air, but I wasn't ready to call it quits just yet.

Getting Out to Go Inward

EPHRAIM – NORTHPORT

9/24/2022

It had been working out so that about every month I made another advance on chasing the waters of the Tomorrow River downstream. September was on the wane, with the first glints of autumn in the tree canopies. The winds would become restless with their southerly tendencies and start changing things up. Good paddling weather would be more and more sparse.

Watching the extended forecast, it looked like southerly winds would hold as the next opportunity to paddle approached. As the day drew near, the wind forecast got better and better. Finally, they called for winds out of the south at 5 mph. Perfect. Rain may or may not be on the menu for the day, but who cares. I had actually pried the money from my wallet for a paddling jacket that would keep me comfortable.

Bridget booked a campsite at Peninsula State Park and we set camp, once again, in the dark on Friday night. I was up with dawn's first light and hauling gear to my launching point on the beach under misty, cloudy skies at 7:00. No wind to speak of and the glassy bay perfectly reflected this fact. The water

240

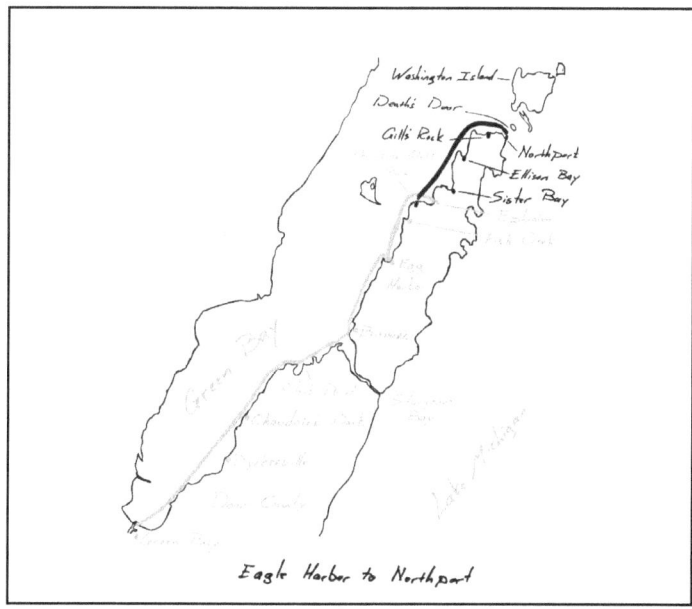

Eagle Harbor to Northport

was also deliciously clear, revealing the sand bottom's mackerel texture. The shoreline bent around to form Nicolet Bay, and bluffs rose to expose the limestone faces of greater Eagle Harbor. The far side of this bay was backed by successive points in the distance. These fading profiles encroached on the watery horizon, terminating somewhere behind Horseshoe Island.

I put in and set a heading for that island. I barely rounded its eastern shore when the far point of Ellison Bluff was revealed. I locked in on it and just started paddling. The grey sky grew darker, and wisps of mist blurred parts of the shoreline as these micro squalls wandered downwind. A few of them caught up to me from the south, passed on, and once again left me alone with my thoughts. A slight southerly breeze popped up. I largely kept pace with it, paddling in relative calm.

The shroud of grey clouds and mist subdued the allure of the shoreline. I passed the town of Sister Bay, wondering if I should not paddle closer to society to better soak in the culture and the landscape. Nope. I was out on the big water, and my journey was inward. Three hours of peace, calm, and repetitive motion.

Kinesthetic Meditation. As I allowed myself to get farther off-shore, I dove deeper within my thoughts and emotions, closer to the root of my current disposition. This was as solitary as I would get, without even any wind-prompted waves to serve as a distraction. And things were in a good state. It had already been a banner year, a welcome change after nearly a decade of increasingly trying times. Changes in habits, companionship with Beege, and determination to find time for paddling had culminated in this moment. Life was good. Even the water, in ever-increasing clarity, seemed to be having a party of its own-rejoicing that it was, at least to a greater extent, free of the sins man had committed upon it back on the Fox River and lower Green Bay.

I made it to Ellison Bay and then Gill's Rock, where I turned the corner from Green Bay, around the north end of this Wisconsin Peninsula, toward Lake Michigan. The bluffs stood as sentinels against the water with short cliffs dropping into turquoise clarity. I still kept away from society and was now just a hop skip and jump from Northport, the place from whence the ferry departs for Washington Island and the rendezvous point with Bridget—also the gateway to Death's Door. We had a notion to paddle the crossing of Port des Morts to the island, and see if it were not possible to venture farther from there.

As I rounded Gill's Rock, the southerly wind backed to the east, where it had come off the lake and curled around the Peninsula. Waves picked up to about a foot, and I texted Bridget to let her know that Death's Door might not be the best idea for her kayak today. It was still calm enough for a snapshot of pillars of rock that support the final bayside point of the Door County mainland, and I leisurely bobbed on the surface. One more bend to round, then a straight shot to Northport and the ferry dock.

As I crossed the last shallow bay and approached a broad arc in the shoreline, I gazed out over the drastically ascending seas. Remnants of larger swells off the lake were becoming increasingly evident. I rounded the bend against wind that was making its presence known, and with about ½ mile to go was pounded by waves of a size I had never before experienced. Endeavor pitched aft and forward as we rode together up, over, and down the back side of waves big enough that my 19 feet of waterline would not ride through. The bow submerged and water washed over the deck, curling around my cockpit in an antagonizing embrace of my vessel and my person. I finally had something to growl back at.

I was meeting the waves head on, rhythmically, with no notion of being pushed to either side, much less capsizing. Endeavor repeatedly plunged into the base of oncoming waves and alternately thrust their bow off each peak. Now, I do not know how to gauge the size of these waves. I had not the presence of mind to see how high their crests were over the horizon while I was in the troughs. I was laser focused on the conditions surrounding me, and connected in the most fiercely responsive way to the nuances that might threaten my ability to stay upright. I would expect they were 5–8 feet, encouraged to grow still more by the wind that must have been a steady 20 mph with gusts doubling that. Welcome to Port des Mort. Farther down the lakeshore, the forecast of the beach warning predicted waves of over 10 feet. So who knows- I was not comparing these conditions to anything else. I was living them for all they were worth and experiencing my boat as it responded to them with poise and confidence. I was in it, living, exceeding the boundaries of anything I had previously experienced. I was holding my life in my hands, with no safety net, insurance company, OSHA rules, instruction manual, or rewind button. I was navigating according to my own means.

So many of the measures put in place to safeguard our safety and health insulate and separate us from life itself. How can we measure it if we don't heft it and wield it ourselves? Not that I was even risking my life, I was just exposing myself to raw elements and dancing with the conditions mustered by the world, in waves I had never interacted with before. I was living.

243

It is these experiences that steer me from the mediocre and mundane drudgery of an uninspiring life. They steer me away from depression, toward valuing life and the interconnections and natural laws of this world. They expose the lunacy that is imbedded in some of our societal structures. They calibrate my inner compass. It doesn't take a life-endangering feat. Venturing for a run in a storm. Walking in the dark. A change of scene. An intimate natural experience. Pushing through mental and physical limits. This is how we live. How we grow. How we thrive.

We start by stepping outside our door, to explore the grass and the trees of the outside. Then we take a walk, venturing out on paths that become increasingly less travelled. We finally leave the trodden trail, following the path of our passions into wildernesses unexplored as we weave the patterns of our own authentic life story and our personal identity. And the path takes us to more and more out of the way places and situations. Rapids previously thought unnavigable become a matter of course. Adventure is sought, but our responsiveness to the elements mitigates our risk. It's intimate, juicy, real. It is life. And it's what we are increasingly separating ourselves from in more and more unbelievable and ridiculous ways.

As we get out there, the lure of the horizon that was once foreboding comes to beckon us like a friend. We don't fear ourselves or our solitude any longer as we search out opportunities to explore ever deeper and hidden coves of our psyches and see how we respond to different situations. We grow and expand and blow the doors off previously held limitations. We embrace and become the best versions of ourselves. And it's inexplicable. We can't impart the feeling to anyone who's never been there. But for those who are intimate with their passions, this level of living and embrace of life is sacred. To others we're nuts, maybe even held in suspicion. Why would anyone in their right mind emerge laughing from a storm?

And then society pulls us back. The job calls. We're accountable to adult responsibilities. We take a respite, which is great, but we're told that risk is to be avoided, that true luxury is leisure without effort. That all things should be provided on a vacation. To rest, relax, and be the subject of pleasures imposed upon our passive minds and bodies. Like zombies, we grow stagnant, disconnected. We're muted. Emotions are drugged out of our bodies. Anger is dangerous and we're bad if we feel it. We shave our bodies, try to emulate some perverted sense of beauty, and are compelled to spend more than we can afford to present ourselves a certain way. We're civilized. And we're sick. We lose focus of what matters. What truly nourishes us. Until we steal ourselves from the stronghold of norms and follow our inner compass. Then, once again, there's hope.

I had reached the threshold of Death's Door. My time in this squall was limited, only a half mile of paddling in the teeth of it. These monsterous (to me) waves had a gentle predictability to them. I was able to roll with them just fine in this waltz I was only just learning. My progress had slowed, but I still made good headway to the breakwaters at Northport. I was cautious not to let my bow get washed beam-to the seas as I eased my way across the path of the waves and wind upon my entry to the harbor. The wind was unrelenting behind the breakwaters, but the waves tamed. The green of their obscured shoals was of a pristine fluorescence I was not accustomed to. I cleared the car ferry that was docked, awaiting its cargo, and paddled toward the protected beach and familiar figure of Bridget, waiting for me there.

I was in my own world as I climbed from my cockpit and cleared gear from the boat. I had sampled the savage waters and my blood was up and senses heighted in an incredible natural high. The waves demanded more poise than force, but I was definitely surly, feeling almost reckless but still in control. One might say, hot as a pistol but cool inside. It felt incredible to be immersing myself in the raw nature of these elements, reuniting with a wilder part of myself I had neglected for way too long. I was truly alive, breathing real air.

A woman who directed traffic for the ferry came down to the beach.

"You're not thinking of going out in these conditions, are you?!?"

"Nope. Just coming in."

Working for the ferry, this woman knew what the lake could do to boats far larger than mine. She gave me a stern look and walked away, probably taking me for a fool for challenging the waters in noteworthy conditions. Often times the storms are scariest when looked upon from a sheltered perspective. She may not be aware that a kayak is actually one of the most seaworthy vessels in these conditions, as this craft doesn't withstand the onslaught, it rolls with it.

We loaded my gear, with no notion to attempt a passage to Washington Island in these seas. We walked out on the battered boulders of the breakwater and took in the storm. A ferry was coming in now from Washington Island, with waves crashing on its bow that splashed over halfway up its three-story cabin. This was going to be a fun boat ride.

So we boarded the ferry to explore Washington Island in the standard way, by vehicle. I was remiss to not make my first venture to this place by kayak, but there's something people say about best laid plans. We had several of what I have termed *miracles,* or *indicators,* that day which marked the significance of the moment. Looking to grab a bite to eat, the first place we found was called the Point Café. The sign over the storefront was scrolled in the same font as Point beer, which is named for the town where Bridget and I both played Rugby over 20 years prior and began our acquaintanceship. We took this sign as a sign and entered.

As we sat down, what was likely someone's online music station could be heard. I could not believe it: familiar boat building tunes by Jimmy Buffet came over the speakers that accompanied me through Endeavor's gestation. In particular, *Boats to Build.* I ordered the last cheese curds on the island as the café was closing down for the season after that day. Then

"Louisiana Saturday Night," the tune that marked my near end to the Big River Trip in New Orleans 15 years earlier, came on. We talked with the manager for a bit and then gave ourselves a little tour of the island. We wrenched every bit of living we could out of that limited time, including history, scenery, running stairs, and a nap on the stones of Schoolhouse Beach that was simply divine. We were cutting it close in making the last ferry to the mainland. Turns out we were the very last vehicle to barely squeeze onto it at the very last minute before departing the island.

On the ferry ride back to the mainland, we were again wind whipped and lambasted by waves. We stood on the upper deck to take it all in. From that elevated view, the waterscape, islands, and mainland all seemed a bit smaller, the horizon more distant (because it was), and less intimate. Oddly, the water seemed more harsh than when I was paddling. Being above the waves rather than in them made them somehow more foreboding. It made me feel just a bit empty for some reason. I was separated from what was going on around me, and the water seemed hopelessly big. I was almost turned off by it, and then I averted my attention rather than follow the notion to its root. I did not want to be intimidated by or lose my passion for the vast water. The root of that feeling holds a bit of mystery for me, one I will surely chase down at some point to see if my hunch about it is right.

With weather cooling and winds shifting, this was likely the last jaunt of this sort for the season. We had certainly made the most of it. Bridget, in addition to offering amazing support to me, got in a hike and some quality time of her own while I was on the water. Of course, I'm still indebted to her. The paddling experience and the indicators afterward were nothing short of magical for me. I could feel myself coming alive again. In some ways, perhaps for the first time.

Thanks Beege.

Now slammed up against October, I figured that was a wrap on the season. By measures personal, temporal, and meteorological, summer was over. Time to shift focus to autumnal exploits like wood cutting with the family, hunting, holidays, and hardening off for winter. The outlying islands at the end of the state may remain yet to be explored, but I had at least made it to the end of the mainland. And with the crescendo of weather, indicators, and pleasure all wrapped into that last leg, another jaunt would likely be anticlimactic. I had gone farther than I ever had reason to hope to. I had definitely lived the dream. Except, there was still a small itch as I thought again of Washington Island. Nothing uncomfortable; I could certainly live with it. But it sure would feel good and make my world right if I could scratch it.

I looked at the calendar for open weekends. Fall was advancing slowly and its colors stretched multidimensionally across the month and landscapes of October. My only shot would be the third weekend of the month. Great. Getting toward the harrowing time when the skies of November turn gloomy. The notion of paddling again was an even longer shot than any trip we did so far. Peninsula State Park reduced their available campsites to one-third of their summer capacity for the winter season, winds became more restless, and water temperatures began to plummet. The bone chilling humidity of the first frosty temperatures had already crept in weeks ago. There was an inch of snow on the ground one morning in the middle of the month. But I watched the extended forecast for Sunday, October 23rd.

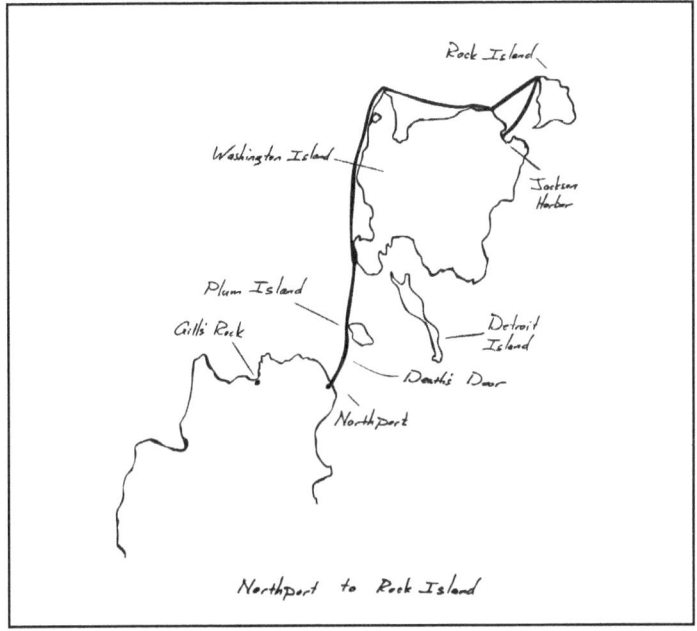

Northport to Rock Island

An Encore

NORTHPORT – ROCK ISLAND, WI

10/23/2022

Bridget texted one day that she booked a campsite that had opened up. Well, we would be in the neighborhood at least. Saturday was my kids' last soccer game, and I would not miss that for the world. If we high-tailed it to Door County from there, we could knock of some miles on the Ice Age Trail, a new endeavor that Bridget is embarking upon, and then head to the campsite for a night's rest before an early day on the water. The extended forecast called for a high-pressure system to maintain stable weather conditions, and the predicted temperature just kept getting warmer. It may be sunny and warm, but what of the wind? At 10 days out, they predicted 10 mph out of the south. Not good. Last time I saw that prediction it was 5 mph, and the reality was quadruple that, with monster waves off Lake Michigan. Well, we'd head up there for some hiking if nothing else. Besides, whatever the wind, we could find someplace to paddle in calm water, on one side of the peninsula or the other.

Saturday morning dawned clear with gloriously warm temperatures in the 50s and calm winds. My son and daughter both scored goals in their last soccer games of the year, so the day was off to an amazing start. Then Bridget and I made the journey to Door County. We dropped the truck on the Ahnapee State Trail, which was also a segment of the Ice Age Trail. The IAT meanders across the state, following the end moraines of the last glaciers that plowed out the landscape about 13,000 years ago. Instead of peddling the trail, we biked through Sturgeon Bay and into Potawatomi State Park where Bridget had hiked the first stretch of The Ice Age Trail with her mom a couple of weeks prior. We locked the bikes and followed the tell-tale yellow blazes of the IAT back toward the truck at the only pace I know with her: breakneck.

We traced the shoreline of Sturgeon Bay, walked through town, and made it to the truck. We had to double back to retrieve the bikes I forgot about, and once again made it into our campsite in Peninsula State Park after dark. Our systems for setting camp becoming routine, we were neatly tucked in the tent within a half hour. Rising well before dawn cracked, we struck camp and left without seeing this portion of the park by the light of day. To meet my objectives, I would need all the time I could get, favorable winds, and yet more logistical support from my partner in this venture. Beege was more than up to the task.

We made it to the place from whence the ferries leave at Northport just as the sun broke the eastern horizon on Lake Michigan. The water was not calm. The steady offshore breeze was about 10 mph, as predicted. I had been pretty sure the day would be a no-go, although that may have been in an attempt to keep myself from being recklessly optimistic and going out in dangerous water. The reality was that the waves crashing on the break water, while formidable, were not insurmountable.

I knew the wind direction and figured the swells to not be overly severe farther out on the open water. The 4-mile passage to Washington Island is interrupted by Plum Island, at about the half way point. From there, the tail of Detroit Island juts to the south to overlap the path of any offshore waves coming between Plum and Washington. . . . I know this is confusing. Suffice to say that I had only 2 miles of open water to worry about, and they lay directly before me-between Northport and Plum Island. Under normal conditions this would be a half-hour paddle. The waters I was seeing I knew I could handle for that time and then some. I was going for it.

There was no conversation as I focused on my gear, clothing, and other preparations. Bridget helped carry my cargo and allowed me to focus on my tasks. In short order I was ready. I posed for a pic before we hugged goodbye, and I took to the water. I knew what I was in for and nervous of it. My hips were too tense to roll with the waves that were hitting me astern, but I rose and fell with them and slowly found my groove. I pointed my bow for the Coast Guard light house on Plum Island and started paddling. The waves grew according to expectation as I put distance between Endeavor and the mainland, but I was comfortable in my craft and handled them easily. Still, I kept a peripheral eye on those oncoming swells as they accosted my starboard quarter. Again, I wondered at their size. They were approaching the scale I remembered the last time I had been in these waters, but not quite there yet. Finally, about 2/3 of the way to the lee of Plum Island, the waves were at their biggest. Many crested above the horizon as I sunk into their troughs, and one was at a significantly inclined line of sight. I was wary of larger water that may be in store, but I was still handling this well. I felt it to be a measured risk I was taking. As I neared the island and was out of the ferry channel, I adjusted my course and paddled straight downwind until I was clear of the shoals that may hide a rogue rock that could capsize my hull. I turned back to the north then, and into the calm waters behind Plum Island.

I'd made the first leg of the passage. Now to venture back out into ascending seas and cross the ferry route once again. I had a vague notion of how far off Plum Island the ferries passed but could not remember for sure. As timing would have it, I saw two of these car-toting vessels simultaneously leaving opposing dockings on the Island and at Northport. I shot straight away from Plum Island and powered across what was their eventual path as quickly as I could. The waves pushed me along, and I was able to surf a bit as I cleared their course. Satisfied to not be a disruption to their route, I relaxed my pace and adjusted my bearing for a protected point on the southwestern tip of Washington Island.

My right shoulder grew tight early in the passage through Death's Door, and then sore. I was paddling hard but also felt restricted in my wetsuit, over which I wore a long sleeve shirt (cotton...what was I thinking!) and then a water tight paddling jacket. That jacket did keep water out, but perspiration in. My shirt had grown wet and clammy, sticking to my shoulders and restricting movement.

Gaining the point on Washington Island, I texted Bridget that I had made it through Death's door. Whew-still some weather to consider, but I likely made it through the worst of it. Now to paddle up the west coast of the island and round the northern tip. I figured it would be all protected waters, and it was, for the first leg anyway. I slipped into a mundane expectation of gaining prominent landmarks on the shoreline, an island, the far side of a bay, a point, and a second point after that. Now 2 hours into the paddle, I made the northwestern tip of the island. Gorgeously clear water, tall cliffs, bright skies, and easy paddling.

I texted once more, shed two layers-now down to my wetsuit, and then turned the corner. My torso was liberated without the encumbrance of wet cotton, and I felt refreshingly cooler without so many layers. I was ready for a stretch that might bring on a touch of headwind as I bore east over the top of Washington Island.

This turned the page on my paddling experience. There were exposed waters to the south in Washington Harbor, and the wind whipped the starboard bow. Moderate waves slapped my hull, washed my deck, and occasionally sprayed my chest and face. *So this is what it's like to paddle into the wind.* It was gnarly water for sure, and the weather helm of my hull kept wanting to drive my bow into the waves. I fought it with tough right hand paddle strokes, but exhaustion was creeping in, especially with my nagging shoulder. I made my way slowly and surely toward the calmer, protected waters on the far side of the bay, but now I was stressed over what might lay in store on the final passage to the tip of Rock Island. That gap, with waters exposed to the full force of what had grown to 15 mph winds off the lake, may not be doable.

Rock Island was the last island in the chain that is part of Wisconsin. As a young George Kennedy might say, "the only thing standing between me and everlasting glory". I resigned to paddle out toward my final destination, just another 3 miles distant, but mentally prepared myself to turn back at any moment should the beam seas become too much for me or my nerves.

No response from Beege indicated that she had not seen either of my texts. I was no longer paddling the mainland; this was its own isolated island whose protection I was about to leave. It was late in the season with questionable weather, and daylight showed in the shallow angles of autumn. It was even Sunday, so time was short on the lifespan of the weekend. There were a pile of reasons for me not to worry as well. I had food and water, a perfectly sound boat, and conditions were not overly threatening. I could go ashore to calmer waters and even bail on the voyage and take-out in the yard of some waterfront property if I needed to. I had a phone and a battery for it, so communication would eventually come round as well. Perhaps it was more than the physical conditions that had me uneasy. This was absolutely the final run of the year. It was the end of the latest chapter of an Endeavor 4 years in the making, with no clear vision of what lay beyond this last horizon. Paddling farther, sharing the passion in other ways, and buying some property (perhaps with Beege) were all pipe dreams that were not yet firmly set. I was at the brink of all these things, and the blustery conditions on this glorious day were the perfect metaphor for it. I was at the threshold of so many dreams coming true, but it was going to take some careful navigation and a whole lot of work to get there.

The waves were smaller than expected as I ventured out into the growing whitecaps from the sanctuary of this northern outpost. I was going for it, springboarding off the last significant land mass, shooting for the final outcropping of Wisconsin in this culmination of waters between Green Bay and Lake Michigan. Endeavor was beam to the swells, and my right shoulder was paying the price of the onslaught. About a third of the way to the point of Rock Island, I figured I was in the roughest of the water. For some reason it still was less severe than I anticipated. Although this went against what I had acquired as some sense of judgement in this realm, I did not dwell on this; I just appreciated it.

Paddling on toward the northern point, the wind and waters predictably bent around the island and more cooperatively approached my stern. I was able to gleefully surf a bit as I slid to my ultimate destination of the summer, the northern point of Rock Island State Park, the tip of Wisconsin, straddling Green Bay and Lake Michigan. A resting place on an Indigenous trade route that has afforded shelter to paddlers for millennia. As I approached the rock face of this point, vegetation came into focus. Humongous birds soared on the winds, venturing out from the overstory above the rock precipice and the exotic, teal-colored waters. Poetically, they were a family of bald eagles.

I rounded to the lee of the northern point and into peaceful waters, bobbing easily on the remnant waves, protected from the wind. I did it. I made my destination. My dream realized. I looked to the north and there was St Martin Island, Michigan territory. It did not call to me. Not one bit. It just sat there on the horizon, content to be left alone, almost shushing me away.

The moment was almost anticlimactic because of exhaustion, thoughts of logistical coordination with Bridget, and the knowledge that a passage was still to be made through hairy water. I was not out of this yet. I tried to drink the occasion in, but as is often the case at the precise moment, I was distracted by the immediate circumstances and could not appreciate its majesty.

One thing I was able to capture, though, was the water. It was clear, bright, vivid, and completely foreign to me. The tropical looking hue created a presentation I have never seen from Green Bay or Lake Michigan. The naked limestone bottom spread out directly below me, with great cracks and fissures etching its surface like the creases of an ancient hand.

The unfamiliar feel of this waterscape was somewhat eerie. Its splendor, in this moment of exhausted distraction, was almost lost on me. It was like stepping in from a rugby match, sweaty, grimy, and gnarly, to an exquisitely formal spread of food and refinement, the subtleties of which a person hardened from the trials of the pitch cannot distinguish. Considering the defilement of my daily life and its effect on our water ways, all the driving, packaging, energy consumed, and general dwelling in excess, I felt like I was not deserving of such pristine surroundings. I knew not what to do with the beauty I beheld. It was more than I could bear, like water flowing off a hardened sponge that, although parched, cannot absorb its succulence. I knew this to be the case, so I snapped a picture in hope of capturing what I knew I was missing. And with that, I left for Jackson Harbor, where Bridget had agreed to meet me with the truck.

Someday, if I could possibly live more gracefully in concert with the providential nature of my surroundings, perhaps I will be able to fully comprehend the magnificence of that wilderness. That is my ultimate aspiration, and to initiate a trend toward the restoration of our hinterlands to that level of purity. It is so tragic that we harden our senses to the degree that we cannot conceive of such beauty and grace as was surrounding me in that moment. And because we cannot perceive it, we cannot be aware that we destroy it. We subside, lost in the smog that surrounds our lives rooted in industry and information, not even noticing the devastatingly putrid shroud of our own making. But that is just one price of our progress, mostly overlooked by the vast majority of society. I felt as though I left a greasy streak of the slovenliness that is consequential of my own life upon the water as I paddled away from that magical spot. I achieved it in the cleanest way I could, but those means are still devastating to the beauty of wilderness lost to the progress of man.

Back to the task at hand. Do I hold to the somewhat protected shoreline of Rock Island as I return south to Washington Island, or do I take a direct route across open water to what I think I can make out as the opening to Jackson Harbor? I monitored conditions, followed the shoreline, and slowly eased my way out into the fray of the wind and waves. As I wandered slowly askew to the shore, the waves again seemed somewhat suppressed. I was now closer to the narrows where the waves of Lake Michigan would wash through and pummel my craft , but they never materialized. They should have been even bigger than on my trip out, due to their confinement. I drew abreast of the slot between the two islands, feeling every bit of the force of the wind, but the waves were like child's play compared to what I was expecting—even smaller than when I made the northbound passage out toward the Rock Island Point. How could this be?

I gazed intently toward the slot between the two islands. I knew from satellite imagery that there was a shoal here, and looking closely, I saw whitecaps. It was shallow enough that the waves off the lake broke as they entered. The turbulence I experienced was only what the wind could stir up between the shoal and my location. That is why the waters were smaller than expected. Still, I had the wind to contend with. Exhausted, and now with my left shoulder being worn down trying to keep my bow pointed toward my destination, I struggled on toward that one particular harbor. I finally made the bay and entered the lighter colored waters of the shoals. I even paused to rest a time or two before making it to the boat landing. Bridget pulled in at about the same time as me, all smiles, congratulating me on achieving a huge goal.

A couple waves of emotion washed over as my fatigue finally took hold, but I stifled it until I was ashore. I stumbled through aches and pains as I extracted my cramped body from the cockpit that had held it captive for the last four and a half hours. Remember that aberration in the foam seat? Well, the feeling in my right buttock was testimony to its existence. I almost toppled over trying to carry Endeavor from the water to a patch of grass where the gear could be transferred to the truck. Bridget went to grab the truck and I began releasing lines and hatches. Amid the activity I was overcome and found myself sobbing in an emotional state of physical and mental release. My vessel, my body, and my psyche had carried me to some pretty far reaches and I was fresh from the moment of that pinnacle. And Bridget's unconditional support was absolutely amazing every step of the way.

We packed the truck together and I could not formulate words to match the level of appreciation, gratitude, and fulfillment I was experiencing. The emotional release, greater than

I could have expected, compiled with aches and exhaustion to be overwhelming. Suffice to say I was a puddle. Bridget drove us back to Nelsonville, home near the headwaters, where in a perfect ending to the experiential leg of this endeavor, I received my kids.

Thanks again for carrying me through on this one, Beege. I love you.

When I was out on the water, I could see St. Martin Island from Rock Island in the archipelago separating Green Bay from Lake Michigan, and it is part of the state of Michigan. It was right there, well within reach. Just another hour's paddle away. But it did not constitute the next horizon of my journey. I was not called to it, not as the waters of Green Bay had teased me to explore farther. I had physically traveled, in the truest sense of the word, far enough. It was time to shift my attention and efforts with this endeavor.

Bridget drove us down-island to Detroit Harbor, from whence the ferry would carry us back to the mainland. As we swayed on the third level of the boat, some 40 feet above the water, I was able to look out upon its vast expanses. That empty feeling crept in, for the second time, and it was a bit foreboding. Retreating back down the peninsula, I saw the bays and open water I had paddled this summer. I could remember the conditions and my disposition at every spot. That emptiness was there every time too, although it remained subtle. It was the same feeling from the ferry that gloomy day the month before. While I had originally attributed it to the weather, as logic would hold, something about it felt deeper than that. It was like I was pushing the limit of what I should be doing at this time. This series of trips has been my own, but they have so far only benefited me. I have reached the frontier of what I should *do* at this time, what I should, as the ARE model holds, *Experience* in paddling these waters. I *Created* this vessel, and I was able to *Share* my passion for boat building and wood working with others. That sharing, however, felt as incomplete as I considered the chasing of the waters, hopefully to the ocean. My gut was telling me it was time to shift gears on this endeavor in a voice that could even be heard outside the hour of sunset. I am learning to heed that call.

Sharing Endeavor: The Next Chapter of Art & Rugby

A Vessel of Multiple Sorts

As were the projects that came into the Barn during Endeavor's creation, this volume is part of the sharing of that project, but not all. As I write this, it has been almost 3 years since the last leg of that trip. Other jaunts will come in good time, but as part of a larger initiative, hopefully to chase the waters from behind the Launch Pad all the way to the ocean. A friend of mine suggested to me when I told him of my plans to build a boat to take down the Mississippi River that I ride a barge down the river and build a boat on the barge as I float. In a sense, that is my intention on the next leg of this endeavor. I'll have this book to share and promote along the way, hopefully building the Art & Rugby (ARE) community as well.

My kayak, Endeavor, is the vessel that carried me through the death of my father, the break-up of my marriage, and the death of one of my best friends, to the reconnection with an old friend whom I fall more in love with all the time as we build a new life together and with my kids. Some aspects of this tale occurred before the construction of the kayak was even under way. Some of the most meaningful moments that came from this project were only indirectly tied to the boat and this undertaking. The folks who visited the barn with all sorts of projects, ideas, and curiosity all left with a few additional skills and a story or two, if not products they could be proud of. The bonding that came with the late nights, toil, and sharing of ideas drew me closer to some really great friends and family. I had the chance to bond more intimately with one of my best friends and he was able to leave a legacy to his family because of this project.

It's about more than just the boats.

Once a functional vessel, Endeavor carried me over 200 miles from Fremont to Rock Island, as I connected the waters between two homes and continued beyond to begin to see where the waters go. The journey itself connected me to the Earth in a way I hadn't been in a long time. Out on the big water, that connection was formed in a new way all together. I am now a broader person for having built and paddled this boat.

As I noted in my journal a few days after completing this final leg, the notion of broadening horizons on the big water was more appropriate than I knew. It felt as if in the household of my psyche and perceived capabilities, a new addition had been annexed. It felt like other dreams were within closer reach than ever before. The victory of this boat and series of paddles made me feel capable of going farther in other aspects of my life and doing more. Now it is time for other people to share that feeling. I look forward to comparing notes with fellow explorers of our hinterlands, with people who have forged beyond the horizons of their own dreams. Those tales of personal ambition and growth are some of the most inspiring of all. That blowing away of perceived limits is the ultimate goal.

Eye Beyond the Horizon

The Art & Rugby model of CREATION, EXPERIENCE, and SHARING, interwoven with *Learning* and *Inspiration,* is the test of a hypothesis that is evolving in pursuit of an authentic experience. So far in the journey, it has exceeded expectations. Of course, the holistic disposition of hindsight will prove the true value of the model. Each component, however, fits nicely with its contribution to the whole. Here is the functionality of where it stands so far:

Create

As we make stuff, anything, we explore interactions with our media through problem solving, establishing and honing our skills, and experimentation that enlightens us to the capacity and limits of the things we work with. Neuro pathways are created as we grow and rejuvenate our minds. It is exciting to learn how the materials we use interact in the physical world.

As we do this, our own self-expression is lent to the physical form we create, and the essence of ourselves is revealed in everything about the product of our labors. The materials we choose, the level of refinement, nuance of style, even our blunders, all speak to who we are as people and where we are on this journey. Our product is a combination of the physical world, the essence of who we are, and the level of skill we bring to the process. It may not always be pretty or graceful, as that comes with practice. This is not some cheap, plastic product off an assembly line of some factory conjured up by the influences of economy and consumerism. It reflects our human spirit, who we are. This product is you. It is not someone else's version of an image that is advertised to be trendy or that creates an image for us to identify with or cling to. It is not a manipulation or perversion of your world view that is molded through some mass production process or filtered to perfection for social media. Every single time, it is a representation of us, and we can know it is real.

Experience

This is our opportunity to take the product we created and see how its performance harmonizes with the forces of nature and society. This is a scary prospect. The boat may not float. There may be all sorts of illusory fears that crop up as the horizon between creation and use approaches. I have found more support than I knew was possible when the time for the christenings came, often from unforeseen places. We can appreciate the performance, the lessons that it provides, and the success of its utility. The way the boat handles the waves and current. Or it could be the feel of a hand wrought clay handle of a coffee mug as it is grasped, the warmth and protection afforded by the intricate cables in a knit sweater. The feeling generated by choreographed, or spontaneous, movements on stage. The productivity of various plants, providing nourishment and decadence throughout the seasons as well as beauty and habitats throughout the year. Experiences are the interface of our passions with this physical existence that we affect and evolve with. They are us at our most vulnerable, but they are also our best opportunities for growth.

Share

We find purpose as others are empowered by our lessons to do things of their own, developing their own interpretations of process, meaning, and stories along the way. It is how we evolve as a society. Communities are knitted more tightly and become stronger, more resilient. Others are provided tools and resources to pursue their passions in a purposeful way farther than previously imagined. It is the interplay of our very essence with society. And we need not be afraid. If it is authentically us then it's beautiful. Because we are light. And light is beautiful at every wavelength when shown in the proper context. As our creations and experiences are accepted and revered and bolster our community, we are fulfilled in our purpose; we strengthen as individuals and society; we heal ourselves and others; we come together as one. Love is cultivated.

Learn, Inspire

Learning and inspiration are woven into the process every step of the way. It starts within and grows and spreads without. We are captivated in the exploration of new interests, which sparks a new light within us and we grow broader in our knowledge and wisdom. We are motivated by our progress. Soon the light of our passions, of our essence, cannot be contained. It spills out to teach and inspire others. And in the same way, love is cultivated within and flows through us. It passes to others and warms the environment, the playing field of our ambitions, to make our inner and outer world a better place. This last bit, hokey as it sounds, is true. How else can one explain the camaraderie that flourished among groups of strangers in a dark, cold, noisy woodshop riddled with cobwebs and dust, slapped together in an ancient barn?

In light of these revelations, would it not be wonderful if someday, somehow, we all managed to begin the pursuit of things that stir passions in our innermost selves? For the sake of the fulfillment and growth of our person, the nourishment of our very soul, it is imperative that we chase down the essence of our passions. It is the scariest thing we can do as we expose the most intimate versions of ourselves, naked before society and the world. To lay ourselves open to the forces of nature and our peers to be tossed among the currents and tempests that are so harshly critical or outright destructive to the fiber of our beings.

But if we remain true to ourselves, it does not matter what these societal forces do to us as we laugh at our blunders and relish in the crash landings. It is how we grow and become more in-tune with our surroundings. The pieces we pick up make a more sophisticated machine for our next approach to the horizon of our dreams. We learn from and even relish the process of self-discovery. And when that horizon is within reach and we are afraid of what unknowns lie beyond it, and there are a zillion things distracting us and pulling us back from the precipice, we have a choice to make. Should we be bold enough to grab that horizon and venture beyond it, we find a fuller, more beautiful, more connected world. If this new growth alienates us from our people, it is because they are afraid of what we are becoming. They were the barriers that held us back. It is now their job to let go of their own bruised egos and fear and embrace their own passions. And it is our job to help them do it. This is how we evolve. With what in my interpretation of this physical world are the prudently applied measures of Art & Rugby toward achieving the essence of our dreams, we reach beyond the farthest horizon to the most distant waters and the communities they feed and tie them all together into a bundle of Home. In so doing we cultivate, spread, and feel the reverberations of universal love.

The experiment that has been Endeavor is working. It works so well I want to grow it. I hope a community can be cultivated out of Art & Rugby Endeavors (ARE), where we can provide resources for each other and hold one another accountable in the pursuit of our dreams. To *inspire* each other to chase curiosity and our interests through the societal hinterlands, artistic undertakings, and the building of skills to explore our passions and tease out their very essence. Collectively, through inspiration and learning, we can evolve as people. Sharing the love of our passions and each other along the way. As this pursuit takes us closer to the Earth and each other, we can begin to heal. Heal ourselves, each other, and this planet we call Home.

I cannot know where ARE will lead in the end. But if we could always see the finish from the start line, it would hardly be worth it to ever run the race. I intend to chase it down like a frisbee. And I hope to meet you along the way, as our respective paths cross en route beyond the horizon of our wildest dreams.

www.artnrugby.com

Acknowledgements

Bridget Mangin, now my wife, snapped the photo used for the front cover. The morning captured here was October 23, 2022, Northport, WI. At the break of day we reached the final put-in of my endeavor to paddle to the end of Wisconsin, a dream of about 4 years in the making. Fall was in the air, the changing of the seasons. I was leaving behind the darkness of the most painful chapter of my life, breaking through personal barriers to brave wild waters and explore new horizons, my ambition unencumbered. The outcome of the day was still unknown with ascending seas driving just offshore, same as with my broader future.

It was the beginning of a new chapter with Bridget as I closed out a phase of chasing down a dream. Waves on the horizon demanded focus in the moment, and the awareness that my personal achievements of the previous years were coming to a climax had me keenly appreciative of where I was. As I paddled this last leg of a journey to the end of Wisconsin in a kayak with an amazing creation story, one chapter gave way to another with the companionship of Beege. As one pinnacle was achieved, I looked forward to incredible camaraderie in navigating the terrain that lay beyond. The tapestry of our interwoven lives is now greater than any expectation I could have conceived and is still growing.

I love you Beege. Thank you so much.

The network of support that has enriched my life afforded the experiences told in this book far more than anything I personally did myself. My family is first and foremost responsible for providing me the latitude to pursue my first and latest flingers. I intentionally held back in this volume from divulging the full story of how tight we all are, as our story is not mine alone to tell. My sister, Mary Beth, had a profound effect on who I am today and still offers advice and encouragement that is most meaningful because it is always kept real. Often joined by my brothers Lew and John on different exploits or encouraged by them, I found success in small things that eventually grew. My parents, often worried, still supported me financially and emotionally. My mom, Carol Mangin, still does to this day.

Others played respective roles. Uncle Tom Kochan read and provided feedback, but most of all encouragement, when I first tried compiling essays and experiences in a story that wasn't yet complete (and rife with cynicism) 20 years ago. The enduring legacies of Rob Ozarowicz and my dad, Les Mangin Jr, motivated me to see this project through. May their adventuresome spirit forever be contagious. The drive that Bill Koepke and Marissa English brought into the boat shop provided an example for me to attempt to emulate in anything I took on. Two people who know what true values are, they are dear friends I look forward to sharing more endeavors with. My dad, Matt Thomas, Cliff Barber, Pat Melotte, and Robert Good are some of the sources of the tools that comprised my shop. Thank you to Rubina Martini and Isaiah Miller for providing the best conceivable location for Endeavor to take shape, not to mention opportunity for carving out the best place I ever lived. Most of the equipment I didn't purchase myself. Again, all these experiences float upon the support provided by others. So often too, others were there with resources or support that was crucial to some element of a silly undertaking in this book. In some respects, I feel guilty of accepting too much of a free ride.

For this writing in particular, support, commentary, and amazing conversation were all provided by several people who took the time to read the various forms of this volume as it evolved. Thomas Kochan, as previously mentioned, encouraged me to never let go of this endeavor. Matthew Brown and George Leopold provided some initial feedback on this iteration, and Donna and Ron Zimmerman took considerable time and offered essential commentary and suggestions. Thank you to Teri Ozarowicz for providing insight and guidance to get right the details and context of the love she shares and character of her late husband Rob.

My cousin, Susan Kochan, shared insights of the publication process and expectations on copy editing as well as tips for searching out agents, should I attempt to go the route of a publishing house. Her knowledge helped me to find my path to publication.

With the geographic focus of so many of this volume's stories, I needed maps. For months I figured I would have to draw my own to extract just the information I needed. I ran into Jeanne Salmon of Salmon Design Co. at a paddling event at the perfect time in order to have her convert my illegible chicken scratchings into something respectable. Thank you to Jeanne for spending a lot more time on a lot more maps than expected.

Dr. Ross Tangedal at the University of Wisconsin–Stevens Point shares his passion for writing every single day. He empowers scores of aspiring authors and students in every step of the publishing process to take their work as far as possible. Ross is a conduit for independent authors to publish their work in an industry with extremely formidable barriers to entry. As a copy editor and designer, he has helped me achieve a higher balance between F. Scott Fitzgerald and Ernest Hemingway. Obviously, I have yet a whole lot of upward mobility in this aspiration. Ross is responsible for taking this work from a manuscript to a published book, a journey that I would not know how to begin.

Personalities of my past have helped shape my values and establish my moral code as I tried to figure out what it is to be a man, and just how relevant that is in today's world. Pete Bloch, John Neumann, and Rob Ozarowicz are a few of the most notable. So many other family and friends through the years have provided motivation, influence, and support that has landed me here today. Thank you all.

Finally, my kids. The trials you weathered and experiences we shared are more personal than I have a right to divulge here. The story of Endeavor is part of who you both are, and I hope like hell it is of more benefit than detriment. In all my victories and blunders as a father, I am doing my best. Thank you, most deeply, for your understanding, trust, and patience.